MAD MEN

AND

PHILOSOPHY

The Blackwell Philosophy and Pop Culture Series
Series Editor: William Irwin

South Park and Philosophy
  Edited by Robert Arp

Metallica and Philosophy
  Edited by William Irwin

Family Guy and Philosophy
  Edited by J. Jeremy Wisnewski

The Daily Show and Philosophy
  Edited by Jason Holt

Lost and Philosophy
  Edited by Sharon Kaye

24 and Philosophy
  Edited by Richard Davis, Jennifer Hart Weed, and Ronald Weed

Battlestar Galactica and Philosophy
  Edited by Jason T. Eberl

The Office and Philosophy
  Edited by J. Jeremy Wisnewski

Batman and Philosophy
  Edited by Mark D. White and Robert Arp

House and Philosophy
  Edited by Henry Jacoby

Watchmen and Philosophy
  Edited by Mark D. White

X-Men and Philosophy
  Edited by Rebecca Housel and J. Jeremy Wisnewski

Terminator and Philosophy
  Edited by Richard Brown and Kevin Decker

Heroes and Philosophy
  Edited by David Kyle Johnson

Twilight and Philosophy
  Edited by Rebecca Housel and J. Jeremy Wisnewski

Final Fantasy and Philosophy
  Edited by Jason P. Blahuta and Michel S. Beaulieu

Alice in Wonderland and Philosophy
  Edited by Richard B. Davis

Iron Men and Philosophy
  Edited by Mark D. White

True Blood and Philosophy
  Edited by George A. Dunn and Rebecca Housel

MAD MEN
AND
PHILOSOPHY

NOTHING IS AS IT SEEMS

Edited by Rod Carveth and
James B. South

WILEY

John Wiley & Sons, Inc.

Published by John Wiley & Sons, Inc., Hoboken, New Jersey
Published simultaneously in Canada

For general information about our other products and services, please contact our Customer Care Department within the United States at (800) 762-2974, outside the United States at (317) 572-3993 or fax (317) 572-4002.

Wiley also publishes its books in a variety of electronic formats. Some content that appears in print may not be available in electronic books. For more information about Wiley products, visit our web site at www.wiley.com.

Library of Congress Cataloging-in-Publication Data:

Mad men and philosophy : nothing is as it seems / edited by Rod Carveth and James B. South.
    p. cm. — (The Blackwell philosophy and pop culture series)
  Includes index.
  ISBN 978-0-470-60301-7 (pbk.)
  1. Mad men (Television program)   I. Carveth, Rod. II. South, James B.
  PN1992.77.M226M33 2010
  791.45'72—dc22   2010005158

Printed in the United States of America

10 9 8 7 6 5 4 3 2 1

CONTENTS

ACKNOWLEDGMENTS

"I Think We Need to Salute That!"

The work on this book required getting into character. Much whiskey, many martinis, and countless cigarettes were consumed in an effort to make the book an authentic companion to *Mad Men*. In the interest of research, liaisons were entered into, suits were worn, and hostile takeovers by other publishers were thwarted.

Putting together a volume such as *Mad Men and Philosophy* requires a team of people working together—a team that deserves to be saluted for their efforts. We would like to thank our contributing authors, who met every tight deadline with high-quality work and good cheer. Unlike Bert Cooper, Bill Irwin, the Blackwell Philosophy and Pop Culture Series editor, offered invaluable assistance every step of the way, and Constance Santisteban at Wiley saw this book through press with all the efficiency and oversight of Joan Holloway.

Rod thanks James for such a great working relationship. Anytime James wants to collaborate on another project, Rod is game.

Rod has two other people he would also like to thank. First, Alana Carveth deserves a lot of credit for putting up with a father who was more distracted and forgetful than usual. It's not easy to raise a parent at seventeen, but Alana really rose to the occasion. Second, Rod would like to thank Nina Spiller. Nina came into his life just as the book project was taking off. A fellow *Mad Men* fan, Nina provided love, support, and encouragement that made editing this volume much, much easier. Rod feels truly blessed to have two such wonderful women in his life.

James would like to thank Beth O'Sullivan and Lula Hopkins, the Allison and Hildy in his life, for putting up with his taking on a new project with the time commitments that entailed. He knows it made their jobs just a bit harder. Working with someone you've never met in person can be tricky. Rod made it very easy, and James enjoyed the collaborative effort.

Last but not least, we want to thank you, the reader, for your interest in the show and in this book. And we want to assure you that no one lost a foot throughout the entire process.

INTRODUCTION

"A Thing Like That"

Take off your shoes. Shut the door. Have a seat. Kick back in your Eames chair. Admire that Rothko print. Pour your favorite drink. And prepare to enter the philosophical world of *Mad Men*, or at least the world of philosophers thinking and writing about *Mad Men*.

Mad Men premiered in July 2007 to immediate critical acclaim. Set in 1960, the series seemed both exotic and nostalgic. It showed a past that many of us had not lived through, and for those who had lived through it, the episodes shined a new light on old experiences. Over the course of the first three seasons, *Mad Men* reminded us of many uncomfortable truths, from the prevalence of drinking and smoking to the systemic sexism, racism, and homophobia that were ever-present in the early 1960s. It also reminded us of a glamour long since lost as we became reacquainted with the fashions of the era, the luxurious civility of airline flight, and the forgotten manners and mores of a previous generation. And *Mad Men* poignantly dramatized the reactions of people to events we still commemorate today. By taking us inside a world in which people struggled to understand these events as they occurred, and

1

showing us those people in their historical context, *Mad Men* helped us understand better both the past and the present.

Few series have distinguished themselves as quickly as *Mad Men*. But the audience didn't need the Golden Globes or the Screen Actors Guild to tell them *Mad Men* was something special, something delightfully disturbing. This show's audience knows quality when it sees it. From the first episode viewers were immersed in a morally ambiguous atmosphere of corporate and family life. We were introduced to likeable characters performing questionable, and at times clearly immoral, actions. Somehow we found ourselves rooting for Don Draper to sell cigarettes, get away with dalliances, and conceal his true identity. And we found Sterling Cooper an alluring and attractive setting, all the while cringing at the subservient role of the women in the office.

The chapters that follow were written by *Mad Men* fans for *Mad Men* fans who can't help but think about the characters, events, and issues long after they turn off the television. Whether you want to think more about the role of women in the series, or the morality of advertising, or the way to lead a meaningful life, you will find guidance in these pages.

Because we didn't have a big advertising budget for this book, we had to write this introduction ourselves. Philosophers aren't known as great salesmen, but hopefully this little pitch was enough to close the deal. Please read on.

PART ONE

"PEOPLE MAY SEE THINGS DIFFERENTLY, BUT THEY DON'T REALLY WANT TO": *MAD MEN* AND PROBLEMS OF KNOWLEDGE AND FREEDOM

One

WHAT FOOLS WE WERE: *MAD MEN*, HINDSIGHT, AND JUSTIFICATION

Landon W. Schurtz

That *Mad Men* takes place in the 1960s is no accident. The creator, Matthew Weiner, could have made a series about modern advertising executives, but he chose not to. By showing us the differences between Don Draper's time and ours, *Mad Men* deftly underscores the ways in which we aren't so different after all. One thing does stand out, however, at least for me. Every time I watch the show, I find myself asking, "Were these people just *stupid*?"

Let me explain myself. I don't *actually* think that the people on the show are idiots. Nonetheless, sometimes they just seem *so dense*. There are things in their world that it seems like they *ought* to know, but, for some reason, *don't*.

For instance, here in the twenty-first century we know that one of the most successful ad campaigns of all times is Marlboro's use of the "Marlboro Man." Cowboy hat pulled low to shade his squinty gaze, he stares into the empty distance, alone in rugged country—the Marlboro Man is still an iconic figure, even though he hasn't been seen in a decade. The campaign traded on the notion of smoking as manly, the smoker as a hardy individualist. It was a runaway success.

Why is it, then, that when advertising genius Don Draper is presented with a similar idea by his firm's research department, he rejects it? Maybe *we* wouldn't have known at first sight that it was a good idea for a campaign, but it seems we could reasonably expect Don to know—yet he doesn't. What's more, Pete Campbell, the junior man on the team, *does* see the potential of the angle. What's going on?[1]

Let's use that case, and others like it, to examine exactly what it takes to *know* something. As we'll see, Don's a smart guy, but what he does and even *can* know is limited by the resources available at his particular time and place in history. Like any effective salesman, though, I need to wind up a bit and get a good lead-in before I can sell you on the bottom line. So before we get to the part where I try to convince you that we're all blinkered by time and place, let's start with something a little more general: What do we mean when we say we "know" something?[2]

"He Could Be Batman for All We Know"

In "Marriage of Figaro" (episode 103), Harry Crane points out to his co-worker Pete Campbell how little they really know about their boss, Don Draper. "Draper? Who knows anything about that guy? No one's ever lifted that rock. He could be Batman for all we know." Pete shrugs the comment off, but Harry's right—they don't know much about Don, because he doesn't really talk about himself. He doesn't give them anything to go on. The junior account executives could sit around making *guesses* about Don if they wanted. But at the end of the day, even if some of their guesses turned out to be correct (without their realizing it), they still wouldn't *know* anything because, right or wrong, they wouldn't have any *reasons*.

The philosophical study of knowledge is called *epistemology*. Epistemologists have long recognized that having *knowledge* involves having *reasons*. Reasons, or—put another way— justification, are one ingredient of what you might call the formula for knowledge. (Philosophers will argue about anything, so I'm necessarily glossing over some quibbles about the details here.) Briefly, we can think of knowledge as *justified true belief*.

Let's take the three ingredients of knowledge in reverse order. When epistemologists talk about "believing" something, they just mean that you think it's true. "Belief" can sometimes carry other connotations, and in everyday speech it's often even set up as an alternative to knowing. That's not how we're using the word here. For our purposes, belief is an *ingredient* of knowledge, not an alternative to it. So to have a belief is, roughly, to just "buy into" something. For instance, after her employee orientation with Joan in the pilot episode ("Smoke Gets in Your Eyes"), Peggy *believes* that if she doesn't butter up the switchboard girls, she won't be able to do her job as a secretary.

The next ingredient is *truth*. You can't *know* what isn't true. In other words, you can believe something false. Betty Draper, for example, believes her husband's name is really Don Draper. She may even think she knows it, but she would be wrong. "Don," as we learn in "5G" (episode 105), is really Dick Whitman. His ruse has fooled everyone, Betty included, into thinking he's someone he really isn't, so that they don't really *know* who he is.

Truth and belief seem pretty straightforward, and they are, indeed, fairly uncontroversial elements of the definition of knowledge. They're also of the least interest to us in trying to answer our initial question. People in all times and places wind up with false beliefs, and therefore come short of having *knowledge*. What we're interested in figuring out is how so many seemingly smart people wound up being so wrong about so many things that seem pretty obvious to us, while still yet apparently believing they have knowledge. To answer that, we need to talk about the last ingredient—justification.

It's one thing to have a belief, and even to be right about it, but it's quite another to have good reasons for that belief. We need reasons to believe the way we do—in other words, justification. Justification is the magic stuff that transforms merely being right into knowing. Earlier, we observed that the junior execs could make guesses about Don all they wanted and they still wouldn't *know* anything about him, even if they somehow came up right on some of the guesses. You can't *know* just by taking shots in the dark. You have to have *reasons*, too.

Of course, reasons aren't enough, not all by themselves— you need justification as well as true belief, and it's very important to understand that having justification doesn't entail having the truth, and vice versa. Betty doesn't *know* her husband is really named Don Draper for the obvious reason that he isn't. That much seems right. But wouldn't we say that she's *justified* in thinking he's Don Draper? Seeing a person use a name on a day-to-day basis, buy a house and conduct business under that name, get married under that name, and so on certainly constitutes good reason to think that that is the person's real name.

Betty's a smart woman, but she's dead wrong about her husband. Still, she's also justified in believing as she does. Can that possibly be right? Perhaps something about how this whole justification thing works can explain how an otherwise smart person who seems to have all the good reasons in the world to believe something is true can somehow wind up with a false belief. If so, then we'll be in a position to better understand why, with the benefit of hindsight, some of these folks from 1960 come across as so obtuse. So let's dig into justification.

"Every Day I Make Pictures Where People Appear to Be in Love. I Know What It Looks Like."

What constitutes being justified? Where do justifications for beliefs come from? The most obvious sources of justification for beliefs are our senses. Some philosophers maintain that we cannot regard beliefs that come about from relying on our senses as justified, but it's clear that what we perceive about the world *must* play an important role in justifying our beliefs. It certainly seems that the chest pains Roger Sterling felt in "Long Weekend" (episode 110) constituted justification for thinking he was experiencing *some* sort of problem, even if it didn't necessarily mean he was justified in thinking he was having a heart attack, specifically.

Another means of justifying beliefs that is a bit more complex than pure sense data, but still pretty basic, is personal experience. In "The Hobo Code" (episode 108), Don observes from their behavior around each other that Midge, his Greenwich Village mistress, and Roy, her fellow beatnik, are in love. "Every day I make pictures where people appear to be in love. I know what it looks like," he says, and he's right. They *are* in love. Don's not justified in thinking that it's true in the same way as he might be justified in reporting some mundane fact about the world around him, like the color of Midge's wallpaper, for instance, but he *is* justified. He can't *see* love in the same way he can see the color of the walls, but, owing to his personal experience, he can nonetheless "see" it when it's right in front of his face.

So far, so good. We can be justified in our beliefs in virtue of what we sense directly and in virtue of what we can figure out based on our own personal expertise. That certainly seems plausible enough. We can imagine we'd accept such first-hand accounts as fairly solid justification for beliefs. But this hasn't helped us answer our initial question at all, or at least not in a satisfactory way.

Normally, if someone doesn't see something that's very obvious to most other people, we think that person is either being careless with the evidence or just isn't "getting it." But all this started when we noted that some things that we regard as obvious are obscure to the *Mad Men* characters. For instance, even the most well-behaved characters on the show are rather startlingly sexist. Their behavior is just wildly inappropriate—it's offensive, intimidating, and unpleasant to a lot of the women on the show. It's hardly surprising that Peggy would come across Bridget crying in the bathroom of Sterling Cooper (episode 102, "Ladies Room")—who knows what she had to put up with that day? So if this is so obvious to us, why don't the characters get it?

On the account I've just given of justification, when someone fails to grasp something it either means that the evidence is difficult to perceive or the person is somehow at fault, epistemically speaking. Since the fact that the behavior of the junior account executives at Sterling Cooper is clearly inappropriate, and would seem so to just about anyone watching the show, it doesn't seem right to say that the evidence isn't clear. But that means the characters must be either very careless or just not very bright. There's something that doesn't seem quite right about that, either. We must be missing a piece of the puzzle.

As it happens, we are. What the preceding account of justification does *not* take into account is that there's only so much we can know first-hand. If we could rely only on ourselves for justification, we'd have relatively little of it, and would therefore know next to nothing. The idea that we must depend on ourselves and only ourselves for justification, and therefore knowledge, is called *epistemic individualism*. Very few thinkers have actually held this view, but for many years, most of the epistemology that was done *acted as if* we were isolated, solitary knowers, focusing solely on the ways in which we were or were not justified with respect to our senses and our own internal mental processes. Relatively little attention was paid to the fact that most of the evidence for our beliefs comes from other people, but that's been changing recently, and this new approach is commonly known as *social epistemology*. Social epistemology recognizes the importance of the social nature of humans in thinking about what and how we come to know things. As a result, it has been able to shed some light on issues that might otherwise be puzzling. Some of the concepts used in social epistemology can help us fill out our picture of justification a little more, and get us closer to an answer to our question that rings true.

"Well, I Never Thought I'd Say This, but What Does the Research Say?"

Testimony occupies a central place in social epistemology. Testimony is a pseudo-religious-sounding term for sincere communication of belief, and social epistemologists have come to understand that it plays a hugely important role in individual knowledge. Freddy Rumsen, Don Draper, and the others didn't do any *personal* exploration of "the Electrosizer" (which made its infamous debut in "Indian Summer," episode 111), but they're nonetheless justified in believing that it gives "sensations" of a certain sort. Why? Peggy told them, and they have good reason to believe that she is in a position to know. Their justification for the belief (and, incidentally, the belief itself) came from her testimony.

So we get a lot of our beliefs through testimony, and likely most of our justification, too. Since beliefs and justification are both required before we actually know anything (the other part, of course, is being *right*), this means that we're remarkably dependent on other people for the ingredients of knowledge. We need other people in order to know much of anything. We depend on other people for knowledge, so maybe it's the case that if otherwise intelligent people fail to know something that seems obvious to us, something's gone wrong in the realm of testimony. So we should ask ourselves, who do the characters on the show depend on, epistemically speaking?

Then and now, one of the best kinds of testimony is expert testimony. After Betty's accident in "Ladies Room," she's very worried because she doesn't know *why* she had the strange attack that caused the car accident. Don, frustrated and worried as well, appeals to the promise of knowledge that experts offer us. "Well, go to a doctor, another doctor. A good one!" Of course, he's also got a healthy sense of skepticism about at least *some* doctors. "That Dr. Patterson is not thorough. I swear when we walked down Park Avenue, I could hear the quacking."

It's all well and good when we can find a qualified so-and-so to answer our queries and be done with it. If any of the secretaries at Sterling Cooper have a question about how the office runs, they can always ask office manager Joan Harris; they do *not* ask Don, even though he's senior to Joan. We may be stuck getting our knowledge from other people, but we can be judicious about who we listen to. What's worrying, however, is when experts in the same area disagree—like Betty's doctors. There's an interesting example of this phenomenon in the first episode ("Smoke Gets in Your Eyes"). It's an incident we touched on earlier—the tobacco ad campaign and Pete Campbell's insight that playing on the danger of smoking could be a viable advertising option.

In case you haven't seen the episode recently, let me refresh your memory. In the wake of widely publicized research revealing that cigarette smoking is linked to various diseases, the Lucky Strike cigarette company is worried about its image. They want an ad campaign that'll still sell a product now known to be potentially dangerous, and they can no longer rely on the dubious doctors' testimonials and vague health claims they'd made in the past. Don Draper is the man in charge of delivering the pitch, and mere hours before the meeting, he still doesn't have any ideas. Grasping at straws, he takes a meeting with Dr. Guttman, a psychologist who works for Sterling Cooper's research department, with Pete Campbell sitting in. The researcher tells him that the best psychological theory available suggests that many people have, on some level, a "death wish," and that it should be possible to sell cigarettes precisely by highlighting the rebellious, death-defying aspect of it. Don sums it up pithily: "So basically, if you love danger, you'll love smoking."

Dr. Guttman is clearly a capable individual who is quite confident about her conclusions. Don, on the other hand, isn't confident. When the big meeting comes, Don doesn't pitch the "death wish" angle, but Pete—without Don's go-ahead—does. As a result, Don's pretty upset with Pete. Not only was it Don's pitch to make, but, as he says later in his office, "If Greta's research was any good, I would have used it."

The difficulty lies in the fact that we have *two* experts in roughly the same area—how to influence consumers—who are saying *opposite things*. What do we do when experts disagree? Some philosophers say that when two people who are epistemic peers disagree, they should both suspend judgment. There are some good arguments for this as a kind of ideal practice, but Don was *not* in a situation that allowed for him to suspend judgment. He had a pitch meeting in just a few hours. He *had* to make some decision. So why make the decision he did, which was to ignore Dr. Guttman's advice?

The answer to this question is going to prove useful to our analysis, but to see it we need to step back a bit. Now, normally, Don's own expertise would be a good reason for having certain beliefs about an ad campaign. Suppose that one of his junior execs, like Ken Cosgrove, had "spitballed" the idea of positioning smoking as "dangerous." If Don's gut instinct was to reject the idea as unworkable, he'd surely be justified, and we'd have no worries about it, either. Why? Well, because while Ken might know *something* about advertising (he'd better, if he wants to keep his job), he's not an expert in the same class as

Don. If Don doesn't listen to his advice, even if Ken happens to be right (as we might know with the benefit of hindsight), we don't think Don's behaving unreasonably, because we don't class Ken as an expert, and neither does he.

Strange as it may seem to us here in the twenty-first century, this may be exactly the same reason that Don didn't use Dr. Guttman's research—he didn't consider her an expert. We're used to thinking of psychologists as having great insight into the human mind, but Don doesn't seem impressed. Maybe it's because he regards psychology as something new and unproven; Roger Sterling's comments in "Ladies Room" make it sound as if psychology is something of a fad.[3] Whatever the reason, Don makes his assessment of the field clear when he tells Dr. Guttman that "psychology might be great at cocktail parties" before dismissing her ideas. To *us* it appears that Don is behaving irrationally, because we have decades more experience with the sorts of insights that psychology can provide us about how and why people do things. As far as Don's concerned, though, research psychology still has yet to make good on its claims—it's "bullshit," as he says in "Ladies Room."

Pete ran with Dr. Guttman's research angle, but he probably doesn't put much more stock in psychology than Don; if he does, we're never given any indication of it. His motivations for bringing out the "death wish" approach are clear enough—he wanted to prove himself where Don seemed to be flailing. As Don told Midge about Pete in the first episode, "There's this kid who comes by my office every day, looks where he's going to put his plants." Pete probably went with the research not because he had more reason to believe that it was correct than Don did, but rather just because he thought it gave him a shot at Don's job.

But there's another instance of Pete going against the popular opinion that doesn't seem to have such a shallow motivation. In "Red in the Face" (episode 107), the Sterling Cooper guys are brainstorming about the upcoming presidential election, assessing Kennedy's chances against their candidate, Nixon. The partners don't seem to think much of Kennedy's prospects. After Sterling notes that Kennedy doesn't even wear a hat, Pete Campbell says, "I don't know. You know who else doesn't wear a hat? Elvis. That's what we're dealing with." The others dismiss his observation.

Pete certainly didn't improve his chances of getting promoted by plumping for Kennedy, so why did he do it except that he actually believed that Kennedy was more of a threat than the others did? Clearly he did, and he was right, too, as we know. He was right because he was able to see something that the others couldn't, something importantly relevant to the situation at hand—Kennedy's youth appeal. Being young, Pete saw what Roger Sterling and Bert Cooper did not. Cooper apparently never even considered the possibility that the vantage point of youth could provide any worthwhile insights. "Remind me to stop hiring young people," he says.

We're now closing in on the real answer to our question. Don didn't grasp the importance of the angle that would eventually come to define one of the most successful ad campaigns ever because he didn't recognize the person presenting the evidence as being appropriately trustworthy. He failed to know because Dr. Guttman's say-so was not enough to provide justification for a belief. Don, along with the other senior execs, failed to know that Kennedy was a threat to Nixon's campaign for the White House because Pete Campbell's insights were not proper justifiers. To them, the opinion of some wet-behind-the-ears junior account executive was just not enough to provide *reason to believe*.

But why would they think that? Wouldn't knowing that Kennedy had youth appeal be pertinent information? Wouldn't being able to understand different viewpoints be of use in forming our beliefs and seeking justification? Some epistemologists have explored that very question. So to get to the bottom of this, once and for all, we're going to look at just a few more examples, this time with the help of an analytical approach known as *standpoint theory*.

"It's Like Watching a Dog Play the Piano"

Standpoint theory, or *standpoint epistemology*, assumes that some individuals in a society are better situated, by virtue of their experiences, to know certain things, even things that it might be impossible for anyone who doesn't occupy a similar place in society to know first-hand. This isn't the same as simply recognizing the importance of expertise, but it is related. Expertise is, in principle, something that anyone can acquire—all things being equal, anyone could work on Madison Avenue long enough to acquire expertise in advertising. The kind of privileged viewpoint that standpoint theory addresses comes from a whole existence that is shot through with the relevant kinds of experiences.

Even the relatively unenlightened characters in *Mad Men* seem to have *some* intuitive grasp of the notion. In "Babylon" (episode 106), Freddy Rumsen and the ad boys use the secretaries to brainstorm for the Belle Jolie lipstick account. They don't have a high opinion of their secretaries' intelligence, referring to them at one point as "morons." The only reason they even bother asking is because they don't know anything about lipstick themselves. Thus they're aware that the girls have *some* information that they don't. But standpoint theory goes further than merely to suggest that some people have access to certain facts that others don't. It proposes that there may be a *great deal* of valuable knowledge that one might acquire from having a particular vantage point, and *that* is something Freddy and his crew never even entertained. When Peggy actually comes up with a good pitch for Belle Jolie lipstick, most of the people in the office are fairly amazed.

It seems obvious enough to us now that things worth knowing are spread out, diffuse in society. In 1960, however, that was hardly the prevailing opinion. *Mad Men* is a world dominated by middle- to upper-class white males. And although things were changing, in their day and age the dominant opinion was that everything that was worth knowing was known, or at least knowable, to those selfsame privileged white men.

This opinion tracks with the notion of epistemic individualism, which, in its extreme form, holds that the only justification available to us is the kind that anyone can, in theory, get ahold of. The idea of justification that only *some* people can have would have seemed frankly bizarre to most ad execs *and* most philosophers in 1960. But here in our day, on the other side of the civil rights movement and the feminist movement and the gay rights movement, it doesn't seem so strange to suggest that not just anyone can really *know*, in a first-hand sort of way, what it's like to be on the other side of sexism, or racism, or homophobia. Although it's far from completely uncontroversial, there's clearly *something* to the idea that people in those situations might have a better understanding of the ins and outs of discrimination, for instance, and that we ought to regard them as experts on the subject whose testimony can justify our second-hand beliefs.

The mistake that Don makes when he rejects Dr. Guttman's research isn't that he's stupid or careless with the evidence. It's that he doesn't recognize her as having the kind of insight on the subject that we think she does. Likewise, the mistake that the senior partners make when dealing with Pete is not recognizing that there are particular, relevant facts that only a young person would be in a good position to grasp. This one in particular is a mistake they do *not* continue to make, as changing times force Sterling Cooper to move to bring on younger creative staff to reach the youth market in "For Those Who Think Young" (episode 201).

There's so much that the *Mad Men* characters seem ignorant of. Isn't it *obvious* that dry cleaning bags are dangerous, Betty? How can you *not* realize that Salvatore is gay, Don?

Don't you all know that you're treating the women in your lives like animals, and that it's just unfair?

And yet, we can't call them *stupid*, because they aren't. They are products of their time, their place in history, right down to what they know and *can* know. Surely by 1960 *some* people have had dry-cleaning-bag tragedies, but until the testimony is out there to be picked up on by Betty Draper, she probably won't have any reason to think they're dangerous unless she has a personal experience with that sort of mishap. There are plenty of gay people around in 1960, but they live such deeply closeted lives, it would take someone who *was* gay to recognize the signs (as in "The Hobo Code"). There's plenty of rampant sexism in 1960 as well, but women's unhappiness is chalked up to "childishness," as Betty's psychoanalyst characterizes her malaise. So, unfortunately, women's insight into the *real* issue at hand goes unheeded. What we can recognize as justifying reasons depends on society, and thus, so do the limits of our knowledge. People in the 1960s weren't dumb—they were just limited by what their era, their culture, would *allow* them to know.

NOTES

1. We need to stop for a moment and acknowledge that while the show's creator, Matthew Weiner, strives for as much realism as possible in *Mad Men*, there are *some* liberties taken. In particular, my central example—Don's negative reaction to a Marlboro Man-style cigarette ad campaign—highlights one such liberty, since the Marlboro Man was created (by Leo Burnett) in the mid-1950s, less than a decade before the setting of the show's first season. Why do I assume this is Matthew Weiner taking liberties, rather than just concluding that my analysis isn't any good, and that Don's reaction doesn't signify what I think it does? Fair question, but there's a fair answer. The whole cigarette ad campaign plot arc is shot through with anachronisms that most viewers wouldn't catch. For instance, Lucky Strike was using the phrase "It's Toasted" to promote their cigarettes in *1916*. There's also Don's dismissive reaction to the use of psychology in advertising, which would be odd given that psychologists were instrumental in the founding of professional advertising in the early twentieth century. I think we're okay in proceeding to take Don's reactions at face value, as I've interpreted them, even though they mark one of the show's rare departures from strict historical fidelity.

2. In order to minimize spoilers for those who are fans of the show, I'll be drawing almost all of my examples from first-season episodes. I'm pretty confident that by now,

every fan should have seen at least *that* much of the show. Later in the chapter, I touch on something that happens in the first episode of the second season, but I don't think it spoils any plotlines.

3. Of course, as already noted, such a reaction to psychology as a tool in advertising would be a bit odd, to say the least, if we were to hold the show to a *strict* standard of verisimilitude. Let's just let 'em have this one, what say?

"PEOPLE WANT TO BE TOLD WHAT TO DO SO BADLY THAT THEY'LL LISTEN TO ANYONE": MIMETIC MADNESS AT STERLING COOPER

George A. Dunn

Authenticity is a word frequently heard in connection with *Mad Men*, a show lauded for the detailed accuracy of its portrayal of the fashions, hairdos, furnishings, office atmosphere, and social mores of Madison Avenue in the early 1960s. Cigarettes everywhere, martini lunches, sexual harassment as an office norm, and even jarring moments such as when Betty Draper scolds her daughter Sally for playing with a dry cleaning bag over her head—not because she might suffocate but because she emptied out the clothes it had contained, possibly all over the floor of Betty's closet!—all these contribute to the show's much admired authenticity, while throwing into relief our own dramatically different habits and attitudes. In many ways, *Mad Men* is as much a mirror on ourselves as it is a window into a bygone era, showing us who we are by reminding us of what we once were and have chosen no longer to be.

But the authenticity of the show involves more than just the social mores of that era. The authenticity applies to material culture as well, all those lovingly restored or reproduced artifacts that grace so many scenes—the IBM Selectric typewriter, the Xerox 914 photocopier, and *The Button-Down Mind of Bob Newhart*. These are antiques to us, but at one time each was "the latest thing," exciting novelties to a generation that hadn't yet become jaded from too much novelty. *Mad Men's* exquisitely crafted sets are like time machines that transport us into a world that no longer exists, but whose shadows and ruins can be seen everywhere around us today, even if we didn't recognize them as such before watching *Mad Men*.

When we praise *Mad Men* for its authenticity, what we mean is that the writers, costumers, stylists, and set designers got it right, that they've accomplished the extraordinary feat of faithfully replicating the look and feel—the façade, as it were—of this fascinating world that existed for a time in the early 1960s. And a captivating and engaging façade it is! It's television at its best. But precisely because it's just a façade— that is, an outer surface designed to make us forget that what we're really looking at are costumed actors reciting lines on a soundstage in some television studio—there's something slightly ironic about the use of the word *authentic* to describe the show, however marvelous its historical accuracy.

Mad Men, "Mad Masters," and Mimesis

The irony stems from the fact that one primary meaning of *authentic* has to do with being the real thing, being in reality just what you are in appearance as opposed to being a mere copy or a fake. Needless to say, in the world of television drama nothing is authentic because everything is simulated or faked. At its best, television is just a copy of real life or, to use a philosophical and literary term of art derived from the Greek word for imitation, it's a case of artistic *mimesis*. Instead of praising *Mad Men* for its authenticity, maybe we should praise it for its extraordinarily accurate and beguiling mimesis of the world it depicts.

Authenticity and *mimesis* are important terms to many philosophers, not just because they're part of the vocabulary we use to describe artistic creations like quality television shows, but also because they're relevant to our assessment of what makes a worthwhile human life and our diagnosis of some of the difficulties we all face in trying to live well. But these two concerns—the creation of art and the conduct of life, *poiesis* and *praxis* in Greek—aren't entirely unrelated, at least not in the mind of Plato (428–348 BCE), the ancient Greek philosopher who over two millennia ago began a discussion about truth, goodness, beauty, and, yes, even popular entertainment that continues to this day.

One of the first and most penetrating critics of popular culture, Plato was none too happy with the popular entertainment of his day: the epic Homeric poems that were recited by professional rhapsodes and the tragedies that were performed on the stage as part of an annual festival held in honor of Dionysus. It wasn't that he thought there was necessarily anything shabby about them from an artistic standpoint. To the contrary, he thought that many of them had achieved a degree of perfection in their artistic mimesis that was downright spellbinding—and that's what he thought was the problem. To put it perhaps a little too simply, Plato feared that the very mimetic perfection of the emotionally riveting dramas to which audiences of his day were drawn impaired the audience's ability to distinguish between reality and theatrical illusion.

Now our initial reaction to this claim is probably to dismiss it as patently ridiculous. After all, we may reel from the intensity and violence of the scene from "Shut the Door. Have a Seat." (episode 313) in which a drunken Don Draper awakens his wife Betty in the middle of the night, yanks her out of bed by her pajama blouse, and snarls "You're a whore" in her frightened but defiant face. But even as we're riveted to our seats, our stomachs knotted with Betty's fear and our jaws tight with Don's anger, we know—intellectually at least—that we're watching two very good actors playing a scene and that nothing bad is really going to happen to January Jones or Jon Hamm. We don't mistake their mimesis for reality. That would be insane and we are, of course, rational beings and not . . . well, not madmen.

Or are we? Plato develops his critique of popular entertainment in the course of his most famous dialogue, the *Republic*, which recounts a wide-ranging, all-night conversation between the philosopher Socrates (469–399 BCE) and a group of his friends and acquaintances. Early in the dialogue, the retired arms merchant Cephalus, at whose home they are gathered, remarks on how old age has finally secured his release from bondage to the "mad masters" that had held him in thrall for most of his life.[1] Those mad masters are his passions, which in his younger days he experienced as tyrants that took his reason hostage and drove him to do things that he would later regret. He makes it sound as if the force of these upstart passions could sometimes be so uncontrollable that they would mow right over his better judgment like some boorish American John Deere tractor over an elegant British foot.[2] No surprise, then, that in the calm afforded him by old age he looks back on his days of bondage to his passions as a time of madness.

Think of Pete Campbell and his sad cycle of indiscretion and remorse, first coercing the German au pair in 14C into having sex with him one night while his wife is away and then, only a short time later, begging Trudy not to leave him alone ever again, clearly afraid of what other shameful deeds his "mad masters" are waiting to lure him into doing the next time she's not there to keep an eye on him.[3] In the throes of his booze-fueled lust (and, as always, looking for a way to bolster his fragile self-esteem), Pete does what *seems* best to his brainless and bloated passions rather than what his reason judges to be *really* best.

In the *Republic*, Socrates cites similar cases of passions prevailing over scruples as evidence that the human psyche is a complex and often internally conflicted entity, something we can envision as being like a political community, albeit not necessarily one that's always ruled by its best members. The best part of us, and the only really sane part, is our rational intellect. In a healthy, stable, and well-integrated personality, the passions always listen to reason. But with an inconstant, emotionally immature guy like Pete, the "mad men"—his powerful but irrational passions—rule the asylum.

Seeing Is Believing

"True enough," you may be saying, "but what has that got to do with Plato's beef with the popular entertainment of his and (by implication) our day?" Everything, as it turns out. We noted before that Plato worried that the undeniable power of artistic mimesis would leave audiences unable to distinguish between reality and illusion. Quite sensibly, we objected that we're rational beings and that only a madman would be unable to tell the difference between television and real life. On that last point, Plato would entirely agree. But he would then remind us that all those gripping emotional dramas to which we turn for entertainment, whether classical Greek tragedies or contemporary television shows like *Mad Men*, owe their primary appeal not to the way they engage our intellects but to the way they arouse our passions and excite our emotions, those parts of our personalities that Plato believed had the potential to become mad when not governed by reason.

None of this is meant to deny that reflection on Greek tragedy has inspired some brilliant philosophical analyses by geniuses of the rank of Georg Wilhelm Friedrich Hegel (1770–1831) and Friedrich Nietzsche (1844–1900). And, of course, *Mad Men and Philosophy*, the book you hold in your hands, is evidence of just how thought-provoking tawdry extramarital affairs, dastardly office politics, and wily business intrigues can be when they involve the men and women of Sterling Cooper. But what makes these dramas work artistically, the reason we're drawn to them in the first place, is the reaction they elicit from that part of our psyches that *feels* rather than reflects and *believes* what it sees rather than seeking the reality behind the appearance.

Our passions don't discriminate between reality and illusion. They respond to carefully crafted mimetic *surfaces*, such as the feigned fear and anger on the faces of January Jones and Jon Hamm, as if they were the real deal. That's why despite what we know intellectually about that disturbing scene in the bedroom between Betty and Don—namely, that we're watching actors and not an actual couple teetering on the edge of a full-blown violent altercation—we're still rattled by it. Ontologically (or in reality), there could hardly be a greater gulf than the one between two professional actors playing a scene and an actual married couple swept up in the emotional turmoil of their unraveling relationship. But that's not a difference we perceive with our eyes; it's a difference we are able to recognize only by using reason. On the surface, they're indistinguishable. And our "mad" emotions react only to the surface, the façade, the appearance.

"Sally, Go Watch TV!"

Now, you may have noticed that we've really identified two distinct ways in which the emotional and passionate side of our nature can be considered mad: First, the passions are often so madly insistent on their own gratification that they deafen their ears to the reproaches of reason, at least until they've spent all their energy on their foolish or shameful deeds. Only then does someone like Cephalus or Pete Campbell hear the voice of reason loud and clear in the form of remorse. Second, like a madman, the passions not only do a poor job of discriminating what's genuinely good from its counterfeits, but they also can't distinguish truth from fantasy, since both *feel* more or less the same.

Combine these two forms of madness and you have the reason why Plato took such a dim view of the sort of dramas performed back then on the stage and nowadays also on our television screens. But that's not all. Plato can also teach us the secret of the mad men, not just the mimetic magic through which the actors bring their characters to life, but also the secret of how the advertisers they portray are so successful at getting us to buy Lucky Strike cigarettes, Right Guard deodorant, Secor laxative, Clearasil pimple cream, and Playtex bras—not to mention how they get us to vote for politicians like Richard Nixon.

But first let's tie up the loose ends of Plato's case against dramatic mimesis. The problem isn't just that for the brief time we spend watching *Mad Men* or a play by Sophocles, reason has relaxed its rule over the rest of the personality and has handed the reins over to the passions. No, Plato believed the problem is that our emotional responses to fictional drama tend to shape how we respond to events in real life, since our passions can't tell the difference between the two. Laughing at Jimmy Barrett's insensitive buffoonery, for example, might make us more prone to say cruel things after we turn the television off. Wallowing in self-pity with Pete Campbell or Roger Sterling could make it easier for us later to indulge that same emotion when facing our own misfortunes. And, as Socrates explains in the *Republic*, the same holds for

> sex, and spiritedness, too, and all the desires, pains, and pleasures in the soul that we say follow all our actions . . . For [dramatic mimesis] fosters and waters them that ought

to be dried up, and sets them up as rulers in us when they ought to be ruled.[4]

We vicariously experience the emotions of characters on the stage or screen, picking up habits of emotional response that we then more or less unwittingly transfer to real life—a further, but in this case unconscious, mimetic operation.

Of course, this wouldn't be a concern if we were exposed only to wholesome models. But, as we dedicated viewers of *Mad Men* know, sensible and sound-minded characters living well-ordered lives just aren't good dramatic material. They're certainly not as exciting as lurid tales of shameful or wicked behavior, or even stories of ordinary people who occasionally lose their grip on their emotions due to life's big and little adversities. Referring to the ubiquitous human tendency to imitate not only the actions of others, but also the desires and emotions on display in their actions, Socrates observes that "imitations, if they are practiced continually from youth onwards, become established as habits and nature, in body and sounds and in thoughts."[5] Mimesis is so powerful—and potentially so dangerous—because it operates prior to reason, taking root in us "before [we're] able to grasp reasonable speech"[6] and continuing to exert its influence throughout our adult lives underneath the radar of reason.

Admittedly, Plato was making a controversial claim when he ascribed to certain forms of popular entertainment such power to shape and even deform the human soul, but it's not entirely outlandish to think that there may be some truth to his view. Would it be all that far-fetched to imagine that the sexism displayed by most of the men at Sterling Cooper, as well as Betty Draper's expectations of married life, may have been significantly influenced by the cinematic depictions of gender roles to which they were exposed in their formative years? And, while pondering that, we might also take a moment to consider what sort of soul-shaping Betty might be unwittingly fostering every time she dispatches her daughter out of the room with the command, "Sally, go watch TV!"[7]

When Plato voiced his concerns about the dangers of popular entertainment, he was probably thinking primarily of its effect on youngsters like Sally and Bobby Draper, as well as on those slightly older but still highly impressionable "spotted masses" to whom Don Draper wants Peggy to "deliver" Clearasil.[8] It's doubtful that he had in mind intelligent, mature, and reflective viewers of the sort who read books like *Mad Men and Philosophy*. In fact, many critics have thought that Plato didn't give enough consideration to the more salutary effects that a good drama can have on its audience, such as educating us about our past, offering insights into our present, and shedding new light on perennial features of the human condition. These are some of the things for which we love *Mad Men*, a show most of us manage to watch on a regular basis without succumbing to the temptation to light up a smoke, toss back a martini, and rush out to commit serial adultery.

Don Draper Knows What Love Looks Like

It was Plato's great student Aristotle (384–322 BCE) who described how the mimetic effects of drama on the human soul can actually be morally beneficial in some cases. But even Aristotle agreed with Plato that we human beings are mimetic animals who take our cues about how to act and feel from others around us, sometimes deliberately but often without much conscious awareness that we're doing so. "Imitating is co-natural with human beings from childhood," wrote Aristotle, "and in this they differ from the [other] animals in that they are the most imitative."[9] So when Don Draper declares, "People want to be told what to do so badly that they'll listen to anyone,"[10] he's making a claim that Aristotle would regard as only a slight overstatement. That's one reason why Aristotle thought it was vital to ensure that people—not just children, but also the general public, whom he, like Don Draper, regarded as highly impressionable and, hence, childlike—have plenty of good role models to imitate.

In order to be virtuous, according to Aristotle, it isn't enough just to honor your contracts, keep your hand out of the till, and play within the rules. If that were the case, then a stuffy penny-pincher like Lane Pryce could be called virtuous, despite his insufferable snootiness. Just as important as the outwardly virtuous actions are the inward dispositions—the feelings, desires, and emotions—that accompany them, since "goodness consists in feeling delight where one should, and loving and hating aright."[11] In other words, the virtuous person is someone who genuinely *loves* virtuous deeds, not just someone who performs them grudgingly. And when it comes to instilling emotions like love, the dramatic arts are much better suited to the task than dry rational arguments that have no power to move the heart.

Presenting noble deeds in a way that inspires our enthusiastic admiration—or, as happens more often on *Mad Men*, base deeds in a way that elicits our derision—is one way that the arts can help to train us in virtue, since, as Aristotle explains, "to acquire the habit of feeling pain or taking delight in an image is something closely allied to feeling pain or taking delight in the actual reality."[12] The upshot is that once we associate pleasurable feelings with an artistically created image of something, say, a virtuous character trait, we automatically transfer those feelings to the real thing, since, as Plato had already observed, our emotions can't tell the difference between (to use the language of a Clairol hair color ad)[13] a real blonde and a fake.

Don Draper understands all too well how to employ this strategy of using images to stir up emotions that we then come to associate with something actual, in his case, a product. Consider, for example, two memorable statements we hear from him on the subject of love. First, speaking to his then mistress Midge Daniels about a photograph he believes reveals her to be in love with her friend Roy: "Every day I make pictures where people appear to be in love. I know what it looks like."[14] Never mind whether Don is right about Midge and Roy. The important thing is that Don not only believes he knows how to create an image or appearance—a mimesis—of love, but is also tacitly conceding that the *appearance* is all he needs to elicit whatever response he wants from the viewer. Of course, on an intellectual level most viewers will understand perfectly well that the people who *appear* to be in love in Don's pictures are *in reality* simply models or actors, but, as Plato argued, mimesis bypasses reason and works directly on the passions, feelings, and desires. We see an image that "looks like" love, and even when we know better, our feelings respond as if we were seeing the real thing.

Let's connect Don's pronouncement to Midge with something else he says on another occasion to Rachel Menken after she's confessed that she's never married because she's never been in love. "What you call love," he tells her, "was invented by guys like me to sell nylons."[15] Obviously that's not strictly true, since the public's preoccupation with love predates the invention of nylons by several millennia at least. But making some allowance for the fact that even the candor of a consummate mad man like Don will often come wrapped in hyperbole, we can recognize a sense in which what Don tells Rachel might be true. What Rachel *calls* love—what love "looks like" to her—may be more profoundly shaped by those "pictures" that Don and his cohorts create than by any brush she may have had with the real thing (which Don cynically denies even exists). And, of course, when the mad men place those pictures in the same frame as nylons—or whatever product they're trying to sell—they hope to get us feeling as excited about their product as we do about love. To the extent that they succeed, Plato and Aristotle help us to understand why.

"All That Is Solid Melts into Air"

Describing the social upheaval created by the unprecedented dynamism of capitalism, Karl Marx (1818–1883) and his collaborator Frederick Engels (1820–1895) wrote in *The Communist Manifesto*, "All that is solid melts into air."[16] Fans of *Mad Men* may have a hard time hearing that line without thinking of the opening title sequence of the show, which depicts the silhouette of a man in a black suit (almost certainly Don Draper) stepping into his high-rise corner office and setting down his briefcase as the pictures on the wall, the blinds on the windows, and even his desk and chairs begin to fall not just to the ground but right through the floor. A moment later, the office is gone and the same silhouette that had been standing bolt upright has joined the other items in free fall, his arms outstretched as his body tumbles through the air. It's as though the unreality of Don's world has suddenly been revealed. It was never anything more than a beguiling illusion, a fragile construct that dissolves the moment it's recognized for what it is.

Don plummets helplessly past endless skyscraper walls on which are superimposed advertising images in soft, diaphanous pastels. Many of them are meant to convey an aura of glamour and sex appeal, but there are also wholesome images of family life tossed somewhat incongruently into the mix. All of these images seem to have been designed to induce some feeling or, more precisely, some variation on the feeling of love: romantic love, erotic love, familial love, even perhaps that form of self-love that goes by the name self-esteem. As Don's body glides past some of the spicier images, it's hard not to think of the old cliché that Peggy Olson in one of her brasher moments makes the mistake of reciting to Don: "Sex sells." He corrects her: "Says who? Just so you know, the people who talk that way think that monkeys can do this." Tossing down a pink construction-paper heart, with dried macaroni glued around the edges and the words "I Love You Daddy" scrawled on it, he clarifies, "You are the product. You *feeling* something. That's what sells. Not them. Not sex."[17] Each of the images we see represents some coveted feeling, in the warm and alluring glow of which the mad men seek to bathe their clients' products. But as these images flutter past like a mobile collage of advertising copy, they become semitransparent to us, both literally and figuratively, and we are able to recognize them as the empty simulacra of real life that they are.

But just as we think that we may be witnessing the final collapse of the world that Don and his fellow mad men have constructed out of captivating images and mimetically induced emotions—and just as we're even beginning to wonder whether there's any reality at all behind the mad men's crumbling illusions—we're greeted with the final image. It begins as a tight shot of Don from behind, in which he initially appears to be still falling, but then the frame widens to reveal him sitting in a relaxed pose, his outstretched arm draped over the back of a couch, cigarette in hand. There he is projecting his trademark air of confidence—or, if not real confidence, then something that looks a lot like it. And in the mad world of the mad men world, that's all that matters.

NOTES

1. *The Republic of Plato*, 2nd ed., translated by Allan Bloom (New York: Basic Books, 1991), 5 (329d).

2. As happens in "Guy Walks into an Advertising Agency" (episode 306).

3. "Souvenir" (episode 308).

4. *The Republic of Plato*, 290 (606d).

5. Ibid., 74 (395d).

6. Ibid., 80 (402a).

7. Betty issues this command in "The Arrangements" (episode 304), sending Sally off to the television just in time to witness the self-immolation of Thích Quảng Đức, who set himself on fire in the streets of Saigon as a protest against the South Vietnamese regime in June 1963.

8. "The Wheel" (episode 113).

9. Aristotle, *Poetics*, translated by Joe Sachs (Newburyport, MA: Focus Publishing/ R. Pullins Co., 2005), 22 (1448b).

10. "Babylon" (episode 106).

11. Aristotle, *Politics*, translated by Ernest Barker (Oxford: Oxford University Press, 2009), 309 (VIII.1340a).

12. Ibid.

13. In 1957 Clairol launched their famous hair color ad campaign that posed the question "Does She or Doesn't She? Only Her Hairdresser Knows for Sure." The campaign was created by Foote, Cone, and Belding.

14. "The Hobo Code" (episode 108).

15. "Smoke Gets in Your Eyes" (episode 101).

16. Karl Marx and Frederick Engels, *The Communist Manifesto* (Bel Aire, MN: Filiquarian Publishing, 2007), 10.

17. "For Those Who Think Young" (episode 201).

CAPITALISM AND FREEDOM IN THE AFFLUENT SOCIETY

Kevin Guilfoy

In the *Mad Men* pilot episode, "Smoke Gets in Your Eyes," the executives from Lucky Strike are all kerfuffled. They believe that the government has manipulated scientific facts to mislead people into thinking cigarettes cause cancer. The tobacco companies have funded their own research, but in this political environment they can't get the truth out. Just when it looks like Sterling Cooper is going to lose the account, Don Draper confronts the central problem of advertising: "We've got six identical companies making six identical products." In a flash of brilliance, Don realizes that truth is irrelevant: "We can say anything we want." There is no basis for a preference among identical products. Advertising is not about truth; it's about creating the unique desire for Lucky Strike cigarettes. Don asks how Lucky Strikes are made. The CEO prattles on about breeding and growing insect-resistant tobacco. (Not sexy.) The tobacco is harvested. (Not sexy.)

And toasted. (That's it!) Don smoothly asserts the new slogan: "Lucky Strike: It's Toasted." It doesn't matter that every other tobacco is toasted, too. Don teaches us what advertising is really about:

> Advertising is based on one thing: happiness. And do you know what happiness is?
>
> Happiness is the smell of a new car. Happiness is freedom from fear. It is a billboard on the side of the road that screams with reassurance, "Whatever you are doing is okay. You are okay."

Happiness? No doubt there is a deep human longing to feel acceptance. Fulfilling that desire would probably make a person happy. But can a cigarette make someone happy? The juxtaposition of the social perspectives of 1960s characters and a twenty-first-century audience makes the manipulative intent of advertising stark. The basic desire to feel okay is deeply human, but if Don Draper can take this generic human longing and create a desire for a particular product, are we genuinely free?

The 1960s of *Mad Men* was a golden age for advertising. America had emerged from World War II and was experiencing unprecedented affluence. The industrial manufacturing base that won the war had turned to mass-producing consumer goods. People had money, time, and the liberty to choose between six identical brands of cigarette. Agencies like Sterling Cooper were there to help people discover what they could do with their newfound wealth. In the late 1950s John Kenneth Galbraith (1908–2006) and Milton Friedman (1912–2006) began a serious study of the problems of affluence. With their economist's understanding of the corporate world depicted in *Mad Men*, Galbraith—a modern liberal—and Friedman—a free-market conservative—debated the origin of our desires, the nature of free will, and the social impact of consumerism. Their books—Galbraith's *The Affluent Society* (1958) and

Friedman's *Capitalism and Freedom* (1962)—are attempts from opposite ends of the political spectrum to describe an America that had found itself suddenly affluent. Not surprisingly, their competing views about what we should do to sustain our affluence and freedom in a capitalist society are played out in the offices of Sterling Cooper.

"She Is . . . Well-off, Educated, with Plenty of Time to Shop"

In *The Affluent Society*, Galbraith coins the term *conventional wisdom*. While conventional wisdom is not always false, it is rarely wisdom. The continued repetition of conventional wisdom makes people feel like they are engaged in a useful and productive activity. According to Galbraith, the conventional wisdom that economists repeat to themselves is that consumer desires are the driving force and final arbiter of success in a free-market economy. This wisdom rests on two propositions. (1) "The urgency of desires does not diminish as more of them are satisfied." The citizens of an affluent society have fulfilled their desires for food, shelter, and basic security. But they nonetheless have urgent desires for luxury items. People aren't satisfied when they get what they want. They want what's next just as intensely. (2) "Desires originate in the personality of the consumer."[1] My desires may be irrational, immoral, and even impossible, but they are my own. A successful business caters to the desires that arise in the characters and personalities of consumers.

As a theory of free will, this conventional wisdom is best described as a kind of compatibilism. That is, if a person is acting on her desires, she is free. If she is acting contrary to her desires, she is not free. There is something commonsensical about compatibilism. When I choose what I want, that certainly seems like a free choice. My desire for a particular product may reflect the values I was raised with. A compatibilist could even think that that these values determine my particular choices. However, if my particular desires have their origin in my own values, they are my own. If the conventional wisdom is true, then consumers' desires are genuine and consumers' choices are free. Galbraith thinks that this conventional wisdom is false and that compatibilism must be modified.

This is part of Galbraith's modern liberalism. He thinks that our desires, perhaps even our characters, are shaped by the complex interplay of social forces, and he thinks these forces can be manipulated. When the government attempts this manipulation, conservatives call it "social engineering." When the business world tries it, Galbraith calls it "advertising."[2] Galbraith believes that Don Draper has the ability to make us want things that we do not really want, want to want, or ought to want. When advertising creates our desires, we are not necessarily acting on our own deeply held values and, thus, are not free.

Galbraith argues that advertising is most effective on the affluent. A person who is uncertain where his next meal is coming from simply wants food and security. The affluent, on the other hand, have food and security, but they still have money and free time. They need to learn to want culinary experiences, and Sterling Cooper is there to help them "discover" these new desires. If the insatiable desire for luxury is created by advertising, then this desire does not originate with the consumer. Both propositions of the conventional wisdom would be false.

Betty Draper agrees with Galbraith. In "A Night to Remember" (episode 208), Betty plans a dinner party for Don, Duck Phillips, Roger Sterling, and a client. She presents her guests with a sophisticated international menu, complete with French wine and Heineken, proudly noting, "It's beer from Holland." Duck, Don, and Roger laugh. Betty has done exactly what Don expected rich suburban housewives would do. He had set up displays of Heineken with "cheese and crackers and little cellophane toothpicks" to appeal to housewives who "think Holland is Paris." Duck explains to the Heineken executives just how successful this was:

> Don's wife, she's a peach of a girl, they had a dinner party. We're talking days after placement. She had this elaborate elegant setup: foods from around the globe and sure enough there was your Heineken: right next to the bone china and the polished sterling. It was incredible. She is exactly who we are after: well-off, educated, with plenty of time to shop. And it is important to her that she is the perfect hostess, the perfect wife.

When Betty chooses the Heineken for her dinner party, she believes that she has acted freely. Betty didn't know it, but Don taught her to want to create a particular culinary experience. She confronts Don later, exclaiming, "You embarrassed me." When he tries to brush it off, she repeats, "You embarrassed me!" Betty thought that she was being sophisticated only to find out she was an unwitting pawn in Don's sales pitch. The advertising taught her that there was something she didn't have—Heineken—and it taught her to want it. Betty feels manipulated.

Galbraith is a "deep-self" or "authentic-self" compatibilist about free will. He believes that all our choices are caused by something. When a choice is caused by factors that are not part of our psychological makeup, the choice isn't free. If someone takes my arm and hits you with it, it isn't my free choice. When a choice is caused by desires that are genuinely our own, the choice is free. One problem is that many of our desires are created by advertising. It would seem, then, that these desires are not genuinely our own, and that the resulting choices do not reflect our genuine wants. If Don Draper can cause us to want something strongly enough, he has *caused* us to choose it. When we purchase the advertised product, we are not acting freely.

A Deeper Bond with the Product

Milton Friedman is a libertarian about economics and free will. As an economic libertarian, he is known to his critics as the godfather of market fundamentalism. Friedman believes that almost all of society benefits when individuals are free to pursue their own financial self-interest.[3] A libertarian about free will believes that human beings make their own choices. We might be influenced. We may act emotionally. Our desires and character are factors when we deliberate about our choices, but nonetheless we are in control of our choices. Unlike Galbraith's compatibilism, Friedman's libertarian view of freedom says that our desires do not determine our actions. In other words, we can act contrary to our desires. When we explain why Betty bought the Heineken, the ultimate answer is: "She chose to." Why? She wanted to be sophisticated and elegant. Why? She wanted to create the best experience for her guests. Why? She wanted to be liked and respected. For a libertarian these are reasons for her decision, not causes of her action. We can keep asking why, but Friedman's answer will never be: "Because Don created the desire and the desire forced her to act." Betty chose the Heineken because she wanted it.

Friedman argues that advertising is informative, not persuasive.[4] Don Draper can't create desire, but even if he could it would not *cause* us to choose. Instead, businesses try to discover what people want and then make a product to satisfy that desire. If they get it wrong, the free market drives them out of business. This is the conventional wisdom: desires originate with consumers, and successful businesses find ways to satisfy those desires. In "The Wheel" (episode 113), Kodak needs an ad campaign for an amazing new product. The desire for the Kodak Carousel did not have to be created. In 1960 people wanted the Kodak Carousel, they just didn't know it yet.

Don's pitch is genius. He begins by telling a story about his mentor, Teddy, who told him that the most important thing in advertising is *new*. *New* creates an itch, and the product is the calamine lotion. So far, Teddy's wisdom exemplifies Galbraith's theory of advertising. Don continues by explaining that Teddy talked about a deeper bond with the product: nostalgia—delicate but potent. Teddy told Don that nostalgia is "the pain from an old wound, a twinge in your heart far more powerful than memory alone." Don then narrates a slide show of his life with Betty for the Kodak team.

> [The Carousel] is a time machine that takes us back to a place we ache to go again. The Carousel lets us travel around and around and back home again, to a place where we know we are loved.

Don doesn't have to create the desire to relive our past. He has touched something deep and real in human nature. Kodak has produced a product that helps us to better satisfy a genuine human desire.

It's too easy to swoon over the Carousel. We're tempted to see this sales pitch as art, whereas the Lucky Strike pitch seemed cynical malice. But Don is in advertising, not poetry. "Teddy" is not really a mentor, but he plays one in the sales pitch. Don's family is as much an image in the show's reality as it is an image on the projector screen. Don Draper is being as authentic as Dick Whitman can. That doesn't matter to Friedman, though. The desire exists; the product is new. The advertiser informs us that the product will satisfy our desire. Our emotions are being appealed to, not created. A good enlightened "fortysomething" viewer of *Mad Men* will feel nostalgia for the Kodak Carousel. My generation grew up with this product. We feel that our own desires are authentic. Other people—smokers, for example—are being manipulated. As Freidman sees it, Galbraith's theory of freedom is just judgmental arrogance. Galbraith claims that people are not free when they make choices we think are foolish. Friedman asks: "Who was [Galbraith] to tell people what they should like?"[5] Friedman informs us that:

> The main content of [*The Affluent Society*] was not really the affluence of society but rather it was devoted . . . to denigrating the tastes of ordinary people . . . who prefer pushpin to poetry, who prefer large tailfins to nice, compact, expensive, little cars.[6]

Friedman has no real love of ordinary people himself, of course. He simply thinks that the desire, say, for a Hummer and the desire for a Prius are equally authentic and must be equally respected in a free society. Liberals and conservatives may argue about which of these desires is created by manipulative advertising to push a product that people don't really want. But Friedman's libertarian answer is that neither desire is created by advertising. While we can denigrate the character and intelligence of people who want things we don't want, their specific desires are genuine and their choice is free. Friedman accepts both propositions of the conventional wisdom. The desire for the Kodak Carousel is as authentically the consumer's as is the desire for Lucky Strike or the desire for a particular car. The intensity of the desire can be gauged by the price the consumer is willing to pay. But the desire is not created or significantly intensified by Don Draper. The consumer is always free to ignore Don's helpful suggestions.

Advertising is just one element in an economy that Galbraith describes as a desire-creation and desire-satisfaction machine. Corporations use advertising to create sufficient consumer desires for their products. Production of these products keeps people employed, which provides them with the money they need to keep buying new products. Galbraith calls this a degenerate spiral into meaningless and destructive individual consumerism. For Friedman, this is the market working to bring people what they want, to satisfy their desires, and to make them happy. Friedman calls this economic growth. As might be expected, the two economists have different assessments of the social consequences of consumerism.

"Mommy, Are We Rich?"

In "The Gold Violin" (episode 207), Don and Betty take the children for a picnic in their new Cadillac. When the meal is over, Don downs one last beer for the road and heaves the can into the bushes. He tells Betty to check the kids' hands. Obviously, he doesn't want them getting his car dirty. Satisfied that the children are clean enough to get in the car, Betty shakes the rubbish off the picnic blanket onto the grass. While the car drives off, the camera stays focused on the pile of garbage they have left behind. The scene is striking to a twenty-first-century viewer; well-heeled people don't do this today. But Don and Betty are playing out the most quoted passages in *The Affluent Society*. Galbraith describes a family outing in which the family has the best of private luxury, including a luxury car and good food. Still they must enjoy this private luxury in public squalor: litter, bad roads, and, worst of all, billboards. When Don and Betty's daughter Sally asks, "Mommy, are we rich?" Galbraith thinks we all should reflect on "the curious unevenness of their blessings."[7]

Wealthier people can afford and enjoy a greater quantity and variety of luxuries. But as private consumption rises, the need for government services rises in step.[8] For example, Galbraith would argue that Don needs good roads in order to enjoy his car and that his famly needs a clean park to enjoy their picnic. Advertisers will, of course, entice people to pay for the best consumer products. But since roads and fields are not consumable by an individual, no one hires Sterling Cooper to entice people to contribute to the common good. There are no commercials showing a beautiful happy family enjoying the patriotic satisfaction of paying their taxes. Galbraith thus claims that we live in a world of private wealth and public squalor.

This theme of public versus private consumption is played out in various *Mad Men* subplots. Only once has Sterling Cooper been approached for a public project. In "Love among the Ruins" (episode 302), the mayor's office wants the new Madison Square Garden built, but there is public backlash. The building will sit on the site of Penn Station, a historic and cultural landmark. Copywriter Paul Kinsey, in full beatnik self-righteous indignation, belittles the project: "The Romans took apart the Coliseum to make their outhouses." Of course fifty years later it is hard to imagine New York without Madison Square Garden. So when the MSG executive responds, "This *is* the Coliseum," he has a point. Don wins the account only to have corporate overlord Lane Pryce tell him to drop it: there is not enough money to be made advertising a public project. This subplot shows Galbraith's most serious critique of advertising and consumer culture. We as a society sacrifice parks, clean streets, and public art on the altar of personal consumption. There is little profit in products that can't be consumed by individuals. So the efforts of mad men are not employed to create the desire for objects such as better schools or good roads.[9]

To pay for these public services, Galbraith would impose a decidedly regressive (and ironically illiberal) sales tax rather than the graduated income tax.[10] This willingness to impose taxes is based in part on his account of freedom. The sales tax adds to the cost of public services, which, inturn, adds to the cost of consumer goods. You can't consume one without paying for the other. This will mean that products are more expensive and there will be items that people can no longer afford. But remember that the desire advertising creates for luxuries is not free desire. And because the choice is not really free, there is no loss of consumer freedom. If some of the money we would spend on luxuries is taxed away, we do not lose anything that we *really* wanted.

Where Galbraith focuses on the loss of public goods with low taxes, Friedman argues that all taxes infringe on our freedom and decrease the incentive to work. His argument is likewise rooted in his beliefs about free will. If consumers' desires are genuine, then taking money from people and using that money for something they would not choose violates their freedom. If people can't do what they want with their money, they simply won't want to work. Friedman's argument is presented in one thirteen-second scene in "Out of Town" (episode 301).[11] Harry Crane is indignant about the progressive income tax. "There is no point in ever making over forty thousand dollars a year if it's just going to be taxed at sixty-nine percent. You're working for them. And God forbid you really make it. Everything over seventy grand is eighty-one percent." Harry also lives out Galbraith's reply to such an objection: people are motivated to work by relative salaries, not after-tax take-home pay.[12] In "The Benefactor" (episode 203), when Harry realizes that Ken Cosgrove has a higher salary, he is not comforted by the fact that the difference is being taxed away. In short, we want the status that comes with the salary; the disposable income doesn't mean that much to us. The fact that Harry exemplifies both sides of the argument is probably a sign that both Galbraith and Freidman are partly correct.

"He'll Never Play Golf Again"

According to Galbraith, Sterling Cooper does not merely create consumer desires. Sterling Cooper also helps to create an image of corporate reality that helps to maintain the larger culture of private consumption. Galbraith is at his cynical best describing the image corporate executives have of themselves. They believe they are heroes and risk-takers who live dangerously. The truth is that while small-business owners may lead a precarious existence at the whim of market forces, top executives in big corporations are largely insulated from those risks.[13]

Sterling Cooper's in-house tycoon, Bert Cooper, imagines that he is one of the few creative supermen. But what does Bert

Cooper actually do? He collects art. He embraces Japanese culture—at least shoelessness. Naturally, he reads Ayn Rand. In "Three Sundays" (episode 204), the staff is called into the office on a Sunday. American Airlines has moved up the pitch meeting and everything needs to be ready Monday morning. Bert Cooper is not at the brainstorming session. He is not in the working groups. We see Bert at the lunch buffet: he has stepped on some gum, and in a rage about manners he fires the only secretary with gum in her mouth. She is shocked; her gum is in her mouth, not on Cooper's sock. Duck quickly takes her aside and thanks her "for getting him out of here for the day." He assures her that Cooper "won't remember firing you." What about Roger Sterling? While the staff is working on the important American Airlines pitch, the other man with his name in the lobby is in a hotel with a prostitute. Roger doesn't even appear on the organizational chart when Sterling Cooper is reorganized.

So what is the essential skill set of the upper executive at Sterling Cooper? We learn that after Guy MacKendrick loses a foot in a freak lawn mower accident in "Guy Walks into an Advertising Agency" (episode 306). MacKendrick is Cambridge-educated, brilliant, charming, and a real "high flyer." None of these skills involve feet. Nonetheless, Guy must be fired: "He'll never play golf again."

Advertising helps to maintain the executive's self-image. The Sterling Cooper conference room sees a parade of self-important executives and their entourages. Clearly, the campaigns are as much about the importance of the executives as they are about the product. In "New Amsterdam" (episode 104), Walter Veith, chairman of Bethlehem Steel, marches into the conference room—he has just beaten Pete Campbell, and his good feet, at golf—and proclaims, "When I come to town I like to do my business and go home. So what do you fellows have for me?" He rejects Don's idea, but Pete convinces him to stay another night. At drinks that evening he is disappointed that Pete didn't bring his redheaded "cousin" to the bar, but he is sure "we can make do with this branch of the family." Pete has a lot of pretty young "cousins" to help executives stay on task. While we rarely see consumers fall for Don's magic, we watch executives get played every week. The campaign that wins Veith over contains the slogan "Bethlehem Steel—The Backbone of America." It beats out Don's first idea, "New York: Brought to You by Bethlehem Steel." This first idea didn't make this executive feel important enough. Veith felt that it was "an ad for cities, not steel." Veith feels that the backbone idea is "concise and strong," just how he would like to feel about himself. Sterling Cooper helps to create and maintain the image business leaders have of themselves as tough, no-nonsense men who pulled themselves up by their own bootstraps. The show plays this for comic effect, but there is a serious social point in the comedy. In Galbraith's writing the false belief of Veith and those like him—that they are hard-working, self-made, and living a dangerous life—is part of the reason people are opposed to taxes and social spending.

Advertising Is Color-blind

Unless you collect antiques, you don't watch *Mad Men* on an Admiral TV. In the 1950s, Admiral was an industry leader, one of the first to offer color sets. In the 1970s the company was broken up and sold. "The Fog" (episode 305) shows Pete Campbell inheriting the Admiral Television account in 1963. Sales are flat nationwide, but he notices that they are growing in Detroit, Newark, Chicago, and other Negro areas. Pete does exactly what Milton Friedman says a good business-man should do: he tries to make money. Friedman's logic is compelling. "There is an economic incentive in a free mar-ket to separate economic efficiency from other characteris-tics of the individual."[14] The business that discriminates puts itself at a competitive disadvantage. A business that misses the opportunity to reach a new market may not be around in ten years. According to Freidman, consumerism can have social advantages. Pete is stunned that no one is willing to accept such compelling logic.

He approaches Hollis, the black elevator operator. Hollis is uncomfortable and unwilling to reveal any insight into Negro TV preferences. When Pete presses, Hollis mildly asserts: "We've got bigger problems to worry about than TV." Pete is shocked: "You're thinking about this in a very narrow way. The idea is that everyone is going to have a house, a car, a TV, the American dream." Hollis turns forward and starts the elevator. All Pete can tell him is the truth: "It's my job." According to Friedman, it *is* his job. Pete had asked if Hollis thought Pete was a bigot, but the answer doesn't really matter. Pete's job is to find out what people want and try to sell it to them. If we just let the market provide people with what they want, everyone wins, he thinks. Why can't Hollis just see that?

Pete brings the idea to the Admiral executives. He shows that they can advertise to Negroes for pennies on the dollar and demonstrates that a small increase in sales in one Negro market would earn as much money as a nationwide sales increase. They don't even need white ads and black ads. They could save money by having integrated ads! This is Friedman's argument: a business that cares about an irrelevant factor like race raises their own costs of doing business while providing a cheaper option to their competition. The soon-to-be-out-of-business Admiral executives are appalled. Their response is astoundingly ignorant: "Who's to say Negroes aren't buying Admiral televisions because they think white people want them?" This is exactly the market intelligence that Hollis wouldn't give up. Freidman thinks that if you know why Negroes like Admiral televisions, then you can craft the right ad and sell more. If Admiral would just ignore race altogether and let the market work, everyone would win! Why can't the executives just see that?

When Pete is called on the carpet by dumbfounded and irate Lane, Roger, and Bert, his only defense is Friedman's: "It seems illogical to me that they would reject an opportunity to make more money." Roger and Bert will have none of it. But Lane realizes that "there is money to be made in the Negro market." At the end of season three, Don wants Pete for their new company because Pete was ahead of the curve on the Negro market. Don and Lane are willing to ignore race. The new agency, Sterling Cooper Draper Pryce, might win. Friedman is not as naive as Pete Campbell; he doesn't expect the free market to solve all problems overnight. But in the long run, Freidman believes, the market can solve these problems.

In the Long Run We're All Dead

If the *Mad Men* storyline were to continue into the new millennium, Peggy Olsen and Pete Campbell's child could be running the agency, and he would have to confront the key issue that Galbraith and Friedman reflected on as they revisited their work before they died: the anticompetitive collaboration between large corporations and the government that emerged in the latter half of the twentieth century. Large corporations have been able to use the government to create regulation that insulates them from the competitive forces of the market. By the 1990s, both Friedman and Galbraith saw this as a serious problem for our economic well-being.

In Freidman's conception, the free market works because consumers are free in the libertarian sense. It is the free choice of consumers that determines a business's success or failure. Theoretically, this means that businesses must be constantly trying to discover and produce what consumers want at the lowest price. Businesses make money, and the consumers are happy. But consumers can be fickle, and businessmen can be greedy. When corporations can shape regulations, they invariably protect themselves from consumer-driven market forces. These corporations no longer have to worry about satisfying consumer desires. For Freidman, corporate control of government means that the market cannot work to the advantage of consumers.[15]

Galbraith's compatibilist conception of freedom fuels his worries. Corporations use advertising to create consumer desires, and we act on those created desires. According to Galbraith, government power is supposed to counter the power of corporate advertising. The government is supposed to tax consumers and provide services that people should want but might not choose on their own. When corporations can control government power, the disparity between private wealth and public squalor becomes more pronounced. For Galbraith, corporate control of government means that resources are devoted to corporate welfare, not the common good.[16]

Bringing Corporations and Government Together

The seed of this problem is planted in "The Inheritance" (episode 210). Don and Pete head out to an aerospace conference. Everyone there will be "trying to figure out how to put a man on the moon. Or blow up Moscow, whichever one costs more." Sterling Cooper's mission does not involve products or even consumers. It needs to sell corporations to congressmen and congressmen to corporations. In the end, Galbraith and Freidman have different reasons, but they agree on one important thing: when Sterling Cooper can bring corporations and government together, consumers will be less happy.

NOTES

1. John Kenneth Galbraith, *The Affluent Society: 40th Anniversary Edition* (Boston: Houghton Mifflin, 1998), 117.

2. Ibid., 124 ff.

3. Milton Friedman, *Capitalism and Freedom: 40th Anniversary Edition* (Chicago: University of Chicago Press, 2002), ix.

4. Milton Friedman, "The Conventional Wisdom of J.K. Galbraith," in *Freidman on Galbraith* (Vancouver: The Fraser Institute, 1977), 15.

5. Friedman, 1977, 14.

6. Ibid.

7. Galbraith, 188.

8. Ibid., 186–ff.

9. Ibid., 112.

10. Ibid., 228.

11. Friedman, 2002, 173.

12. Galbraith, 68.

13. Ibid., 84.

14. Friedman, 2002, 109, and ff.

15. These reflections are not in the introduction to Freidman, 2002. Freidman made the remarks in a 2006 interview that can be found online at the Library of Economics and Liberty, www.econlib.org/library/Columns/y2006/Friedmantranscript.html. In the interview, Freidman cites an unpublished lecture, "Suicidal Impulses of the Business Community."

16. Galbraith, xi.

PART TWO

"THERE IS NO BIG LIE, THERE IS NO SYSTEM, THE UNIVERSE IS INDIFFERENT": *MAD MEN* AND THE PROBLEM OF MEANING

PETE, PEGGY, DON, AND THE DIALECTIC OF REMEMBERING AND FORGETTING

John Fritz

Blessed are the forgetful: for they get over their
stupidities, too.

—Friedrich Nietzsche (1844–1900)[1]

More than anything else, *Mad Men* is a television show
about remembering and forgetting. But while memory and
remembering have a rich history that spans from the ancient
Greeks to contemporary philosophers, remembering's conceptual opposite—forgetting—has not fared as well. Friedrich
Nietzsche, however, provides us with a potent explanation of
the positive power of active forgetting that can illuminate the
characters of Pete Campbell, Peggy Olson, and Don Draper.

Pete Campbell and Remembering

"Why can't I get anything good all at once?"

—Pete Campbell in "Out of Town" (episode 301)

Pete Campbell is unable to forget the past. His pettiness, jealousy, and constant temper tantrums are a direct result of his unhealthy memory. Nietzsche, in the second of his *Untimely Meditations*, titled *On the Uses and Disadvantages of History for Life*, challenges the idea that history and its remembrance are unqualifiedly good. He claims that too much history, too much remembering, can ultimately destroy the present and the future, saying that "there is a degree of sleeplessness, of rumination, of the historical sense, which is harmful and ultimately fatal to the living thing."[2] We can see this in people we know who "live in the past," especially when they cannot move forward with their lives. When we remember *too much*, our pasts can hinder us; the future is annihilated, and the present only exists in constant reference to our memories. The past has value for Nietzsche, though, only insofar as it *serves* the present and the future, insofar as it *serves life*. The past and its remembrance loom as a constant threat to the health and strength of an individual. As Nietzsche says, "Man . . . braces himself against the great and ever greater pressure of what is past: it pushes him down or bends him sideways, it encumbers his steps as a dark, invisible burden."[3]

One extreme of the dialectic of remembering and forgetting now reveals itself. The person who is unable to forget his or her misfortunes, who is constantly "bent" and "pushed" by the past, is unable to fully embrace the present and the future in a robust and healthy way. Nietzsche compares the person who cannot forget to a dyspeptic, someone who stews in their own juices because "he cannot 'have done' with anything."[4] People who cannot forget are condemned to the past and to never being able to move forward with their lives. They allow even the smallest transgression to eat them alive and are constantly tortured. This is Pete Campbell.

Pete is motivated mostly by petty, reactive instincts. He feels the world owes him something, even when he actually doesn't deserve it. He cannot "have done with anything." Occurrences that would normally be non-issues for strong, healthy people cause the deepest pettiness and resentment in Pete toward those he blames for the things that go wrong in his life. He feels supremely entitled, despite never having accomplished anything of note. The inability to forget drives his actions. We learn in "New Amsterdam" (episode 104) that Pete's "aristocratic" parents do not value his profession and that they have neglected to give him the same help throughout his life that they gave to his brother. Perhaps this causes his outlook, his long memory, and the rancor that motivates many of his actions.

A case in point is in "5G" (episode 105) when Ken Cosgrove's short story is published in the *Atlantic Monthly*. A strong, forgetful, healthy person might congratulate Cosgrove while perhaps feeling a slight sting of jealousy. We know that everyone at Sterling Cooper is a failed artist, but Cosgrove's stories are actually good enough to be printed in a reputable publication. Upon hearing this, Pete is eaten alive by his jealousy. Cosgrove's success comes at the expense of Pete's feelings, which are hurt as a direct result of his deep lack of character. He is unable to forget the feelings of inadequacy and impotence that are caused by his coworker's success, all while feeling entitled to his own legitimate success, despite not legitimately deserving it.

Cosgrove's success causes Pete to try to force his new wife to get his own ludicrous story about a talking bear published, all to nurse his wounded pride. What makes this even more ridiculous is that for his wife to get his story published, she has to bargain with the man who took her virginity, which is a compromising situation to say the very least. *And Pete knows this*. But his petty jealousy and ambition know no bounds. A magnanimous, strong person would simply congratulate Cosgrove and forget the incident or work harder at writing if that is what he really cares about. We even get the feeling that it isn't success as a writer that Pete cares about, but the fact that Cosgrove succeeded and he failed. But Pete feels no qualms about forcing his wife into an incredibly awkward situation to satisfy his desire for success. When she does come through with an offer for publication in *Boys' Life*, Pete is further enraged because that isn't good enough for him.

This tension between Pete and Ken Cosgrove is amplified at the beginning of the third season in "Out of Town," when both men are promoted to share the same head of accounts position. While Cosgrove's attitude toward the situation shows character, Pete is totally infuriated at the prospect of sharing the position. Cosgrove sees that management's plan is for him and Pete to compete for the permanent position, causing them to hate each other. While Cosgrove "refuses to participate in that," Pete is filled with such rancor that he responds by saying that he will not be "holding hands" with Cosgrove as they move forward.

Pete's pettiness is clearly on display in his treatment of Peggy during the first season. After Peggy and Pete's illicit hookup, from which they have an illegitimate "love child," Peggy gets her first real victory with the Belle Jolie lipstick campaign in "The Hobo Code" (episode 108). Here again, Pete is jealous of Peggy's legitimate success, which came through insight and hard work. Pete is insecure and deeply disturbed by the fact that this secretary with whom he just had a fling could do work that is as deserving of praise as anything of which he is capable. His resentment of Peggy's success, partially motivated by sexual stereotypes, continues as she moves up the ladder at Sterling Cooper. He is infuriated when Don promotes her to work on Clearasil, and he actively tries to get Don to ignore her work on the Rejuvenator. Pete is unable to be happy for anyone, including himself, because he is unable to forget their success and his inadequacies.

Peggy Olson and Forgetting

While one extreme is an individual who is unable to forget (Pete Campbell), another extreme is an individual who is *too* able to forget (Peggy Olson). In writing about the latter, Nietzsche talks about children, who literally have no past to encumber them.[5] Here, as elsewhere, Nietzsche connects the idea of forgetting with happiness, strength, and vitality. This runs parallel to his connection of an excess of remembering with unhappiness and self-laceration. Nietzsche writes: "It is always the same thing that makes happiness happiness: the ability to forget. . . . He who cannot . . . forget all the past . . . will never know what happiness is"[6] It is necessary to forget the past, at least to a degree, in order to embrace the present and, especially, the future. The individual who forgets to an extreme degree is not hindered by the past at all, but rather must live *only* for the present or the future. While Nietzsche tends to praise individuals who are capable of forgetting their pasts as powerful, in Peggy we can see the obvious complications that can be caused by forgetting.

Peggy's extreme, active forgetfulness is manifested mostly in season two, but there is also perhaps one major example of active forgetting in season one. Peggy's ambition and strength result in her ability not only to block out the past but to alter her present as well, all for the sake of the future. Similar to Pete's situation, Peggy's ambition and her dissatisfaction with her status as a secretary at Sterling Cooper drive her character arc. After experiencing several professional victories throughout season one, it becomes clear that Peggy is destined for a greater role at Sterling Cooper than secretary. Season one culminates with the realization that Peggy is pregnant with Pete Campbell's child. The biggest surprise was not that Peggy was able to ignore her tryst with Pete and continue climbing the ladder at Sterling Cooper, but that she was able to forget the present state of her own body because of the threat her pregnancy posed to her own advancement. Dresses were ripped, after all. Vicious jokes were made by the men in the office. Cosgrove called Peggy a "lobster—all the meat's in the tail" ("Shoot," episode 109). Her pregnancy was made all but apparent to the viewer. The changes in her own body would seem obvious to a person directed in some sense toward their past or their present. But it takes the doctor forcing Peggy's own hand to her stomach to convince her that she is actually pregnant.

Peggy feels no connection whatsoever to her baby, even going so far as refusing to hold the child. Peggy's orientation toward her future and her uncanny ability to forget are the only explanations for how she could be nine months pregnant without even an inkling of the impending birth of her son. Since the meaning of that birth would be the logical equivalent to the termination of her budding career as a copywriter at Sterling Cooper, she is able to forget not only the past but the present, as well. At this point Peggy is a character who lives completely outside of herself, oriented entirely toward the future and the object of her ambition.

A more obvious case of active forgetting is the way that Peggy acts (or doesn't act) in season two in regard to the child she gave up for adoption. We find out at the end of that season that Peggy gave the baby away (after viewers were deliberately misled by the writers to believe that Peggy's sister Anita was raising the baby). She confesses this fact to Pete, though her face betrays little or no emotion. It seems obvious that Peggy *does not regret* how things went. She tells Pete that she could have had him in her life if she had wanted that. When Pete doesn't understand, she says, "You got me pregnant. I had a baby. And I gave it away."

"What?"

"I had your baby and I gave it away. *I wanted other things.*"[7] Even in remembering and confessing her past to the father of her child, Peggy remains relatively unaffected. She admits that it was her desire for success that drove her actions. She wanted other things. And she is only a little more emotional here than someone recounting a disappointing meal they had a few days earlier. Like Don, Peggy is hardened. To forget is not necessarily to be entirely ignorant of the past. Rather, to forget means that the past no longer affects you in any meaningful way, that it has lost its affective meaning.

In "Flight 1" (episode 202) Peggy twice comes into contact with her sister's child, born around the same time as her own. This might cause regret or at least some show of emotion from someone whose past remains affective in their present. But in both cases—when she sees the sleeping children in their beds at her sister's and when she is forced to hold her sister's screaming child while her sister receives communion—Peggy's face tells no story. It tells no story because there is no story. The past is irrelevant. It has been forgotten.

Peggy's sister describes her best when confessing to Father Gill in "Three Sundays" (episode 204). Anita feels that Peggy "does whatever she feels like with no regard at all." In her confession to Father Gill she says, "I'm so angry at my little sister . . . she had a child out of wedlock . . . she seduced a married man . . . it's a terrible sin and she acts like it didn't even happen . . . she goes on like it didn't even happen . . . nothing at all." Anita is distraught over her sister's actions and the attention that she has received because of her work. But if Peggy "goes on like it didn't even happen," it is not simply because she is mendaciously using her psychological state leading up to, during, and after her pregnancy as a cheap excuse to avoid any type of responsibility for her actions. It is because Peggy, like Don, has forgotten the past because it is necessary to move on. She wanted other things and she chose other things. Raising Pete's baby was incompatible with continuing her career. She chose her career and forgot about everything except her future.

Interestingly, the deliberate advice to actively forget her past comes from the show's main character, Don Draper. In one of the pivotal scenes of season two, we find out in a flashback that Don visited Peggy while she was in forced psychiatric care after the birth of her baby. Peggy can clearly answer questions about the year and the place, but she has no idea why she is there, despite the doctor repeatedly explaining to her that she had a baby. Don, perhaps seeing Peggy's potential, sings the Nietzschean song of forgetting to her as she lies in her hospital bed. "Get out of here and move forward. This never happened. It'll shock you how much this never happened."[8] We find out that it was Don's advice that allowed Peggy to actualize the ability to forget in a willful way, whereas the first instance of her forgetting (the fact that she was pregnant) was accidental or unconscious or perhaps even caused by genuine ignorance. Don counsels Peggy to forget the past, and, unlike Pete, Peggy has enough *strength* to do so.

This idea of Peggy's forgetfulness is a minor theme throughout the rest of the season. After cleaning up Don's mess with Bobbie Barrett, she tells him, "You'll have to believe me that I'll forget this. I don't want you treating me badly because I remind you of it. This can be fixed."[9] Similarly, she tells Bobbie Barrett, "If you're lucky, it'll just disappear," in reference to the same situation. Peggy wills herself back to her career at Sterling Cooper. She gives the baby away. And she remains more or less unaffected through the rest of the season because of the positive power of active forgetfulness that was revealed to her by Don.

Don Draper and the Dialectic of Memory and Forgetting

Pete Campbell represents the one extreme of remembering, and Peggy Olson represents the contrary extreme of forgetfulness. If we understand the extreme positions, forgetfulness and memory, the third position reveals itself as an interplay or relationship between the two, with Don Draper sometimes being forced to remember, sometimes successfully forgetting. It is this tension between forgetting and remembering the past that produces most of the complexity in Draper's character. He knowingly worships at the altar of forgetfulness, but he is always recaptured by his past. It is his greatest wish to forget the past because only this would allow him to move on. But other characters, incidents, and seemingly insignificant occurrences reawaken Don's past in a way that constantly threatens his present and his future.

In Nietzsche's later work, *On the Genealogy of Morals*, he writes: "To be incapable of taking one's enemies, one's accidents, even one's misdeeds seriously for very long—that is the sign of strong, full natures in whom there is an excess of the power to form, to mold, to recuperate and to forget. . . . Such a man shakes off with a *single* shrug many vermin that eat deep into others"[10] Here it is not just health that concerns Nietzsche, but *strength*. He seems to indicate that strong individuals are more forgetful than individuals who are eaten alive by their own pasts, like Pete Campbell. Rather than a mathematical equality of remembering and forgetting, Nietzsche presents the strong individual as one who is able to forget more than he remembers. Nietzsche writes: "It will be immediately obvious how there could be no happiness, no cheerfulness, no hope, no pride, no *present*, without forgetfulness."[11] Don ultimately sides with Nietzsche in privileging forgetfulness over memory. He knows that forgetting is essential to the robust expression of his vitality and his life. But Don is *constantly reminded* and can never truly escape a past that he would like only too well to leave behind. Don *knows* that forgetting is essential for life. But despite his best efforts, the past looms too close behind him, threatening to devour his new life.

That Don ultimately takes a Nietzschean stance on the value of forgetting should be obvious to any viewer of

Mad Men. After all, it is Don who counsels Peggy to do whatever it takes to get out of the hospital, to move on, because "this never happened." Don's advice is indicative of his own strategic employment of forgetfulness. Further, it shows us that Don does not simply have a bad memory, but that he is *aware* of the value of forgetting. In telling Peggy to move forward as if the past had never happened, Don tips his hand and reveals what we should have already realized: he uses forgetting as a tool to relieve the pressure of the past, which threatens to destroy his present and his future.

In season one we learn that Don Draper's real name is Dick Whitman, that he has stolen another soldier's identity to escape his own past, and that he is totally reluctant to even discuss, much less truly revisit, his own past. When asked about his upbringing in "Ladies Room" (episode 102), he says, "Just think of me as Moses. I was a baby in a basket." Later in the same episode he tells his wife Betty, in reference to his past, "It's like politics, religion, and sex. Why talk about it?"

In "5G," Don's brother Adam discovers that Don is actually alive and well, which is what he had always suspected. At first Don denies even knowing Adam, claiming that he is mistaken. When this strategy fails, Don meets Adam for lunch and tells him that revisiting the past and having a relationship with Adam are both out of the question. "I'm not buying your lunch, because this never happened." Later, after Don burns the picture of himself and his brother, he makes it even more evident how much it is worth to not to confront the echoes of his past: $5,000. He offers Adam the money if he will forget that he ever discovered Don's true identity. As Don explains to Adam in one of the hardest scenes to watch in the series, "I have a life—and it only goes in one direction—forward."

After getting high with his mistress in "The Hobo Code," Don has a flashback to his childhood when his father's farm was visited by a hobo, a "gentleman of the rails." In what is surely a formative moment for the young Dick Whitman, the hobo explains to him that because he moves from town to town, every day is brand new. He has severed the tie with his own history and has completely escaped his previous life. The hobo "sleeps like a stone" because he has freed himself of the pressures of his past. This is meant to show a moment in Don's childhood that deeply influences the way he lives his life as an adult. In forgetting his childhood, his family, and his past, Don lives like the hobo, not bound to conventional codes of morality or obligations because he has annihilated the very thing that gives power to those codes—the past.

Don is sometimes too successful at forgetting. In "The New Girl" (episode 205), after Peggy handles the incredibly delicate situation that results from the car crash with Bobbie Barrett by bailing Don out of jail, Don truly forgets the trouble that Peggy went through for him *by the next day*. Peggy put up a significant amount of money to bail Don out of jail after the crash. In the office the next day, when she is ill-prepared for a client but expects Don to remember that she was busy saving his ass all night—going so far as to house Bobbie Barrett after the crash—Don heartlessly scolds Peggy in the presence of other coworkers for not being ready for her meeting. When Don and Peggy are alone, in what must have been a true test for Peggy, she confronts Don, asking him to return the large amount of money she lent him for his bail. Don *genuinely forgot the whole thing in the span of one night*, despite wearing a cast on his arm from the accident. He halfheartedly apologizes to Peggy and gives her the money, saying, "I guess when you try to forget something, you have to forget everything."

These incidents and the general theme of the show should be enough to convince us that Don knows that in order to be strong, forgetting his past is essential. But Don is more complicated than either Peggy or Pete. While he knows that it is essential to forget the past, he cannot always do so because he is sometimes *forced* to remember it. He remains incapable of truly actualizing the Nietzschean ideal of forgetfulness because the past eventually does find him, again and again.

Don's memories are always triggered externally. We never find Don simply contemplating his past. A circumstance, an object, or a line delivered by another character seems necessary to force Don to reactivate his past. We see this in the hobo flashbacks, when smoking pot causes Don to remember his life on the farm because he looks into the mirror in his mistress's bathroom. We see this again at the beginning of season three when Don is warming milk for the pregnant Betty, which forces him to reflect on the disreputable circumstances of his own birth. This dynamic is also at work with Adam's "suicide box," which is literally a box of memories.

The theme of Don's remembrances always being externally triggered is perhaps most obvious in the thrilling finale of season one, "The Wheel" (episode 113), when Don pitches the Carousel to Kodak. Don uses the touching photographs of his own past to sell the idea. But being confronted with the actual images of his own happiness with his real family forces Don to remember and to realize what he stands to lose by not going with Betty to her family's house for Thanksgiving. He rushes home to go with her and the children, even imagining what it will look like. In probably the most perfect use of music in film since the Pixies' "Where is My Mind?" played at the end of *Fight Club*, Bob Dylan's "Don't Think Twice, It's Alright" plays as Don sits on his staircase, alone, realizing he has missed and is missing his family.

"Have Done" with the Past

In the end, Peggy Olson is the true Nietzschean. Her active forgetfulness, inspired by Don's advice, allows her to move forward despite having given up a baby fathered by Pete Campbell. While she eventually tells Pete this, she does not seem affected because she has forgotten her past. It has no effect on her present, even when recounting it to Pete. Campbell, on the other hand, constantly proves that he is unable to forget even the slightest transgression and that he is doomed to allow "small vermin" to eat deep into him because of his lack of forgetfulness. Don Draper knows that it is necessary to "have done" with the past, but nonetheless he is constantly reminded of it by external factors, making him incapable of truly forgetting, forcing him to always be caught up in the dialectic of remembering and forgetting.

NOTES

1. Friedrich Nietzsche, *Beyond Good and Evil*, translated by Walter Kaufmann (New York: Vintage Books, 1966), 217, 146.

2. Friedrich Nietzsche, "On the Uses and Disadvantages of History for Life," in *Untimely Meditations*, translated by R. J. Hollingdale, edited by Daniel Breazeale (Cambridge: Cambridge University Press, 1997), 62, italics in the original.

3. Ibid., 61.

4. Friedrich Nietzsche, *On the Genealogy of Morals*, translated and edited by Walter Kaufmann (New York: Vintage Books, 1987), Second Essay, 1, 58.

5. For instance, see Nietzsche, "On the Uses and Disadvantages of History for Life," 61.

6. Ibid., 62.

7. "Meditations in an Emergency" (episode 213). Italics added by author, obviously.

8. "The New Girl" (episode 205).

9. Ibid.

10. Nietzsche, *On the Genealogy of Morals*, First Essay, 10, 39.

11. Nietzsche, *On the Genealogy of Morals*, Second Essay, 1, 58.

THE EXISTENTIAL VOID
OF ROGER STERLING

Raymond Angelo Belliotti

Exquisitely portrayed by the actor John Slattery, Roger Sterling is one of two senior partners of Sterling Cooper. His father founded the firm with Bertram Cooper, with whom Roger has had a long personal relationship beginning when he was a child and Bertram was in his early twenties. Cooper's deceased wife introduced Sterling to Mona, the woman he married.

Sterling is an avid consumer of alcohol and cigarettes and an unrepentant womanizer. Although two heart attacks caused him to reassess his lifestyle, the phases of superficial intro-spection passed and he resumed his hedonistic patterns. He soon after divorced his wife, struggled to find a suitable role in his daughter's upcoming wedding, and convinced twenty-year-old secretary Jane Siegel to marry him. Anticipating his costly divorce and upcoming nuptials, Sterling supported the Putnam Powell and Lowe takeover of Sterling Cooper. Although often strikingly blunt with his institutional subor-dinates, Sterling exudes a dry wit and buttoned-down charm.

His face betrays his excesses: he appears significantly older than his chronological age.

At first blush, cynical viewers are tempted to dismiss Roger Sterling as a man "who was born on third base and thinks he hit a triple."[1] While he exudes an unshakeable smugness and an imperial sense of entitlement and relishes aristocratic privilege, he cannot be defined so neatly. Roger is also uncommonly intelligent and disarmingly frank and brandishes a stiletto-sharp wit. Although viewers may be hard-pressed to chronicle how Sterling fills his work day—other than by strolling from office to office cadging alcohol, ogling female employees and clients, and targeting victims of his barbs—he serves an important corporate function as Sterling Cooper's troubleshooter. Roger mollifies ruffled clients, deflects potential lawsuits, and blows just enough smoke to remain credible while maximizing firm profits.

Philosophical analysis can help us understand the complicated, concealed, enigmatic inner life of Roger Sterling. Does his life exemplify existential values such as intensity and authenticity? Does he understand and exercise his radical freedom? Or is he mired in "everydayness" as he strolls unreflectively through a life of habit and routine punctuated only by hedonistic diversions? Do his entrenched behaviors betray his consuming existential anxiety over his mortality? In short, is Roger Sterling simply a stereotypical 1950s/1960s bureaucratic man or can he be reasonably viewed as an existential hero?

The Relentless Hedonist

The existential philosopher Søren Kierkegaard (1813–1855) sketched three stages of life, processes by which we make choices, act, and define ourselves.[2] Kierkegaard's first stage, the aesthetic stage, fits Roger Sterling more crisply than one of his own custom-tailored three-piece suits.

The person in the aesthetic stage basks in the immediacy of the moment. The pursuit of sensations and feelings rooted in particular pleasures defines this stage of life. Detached from firm commitment to the extent possible and governed by sense, impulse, and emotion, Kierkegaard's aesthetic person recognizes no fixed, universal moral standards. Instead, aesthetic persons strive for the absence of all limits, except those imposed by their own tastes. Boredom is taken to be the worst evil. Immersing themselves in pleasure, whether sensual or intellectual, aesthetic people live overwhelmingly for the moment, in search of yet another self-gratifying experience.

Let the words of Roger Sterling consign him to Kierkegaard's aesthetic lifestyle. First, Sterling distances himself from personal commitment to the extent possible. On the topic of intimacy, love, and friendship: "I have a very good friend . . . cannot remember the guy's name."[3] On lasting commitment: "I'll tell you the same thing I told my daughter. If you put a penny in a jar every time you make love in the first year of marriage and then you take a penny out of the jar every time you make love in the second year, you know what you have? A jar full of pennies."[4]

Second, Sterling luxuriates in the immediacy of the moment and in hedonistic self-gratification. On the topic of pursuing pleasure in the present: "Don't you love the chase? Sometimes it doesn't work out, those are the stakes. But when it does work out, it's like having that first cigarette: head gets all dizzy, your heart pounds, knees go weak. Remember that? Old business is just old business."[5] On concern for others, when Don Draper asks Sterling what women want, Roger replies, "Who cares?"[6] On the drinking life: "You do not know how to drink. Your whole generation, you drink for the wrong reasons. My generation, we drink because it's good, because it feels better than unbuttoning your collar, because we deserve it. We drink because it's what men do."[7] As he recovers from a heart attack, Roger evaluates his adulterous relationship with Joan

Holloway: "Look, I want to tell you something because you're very dear to me and I hope you understand it comes from the bottom of my damaged, damaged heart. You are the finest piece of ass I ever had and I don't care who knows it. I am so glad I got to roam those hillsides."[8]

Third, the mere thought of boredom leads Sterling to break out in hives. Again, after surface reflection on his own life as he recovers from a heart attack: "Jesus! I've been living the last twenty years like I'm on shore leave. What the hell is that about?"[9]

Fourth, Sterling detaches himself from moral reflection and adherence to firm moral principles. On the proper treatment of institutional subordinates: "Throw him a token sum, watch a wave of pathetic gratitude wash across his gormless mug, and send him back to the salt mines, ignorant of the knowledge that you spend the equivalent of his yearly salary on a week's worth of hookers and vodka. And make a point of not remembering his name the next time you see him."[10] When Guy MacKendrick—Putnam, Powell and Lowe's anointed fair-haired boy—arrives from London to assume leadership of Sterling Cooper Putnam, he is seriously injured at an office party when one of the secretaries accidentally drives a John Deere vehicle over his foot. When Roger Sterling is told that MacKendrick will probably lose his foot, he doesn't miss a beat: "Right when he got it in the door."[11]

We should be cautious about placing too much stock in Sterling's quips. Surely none of us should be evaluated entirely on a few miscellaneous remarks uttered when we are cracking wise. And, of course, we can cite evidence undermining the conclusion that Sterling is a prime example of Kierkegaard's aesthetic man: Roger was married for over twenty years to Mona. Unlike Kierkegaard's flighty aesthetic man, Roger Sterling was committed to family life and was also committed to his career. Moreover, Roger is now committed to Jane. He, not she, was pressing for the marriage. Accordingly, perhaps

I have only randomly selected a few similarities between the aesthetic man and Roger Sterling. Perhaps we should not exaggerate the comparison.

I would rejoin that the quotes from Roger Sterling are not peripheral to, but mirror, his lifestyle. His quips provide sharp commentary on his behavior. Sterling's professional and personal actions provide scant evidence that he is concerned with honoring moral principles. His career was staked out for him by his father and represents the easy, lucrative path of a scion born, after all, on third base. His marriage to Mona hardly rises to the level of Kierkegaard's subjective, existential truth. The marriage has never impeded Sterling's roving eyes and roaming hands. He admits on several occasions that passionate commitment was extinguished early in the relationship, and he has remained married largely because of social expectations, not because of a passionate, internal commitment. For Kierkegaard, subjective, existential truths require internal performances. The test is *how* a truth is held and the relative importance of the *way* a person's choice was formed. In an objective (nonexistential) sense, Sterling was married to Mona for over twenty years. The proposition that Mona and Roger were married is objectively true. But existentially, Sterling's commitment lacks the passionate inwardness that characterizes Kierkegaard's understanding of subjective, existential truth. Accordingly, the marriage was inauthentic: it lacked the internal commitment and emotional judgment that constitute existential truth. Although formally wed, the couple were not existentially united.

What should we predict about Roger's subsequent marriage to Jane? Is this only Roger's latest desperate attempt to soften the fear of his looming mortality? Is Roger finally happy? Or is he, in Don Draper's words, simply "foolish"?[12] If Kierkegaard were a betting man, he would cast his lot with Draper.

For Kierkegaard, aesthetic people such as Roger Sterling cravenly flee boredom, despair, and the burden of self-creation.

Continually pursuing more intense pleasures, the aesthetic person is doomed to collapse back into boredom and despair. Living in the present can, at best, provide only a partial attitude toward life. By never forging bonds, by weakly committing to projects, and by making only transitory choices, the aesthetic person is a spectator in the world and fails to define his own life sharply. His chosen end is his own beginning: vague dissatisfaction, a sense of no remedy, no salvation, a foreboding of nothingness. Kierkegaard insists that the aesthetic person's choices are to either remain in despair at this stage or to make a transition to the next one—the ethical stage—by choice and self-commitment. The ethical stage, among other things, embraces universal moral standards and is exemplified by congenial family life. It's hard to imagine that Roger Sterling will ever make that kind of commitment and live that kind of life.

The Last Man and the Will to Power

Friedrich Nietzsche (1844–1900) calls "the most despicable" creature the last man.[13] He describes the last man as a seeker of happiness defined by pleasure; a conformist geared primarily to adapting to and reflecting his environment; a person aspiring to comfort, the absence of obstacles, and the assumption of few risks; a relatively unreflective being who shuts out reality and eases his pain through "drugs" such as religion and subscribing to dominant social ideas; a timid soul who lacks the spirit of robust adventure and who pursues only simple goals.

Does this description fit Roger Sterling, the lovable reprobate? Surely, Roger defines happiness hedonistically and seeks material comfort. When he is asked what type of advertising agency he prefers, Sterling responds, "The kind where everybody has a summer house."[14] He drinks to anesthetize his pain, to massage his aristocratic sense of entitlement, to experience pleasure, and to facilitate communication. Sterling accepts conventional, dominant images of human success: material accumulation and authority over others. He unsqueamishly relishes his advantages and revels in his place in the agency's hierarchy. When Herman "Duck" Phillips, director of account services, requests more responsibility and remuneration, Sterling informs him that he'll have to advocate for himself at the partners' meeting. Duck accepts readily and says he would be honored to present his accomplishments. Sterling coldly and imperially answers, "Good, because I am at a loss."[15]

Roger Sterling is not involved in the creative end of advertising. Having simply assumed a career carved out by his father, Sterling is rarely introspective, and even when he is, his analysis is superficial and fleeting. He bears the stigmata of the last man, yet he may not be one. Whether or not his adventures are timid and his goals simple is debatable.

For Nietzsche, the greatest human beings do not strive for happiness grounded in maximizing pleasure and minimizing pain. Instead, they pursue power. The most refined pleasures are those accompanying our conscious reflection of the ascendancy of our strength.

Contentment, peace, and serenity are false idols. Genuine happiness requires struggle and grand obstacles. To increase power is to seek and overcome obstacles. The human needs for love, friendship, respect, and honor are manifestations of the will to power, not independent, conflicting impulses. Whereas "last men" live in order to survive, the greatest among us strive for distinction, even perfection. Both aspirations flow from the will to power, but the muted ambitions of last men—reflected primarily in their self-image of unthreatening, domesticated, and acceptable herd animals—are unworthy. The greatest among us assume responsibility for the challenging project of self-creation, take risks, and live according to self-imposed values.[16]

Although Roger Sterling embodies an aristocratic mentality, he falls far short of Nietzsche's grand creator. His work at the advertising agency requires "telling good jokes and lighting up smokes" more than ingenuity, innovation, and production. When Guy MacKendrick unveils Putnam, Powell and Lowe's new organizational chart, Roger Sterling's name is not included. When the error is pointed out, MacKendrick brushes it off as an oversight. Unsurprisingly, Sterling offers an ego-saving one-liner: "I make my job look too easy."[17] Moreover, nothing in Roger Sterling's personal life—surely not his banal seduction rituals and general tired, predictable approach to women—suggests grand creativity that would transform him in salutary ways. Sterling is less of a Nietzschean grand transcender and more of a man on a perpetual pendulum, covering the same ground as he oscillates between frustration (when his immediate desires are unsatisfied) and boredom (when his desires are satisfied and spawn a momentary euphoria that soon deflates). Whereas the grand transcender defines creativity as sculpting the self in ever more glorious and powerful ways, Roger Sterling traverses the same terrain in increasingly robotic fashion. As such, Sterling only reaffirms his past self instead of transcending to a higher form.

For Nietzsche, the will to power is not fulfilled unless it confronts struggle, resistance, and opposition. Pursuing power, in the sense of increasing influence and strengths, requires intentionally and actually finding obstacles to overcome. Indeed, the will to power is a will to the precise activity of struggling with and overcoming obstacles. Because suffering and pain attend the experience of such struggle, a robust will to power must desire suffering. The resulting paradox is that the fulfillment of the will to power—the overcoming of resistance—results in dissatisfaction, as the struggle has (temporarily) concluded. The will to power actually requires obstacles to the satisfaction of its specific desires because beyond specific desires, the will to power has a more fundamental desire to struggle with and overcome obstacles. In sum, the will to power deeply desires resistance to the satisfaction of its own specific desires. Accordingly, the will to power cannot embrace final serenity or permanent fulfillment. The satisfaction of one specific desire brings both fulfillment—a feeling of increased strength and influence—and dissatisfaction—as resistance has been overcome and is no longer present. Only endless striving and continual conquests fuel a robust will to power.[18]

Roger Sterling's will to power centers on hedonistic pursuits that Nietzsche would judge unworthy. He confronts resistance only in muted forms: women who are initially reluctant to succumb to his overtures, subordinates who are disturbed by office arrangements, and clients upset with service rendered. A surface reading might conclude that a strong parallel exists between Sterling's continual pursuit of seduction and Nietzsche's grand transcender who cannot attain fulfillment once and forever. But the grand transcender is Nietzsche's exemplar for reasons beyond simply being a relentless striver who cannot reach final serenity. The type of resistance the transcender confronts, the quality of the projects he pursues, the level of creativity he manifests, the products that result, and the self-transformation that occurs are all crucial. Judged by such criteria, Roger Sterling strikes us more as a man who is getting nowhere slowly than a grand transcender striving for self-mastery.

Authenticity

Martin Heidegger (1889–1976) gave to existentialism the terminology of authenticity. He described inauthentic human living as distinguished by wrongly denying freedom and succumbing to false ideas of inevitability. He suggests at least five partially overlapping ways in which I might be living inauthentically, denying my individuality.[19]

> I am *sunk in everydayness* if I live in the "they" and consider myself as *das Man*—which translates roughly to generic

humankind; thinking and acting in accord with "what one does" or "what people do"; subjugating myself to the mass of others; regarding myself as a member of a kind or type. If I accept the seductions of conformity, then a banal life of habit and routine, punctuated by diversions, follows. A particular example of this is distancing myself from reflection on my mortality. If I recognize abstractly that all human beings are mortal, but insist that my death has nothing to do with me now, then I prevent myself from consciously and continually creating who I will be. Heidegger calls this a mark of *falling*.

I am *denying my freedom and transcendence* if I think of myself as *necessarily* being who and what I am. Regarding the roles I play and the categories to which I belong as necessarily part of who I am reneges on my capability of transforming who I am.

I am *kneeling before false necessity* if I take my decisions, choices, and actions as being the appropriate, natural, inevitable result of the kind of person that I am. Doing so relegates my future to my unalterable nature.

I am *clinging to fixity* if I accept that I have a fixed, unalterable essence. Doing so denies my transcendence—my freedom and capability of transforming who I am—and overly empowers my facticity—my givenness, aspects of me that cannot be changed, such as my birth date, biological inheritance, birth parents, and the like.

I am *settling for chatter* if the overwhelming bulk of my conversation with others centers on small talk, babble, gossip, and shop. I am merely squandering time in nonthreatening ways. I avoid profound issues such as politics, religion, philosophy, and race because discussing such topics jeopardizes my acceptance by *das Man*. In sum, *das Man*, necessity, fixity, fallenness, and chatter are the standard bearers for inauthentic living.

Roger Sterling clearly settles for chatter. If he has ever had a serious discussion with anyone on a profound matter, viewers have not been privy to it. His actions suggest, but do not fully determine, that he clings to fixity, denies his freedom and transcendence, and kneels before false necessity. Outside of a few quickly passing moments of reflection while convalescing from heart attacks, Sterling displays no awareness of or predisposition to exercise his power to change.

Whether he is sunk in everydayness is less clear. His reflections on his own mortality were fleeting and conjured for the moments of his recovery while in the hospital. He unreflectively embraces conventional measures of success congenial to *das Man*. Sterling may or may not view himself as a member of a specific kind or type. He often flees from his freedom by blaming others, particularly Mona, for his problems. His relationship with Jane may be a reaction to his two brushes with death, but is not undertaken consciously in that vein.

For Heidegger, authentic human living focuses on transcendent self-creation in the context of one's facticity. I must *recognize my uniqueness* and not identify as a member of a kind or type. I must embrace *consciousness of my particular death* by heightening my awareness of my mortality instead of regarding mortality abstractly as universally pertinent. I must *embrace my freedom* by concentrating on the decisions, choices, and actions that constitute my life and that help form my self. I must *shape my future in context* by denying that I am a fixed essence, by accepting the limits of my facticity, and by understanding my transcendent possibilities. I must *appreciate the contingency of kinds and types* by viewing them as accidental memberships subject to reimagination and revision. Although none of us is entirely authentic or inauthentic, we differ in degree, and those differences distinguish the quality of our being.

Judged by Heidegger's criteria, Roger Sterling's life seems significantly more inauthentic than authentic. Critical to this judgment is the undeniable observation that Sterling neither displays a conscious desire to change in salutary ways nor participates in new projects or relationships that might have that effect.

Existential Values

The primary existential values are authenticity and intensity. Embracing a tragic sense of life, reaffirming the beauty of life while honestly facing its horrors, recognizing that suffering and anguish are required for fully human life, accepting our freedom and taking complete responsibility for our choices and actions, distancing ourselves from the petty fears and hopes of the faceless masses, heightening our consciousness of the human condition and of our own mortality, and bestowing our energies and enthusiasms upon the world are all paramount ways of manifesting and sustaining those values.[20]

When Roger Sterling is on his knees in blackface, crooning "My Old Kentucky Home" to Jane at a country club party they are hosting, Don Draper intuits that the performance is painfully inappropriate even for the early 1960s. Draper whispers to his wife, "Can we go?"[21] Viewers share Draper's uneasiness. They, too, flinch and are disappointed when Betty wants to remain at the party. Later in that same episode, when Sterling, with ashen complexion, world-weary eyes, and a lifeless glare, coolly accuses Draper and others of resenting his happiness, we are tempted to respond, "Happy, Roger? You could have fooled us!"

NOTES

1. A line famously uttered about George H. W. Bush by the former Texas governor Ann Richards at the 1988 Democratic convention. The origin of the quote is contestable, but *Time* magazine's Susan Fraker penned it in the May 30, 1983, issue, referring to the Superior Oil leader Howard Keck.

2. Søren Kierkegaard, *Either/Or*, translated by Alastair Hannay (London: Penguin Books, 1992).

3. "Six Month Leave" (episode 209).

4. "The New Girl" (episode 205).

5. "Three Sundays" (episode 204).

6. "Ladies Room" (episode 102).

7. "New Amsterdam" (episode 104).

8. "Indian Summer" (episode 111).

9. "Long Weekend" (episode 110).

10. "The Benefactor" (episode 203).

11. "Guy Walks into an Advertising Agency" (episode 306).

12. "My Old Kentucky Home" (episode 303).

13. Friedrich Nietzsche, *On the Genealogy of Morals*, translated by Walter Kaufmann and R. J. Hollingdale (New York: Vintage Books, 1967); *Thus Spoke Zarathustra*, translated by Walter Kaufmann, in *The Portable Nietzsche* (New York: Viking Press, 1954); *The Gay Science*, translated by Walter Kaufmann (New York: Random House, 1967); *The Will to Power*, translated by Walter Kaufmann and R. J. Hollingdale (New York: Vintage Books, 1968).

14. "Flight 1" (episode 202).

15. "The Jet Set" (episode 211).

16. Nietzsche, *Thus Spoke Zarathustra*, Part I, "Zarathustra's Prologue," 5; Part I, "On the Three Metamorphoses."

17. "Guy Walks into an Advertising Agency" (episode 306).

18. Nietzsche, *The Will to Power*, section 1067; *Thus Spoke Zarathustra*, Part I, "On the Thousand and One Goals"; Part II, "On Self-Overcoming"; Part II, "On Redemption."

19. Martin Heidegger, *Being and Time*, translated by John Macquarrie and Edward Robinson (New York: Harper & Row, 1962).

20. Nonexistentialists take these values and their subordinate prescriptions as, at best, necessary but not sufficient conditions for leading a good human life. After all, we can easily imagine a person who is existentially intense and authentic, but still a thoroughly immoral person who causes much unjustified injury to others.

21. "My Old Kentucky Home" (episode 303).

EGOLESS EGOISTS: THE SECOND-HAND LIVES OF MAD MEN

Robert White

Don Draper removes his shoes and enters the office of Bertram Cooper, senior partner of the advertising firm Sterling Cooper. Draper takes his seat. Cooper points to a novel displayed proudly on a shelf next to a bonsai tree by the window, "Have you read her?" he asks. "Rand. *Atlas Shrugged.* That's the one."

Draper agrees.

Cooper states that he knows what kind of person Draper is, because Draper and he are alike: "I mean you are a productive and reasonable man, and in the end completely self-interested" ("The Hobo Code," episode 108). Rand is Ayn Rand (1905–1982), the Russian-American novelist and philosopher. Rand was notorious in 1960s New York for her novels *The Fountainhead* (1943) and *Atlas Shrugged* (1957), in which she defended the morality of self-interest.[1] Rand would later edit a nonfiction anthology on ethics, *The Virtue of Selfishness* (1964). So it's not surprising that Cooper would recommend Rand to someone he believes to be completely self-interested.

But Cooper is mistaken. Draper is not at all self-interested. He represents the opposite of Randian self-interest; in fact, he embodies the conventional image of self-interest Rand sought to challenge through her novels and nonfiction writings.

Objectivism 101: A Brief Introduction

Like C. S. Lewis (*The Lion, the Witch, and the Wardrobe*), Jean-Paul Sartre (*Nausea*), and Iris Murdoch (*The Black Prince*), Rand was a philosopher as well as a novelist. Rand named her philosophy Objectivism because it emphasizes adherence to reality. Rand stresses that she is not primarily a defender of self-interest, but of reason. The self-interested person, according to Objectivism, is not the person who indulges his whims; he's the person who sustains and nourishes his own life through living in accordance with his nature as a rational animal. To appreciate Rand's argument for self-interest, we must first consider the key foundational principles of Objectivism.

Existence Has Primacy over Consciousness[2]

What is, is, regardless of what we believe or want to be true. There was a time when most people believed that the Sun revolved around Earth; this belief did not affect the movements of the Sun or Earth. Rand argues that we must, therefore, conform to existence; we cannot expect existence to conform to us. In season one of *Mad Men*, Peggy Olson did not know she was pregnant until her water broke; she thought overeating had caused her weight gain. Peggy's ignorance of her pregnancy did not alter the fact that she was pregnant. Almost nine months after conception, the baby still came out, as it had to given the facts of female biology (and barring complications).

Human Beings Are Rational Animals[3]

Rand agrees with Aristotle (384–322 BCE) that "man is a rational animal." Like Aristotle, Rand does not mean that human beings are always rational; she means that reason is the human means of consciousness. Rand agrees with Aristotle that human beings alone possess the capacity for reason; however, Rand does not place any weight on this observation. Even if it turned out that other animals also possess reason, reason would still be the human means of consciousness. Today, reason is often equated with the capacity to calculate means to ends. Rand, however, stresses that reason is primarily the capacity to conceptualize our perceptual observations. Reason, Rand argues, is the human means for grasping the facts of reality, including our own nature and the natures of that which exists. The human capacity for reason makes possible organizations such as Sterling Cooper. Advertising is a conceptual means of communication. Advertisers sell products to consumers through means of a "product concept."[4] Naming Kodak's new slide projector the Carousel (rather than the Wheel), for instance, invokes nostalgic memories of childhood, the very memories that the slides capture in photographic form. Only a conceptual being possesses the capacity to see memories of his past in the scribbling of lines on paper.

Human Life Is the Standard of Moral Values[5]

Rand argues that the fact that life is a conditional form of existence gives rise to the phenomenon of values. (*Value*, for Rand, is a noun, not a verb. A value is that which is of value to a living organism, not necessarily that which the organism values.) Rand observes that there's a fundamental difference between life and inanimate matter: the existence of life is conditional; the existence of inanimate matter is not. When Betty Draper smashed a chair in "A Night to Remember" (episode 208), the chair ceased to exist, but the matter that constituted the chair remained in existence. Only the chair's form changed. If Betty, however, had shot one of her neighbor's pigeons ("Shoot," episode 109), killing it, the life of that pigeon would not merely have changed form, like the material constituents of the chair; the life of the pigeon would have gone out of existence. Rand argues that life is a continuous process of an organism living in accordance with its own nature in order to sustain its existence. Pigeons sustain their existence by living in accordance with their own nature as pigeons. Similarly, as human beings we sustain our existence by living a properly human life. We could not sustain our existence by living, for instance, the life of a pigeon. Rand argues that all living organisms have values. Most organisms, however, have no choice but to live in accordance with their own nature. Human beings, by contrast, have a choice, and thus we have moral values. Unlike most other organisms, *we must choose* to live in accordance with our nature; that is, we must choose to live as human beings.

The Virtues Are Constitutive of Living a Human Life[6]

Rand argues that the primary virtues that sustain and nourish human life are the virtues of rationality, independence, integrity, honesty, justice, productiveness, and pride. Rand is not claiming that these virtues are instrumental means to human sustenance, but rather that they are constitutive of living a properly human life. A person does not obtain life as a consequence of being virtuous; rather, in being virtuous, a person is living his life.

Consider the virtue of productiveness. Peter Campbell's mother, Dorothy "Dot" Dyckman Campbell, comes from old money. She had a trust account her husband squandered on oysters and country club memberships ("Flight 1," episode 202). Dot did not produce this wealth herself; it was bequeathed to her. Rand's point is that Dot may be able to subsist through her ancestors' productive efforts, but for Dot to sustain and nourish her life, she must be productive. Dot must live her own life. Dot's ancestors cannot live her life for her. As evidence, observe that Dot does not appear capable of looking after her own affairs ("The Inheritance," episode 210). Productiveness, Rand argues, sustains and nourishes life not only through the wealth a productive person produces, but, more fundamentally, through the very act of being productive.

We are now in a position to appreciate Rand's defense of self-interest.

The Virtues Should Benefit Their Possessor

Egoism is the ethical position that each person ought to pursue his or her own self-interest. While egoism is usually taken to be an answer to the question "What, fundamentally, ought one to do?"[7], Rand takes egoism to be an answer to the question "Who ought to benefit from what one, fundamentally, ought to do?"[8] In the Objectivist ethics, human life is the standard of moral values, not self-interest. Thus Peggy Olson's nature as a human being, for instance, establishes what values and virtues she ought to benefit from; the benefit is not the standard of her values and virtues. Self-interest affirms that a person ought to benefit from those values and virtues that sustain and nourish his or her life. Self-interest does not establish what sustains or nourishes a person's life. Other ethical principles within the Objectivist ethics address this issue.

Egoism, in the Objectivist ethics, means that each person is the proper beneficiary of his own moral actions.[9] The key word here is *moral*; an individual should benefit from his *moral* actions, not his *immoral* actions. Rand is not claiming that a person should do anything that benefits himself. Rather, Rand's claim is that a person ought to benefit from those virtues constitutive of living a human life, that is, the virtues of rationality, independence, integrity, honesty, justice, productiveness, and pride.

Consider Roger Sterling's extramarital affair with Joan Holloway. Sterling and Holloway may be seeking their own benefit; however, this does not mean that they are virtuous by the standards of the Objectivist ethics. Rand would likely object to this affair, not because Sterling and Holloway are seeking to benefit themselves, but because they are seeking to benefit from living their lives contrary to the virtues that sustain and nourish their lives. Sterling and Holloway are unethical, according to the Objectivist ethics, not because they are self-interested, but because of what they regard as being in their self-interest. Rand defends self-interest, but self-interest is one principle within a much broader ethics. Other principles within Rand's ethics provide the basis for differentiating ethically between the various ways a person might benefit himself.

In *Kings of Madison Avenue*, the author Jesse McLean implies that Draper is self-interested (in Rand's sense) because of the "ruthless acts that he commits in the name of business or protecting his secrets."[10] However, this is not Rand's egoism. Rather, it's the conventional image of the egoist, ruthlessly sacrificing others to advance his own interests. Rand observes that this conventional image of self-interest is based on the assumption that we must choose between sacrificing self to others (which most people call "altruism") or sacrificing others to self (which most people call "egoism"). Rand argues that this is a false alternative: either way someone is sacrificed, and the debate is merely over who should be the victim. Rand proposes that if human life is the standard of moral values, we should be opposed to sacrifice as such, whether of self to others or others to self.[11] The self-interested person, Rand states, should seek to live as a trader, exchanging value for value with the expectation of mutual benefit.[12]

Don Draper may be motivated by his own self-interest, but this does not mean that Draper is completely self-interested. Being *motivated* by one's own self-interest is not the same as *acting* in one's self-interest. An alcoholic, like Duck Phillips, for instance, may be motivated by his own self-interest to drink immoderately. This does not mean, though, that immoderate drinking sustains or nourishes the alcoholic's life. For Draper to be self-interested, in Rand's sense, he must be seeking to benefit from that which actually sustains and nourishes his life. That is (if Rand is correct), he must be seeking to benefit from a life lived in accordance with the Objectivist virtues. We cannot examine all the virtues here. So let's focus on two: the virtue of honesty and the virtue of independence.

Don Draper Is Not Don Draper: The Vice of Dishonesty

Dick Whitman served next to Don Draper in the Korean War. There was an accident, killing Draper. Whitman took this opportunity to break with his past. He switched dog tags and took over Draper's identity ("Nixon vs. Kennedy," episode 112). The Don Draper we know is not the real Don Draper; he is, in fact, Dick Whitman. Whitman/Draper's life is a lie. There's nothing dishonest in changing names or breaking with a horrific home environment. Whitman had good reasons for wanting to forge a new life for himself. The dishonesty is in how Whitman broke with his past. Whitman did not merely change names; he took another man's identity. Every day, Whitman/Draper lies to his wife, his children, his in-laws, his clients, his colleagues.

Philosophers traditionally oppose dishonesty on the grounds that we have a moral duty to others to tell the truth. Rand, however, grounds the virtue of honesty in the primacy of existence.[13] What is, is, regardless of what we believe or want to be true and regardless of what we persuade others to believe to be true. In Hans Christian Anderson's *The Emperor's New Clothes*, the emperor is naked despite the fact that people praise his new clothes. Rand stresses that pretending something is true is not the same as it being true: a pretend house will not provide shelter to the homeless; a pretend meal will not feed the starving; a pretend umbrella will not provide protection from the rain. Honesty is a virtue in the Objectivist ethics, and dishonesty a vice, because the nonexistent cannot sustain or nourish human life.

Consider Whitman/Draper's relationship with his wife. Betty Draper is not married to Don Draper; she's married to the man Dick Whitman pretends to be. Rand recognizes that human beings have a profound need to make a connection with others. This connection, Rand argues, consists in mutual psychological visibility. When we look at ourselves in the mirror, we observe our physical self. However, we cannot similarly observe our psychological self. We can only observe our psychological self through the reactions and responses of others.[14] Other people are mirrors to our souls, but sometimes the reflection is distorted. When other people react and respond to us in a way that is at odds with our conception of ourselves, it can be like looking into a fun house mirror. We don't see our expected selves reflected back, so we feel invisible.

Whitman/Draper is invisible to his wife. Mutual psychological visibility is only possible between two (or more) people who genuinely see each other. Betty Draper cannot make a connection to her husband because the man she's reacting to and responding to does not exist. For Betty to make this connection, she must see the man her husband in fact is, not the man he pretends to be.

Psychological visibility reaches its height in romantic relationships; however, Rand's observation applies to all our relationships. (An elevator operator, for example, can experience invisibility if he's treated like a machine rather than a person.) Observe that Whitman/Draper does not appear to have any genuine friends. This is not surprising. Whitman/Draper's clients and colleagues are reacting and responding to Draper, not Whitman. Whitman/Draper has to move through his days invisible to all those around him. As evidence, observe that the one person Whitman/Draper appears to have a genuine connection with is Anna Draper, widow of the real Don Draper. With Anna, Whitman/Draper appears relaxed, even happy ("The Mountain King," episode 212). Whitman/Draper is able to make this connection to Anna because Anna is the only person who sees Dick Whitman. Anna is reacting and responding to *him*, not the man he pretends to be.

A Night to Remember

In "A Night to Remember," Betty Draper accuses her husband of having an affair. Betty knows Don has been lying to her, though she does not yet know the extent of his dishonesty. Betty is angry at Don's betrayal of their "perfect marriage."[15] Yet Don and Betty never had a perfect marriage. Betty believed she was married to Don Draper, a faithful husband and hardworking advertising executive. But what is, is. Betty believing her husband to be Don Draper does not alter the fact that he's Dick Whitman, a philanderer, who spends many of his days either drinking alone in a bar or in the beds of his mistresses. Betty discovering the truth cannot end that which never existed. Draper's betrayal does not consist in ending their "perfect marriage" but in having built their marriage on a foundation of lies.

Rand's argument for honesty places no weight at all on the dishonest person being found out. Rand does not appeal to a cost-benefit analysis, in which she weighs the chances of being caught against the benefits of being dishonest. Rand's point is that such a cost-benefit analysis is not possible, as there are no benefits to be derived from dishonesty; one cannot weigh possible costs against nonexistent benefits. Nonetheless, Rand observes that the likelihood of being found out is inherent in the nature of dishonesty. The dishonest person has to come up against one immovable obstacle: facts. What is, is, so pretending otherwise will not alter relevant facts. No matter how skilled a liar someone is, he cannot rewrite the facts of reality, and so every lie must constantly come up against facts that contradict, and thus threaten to blow, his deception.

Facts are a constant threat to the dishonest person. Draper takes the train to work, and someone recognizes him as Whitman ("Marriage of Figaro," episode 103). Draper's photo appears in the newspaper after he wins an advertising award, and Adam Whitman recognizes the half-brother he thought dead ("5G," episode 105). Draper is sent a parcel of Dick Whitman's mementos, but Peter Campbell receives it instead and learns Draper's true identity ("Nixon vs. Kennedy"). Draper has dinner with one of his mistresses, and on the way back to her apartment they have an accident ("The New Girl," episode 205). The honest person has nothing to fear from being recognized on a train, or having his photo appear in a newspaper, or having a parcel mistakenly delivered to a colleague, or being in a car accident. For Draper these ordinary events of everyday life pose a constant threat.

From a Randian perspective, Draper necessarily finds himself in the position of having to take ruthless acts to protect his secrets, because he's in a constant battle with reality. From spurning his younger brother ("5G"), to firing a secretary who failed to cover for him ("The Benefactor," episode 203), Draper's ruthlessness is a product of his own vices. Rand would argue that this is a battle Draper cannot win, as whatever lengths he goes to protect his secrets, he cannot alter the fact that what is, is.

The Nonconformist

Bertram Cooper makes Draper a partner in order to restore faith to their clients after Roger Sterling suffers a second heart attack. Draper insists that there be no contract. "Beware the nonconformist," says Cooper. He turns to leave. "I'm going to introduce you to Miss Ayn Rand. I think she'll salivate"

("Indian Summer," episode 111). Presumably, Cooper believes Rand to be a defender of nonconformity. However, Cooper is mistaken. Rand defended the virtue of independence. The independent person is primarily oriented to reality, rather than to other people.[16] Such a person is independent in the sense that he has a first-hand grasp of the facts. His primary concern is with what is true, not with what other people think is true. The conformist and nonconformist, in contrast, are primarily oriented to other people, rather than to reality. The conformist conforms to what other people think is true. The nonconformist is concerned not with what is true, but with reacting against whatever other people think to be true. The independent person will sometimes swim against the current, like the nonconformist, because his concern is with the truth. Unlike the nonconformist, however, he does not swim against the current because it's the current.

Rand stresses that independence is the *means* by which one grasps the truth, it is not the *standard* of truth. A person must grasp for himself the basis in fact of his ideas and convictions. He holds to them, not because they are *his* ideas and convictions, but because they are grounded in the relevant facts. Thus the independent person will hold to his ideas and convictions in the face of opposition from others, yet he will just as easily abandon his ideas and convictions if others offer a basis in fact for thinking him mistaken. The emphasis, for the independent person, is not on what *he* thinks to be true, but on what *is* true. In "The Hobo Code," Draper explains how he deals with reluctant clients: he seduces them, then forces them. An independent person does not force others to accept his position. He respects their independence by appealing to their rational capacity to grasp the same facts he does.

Rand contrasts the independent person with the second-hander. The second-hander is second-hand in the sense that he has a second-hand grasp of reality. Consider Peter Keating, from *The Fountainhead*. Keating is living a second-hand life.

Keating did not want to become an architect. He would have preferred to become an artist, but his mother thought architecture a more respectable profession. Keating rises through the ranks of the architectural profession, not on the basis of his talent (he has little), but through schmoozing and scheming. Keating rejects the woman he loves in order to marry a woman he does not, so as to advance his career. Rand describes Keating as "a perfect example of a selfless man who is a ruthless, unprincipled egotist."[17] (By "egotist," Rand here means "egoist.") This sounds like an odd claim. How can a person be a selfless egoist? Rand's point is that Keating is an egoist because he's seeking to advance his own interests, yet he's nonetheless selfless because others dictate his interests. He has no real self. Keating's primary orientation is to other people, not to reality. He seeks greatness in other people's eyes. He does not want to be great. He wants others to think him great.[18]

Most, if not all, of the characters in *Mad Men* live second-hand lives. Betty Draper is a housewife and mother, not because this is her chosen profession (she would rather be a model), but because this is what was expected of women in 1960s America. Harry Crane's wife, Jennifer, is pleased her husband has become the head (and only member of) the television department at Sterling Cooper, not because this is good for him, but because this will impress her friends ("The Benefactor"). Peggy Olson smokes a cigarette and drinks beer while on a blind date, not because she likes cigarettes and beer, but in order to look "Manhattan" ("Indian Summer"). Peter Campbell thinks he's qualified for the position of account manager, not because he would do the job well, but because he has the right social connections ("Nixon vs. Kennedy"). Perhaps most tragically, Salvatore Romano is a closeted homosexual man married to a woman. As a result, he regularly makes macho remarks in order to persuade others of his heterosexuality. These characters are conformists. If Cooper is correct, Draper is a nonconformist. However, Draper and the other characters of *Mad Men* are united in their rejection of independence. They are all primarily oriented to other people, not to reality. In a sense, they are all Peter Keatings.

The Whore-Child

Rand argues that the independent person grounds his self-esteem in his objective estimate of himself, not in others' estimate of him. Self-esteem is a person's appraisal of his own moral worth; a positive self-appraisal is the reward for having lived a virtuous life.[19] The independent person is concerned with being good, not with others thinking him good. When the independent person receives praise from others, his estimate of the other person goes up; his estimate of himself does not change. The independent person recognizes that his character is what it is independent of what others think of him. Contrast this with Harry Crane's reaction when he discovers that Ken Cosgrove earns one hundred dollars a week more than him ("The Benefactor"). Crane's self-appraisal is based not on his actual job performance, but on how his paycheck compares to someone else's.

The second-hander bases his self-appraisal not on what he is, but on how others see him. Whitman/Draper is living a second-hand life, not because he took over the real Don Draper's identity, but because he did so in order to manipulate others' perception of him. Whitman/Draper had a horrific childhood. He was the son of a prostitute and a drunkard. His mother died in childbirth, so his father and his father's wife raised him. Those raising Whitman/Draper (I'm loathe to call them his parents, as they did not live up to that position) referred to him as the whore-child ("The Hobo Code"). Whitman/Draper was not responsible for his mother's profession or his father's infidelity, and to hold him responsible was clearly unjust. A child lacks the intellectual maturity to evaluate himself rationally. As Whitman/Draper matured into an adult, however, he was in a position to make this assessment (or, if there was too much emotional baggage to overcome, to seek professional help). Instead, the adult Whitman/Draper accepted others' evaluation of him as the standard of his own self-worth, and so sought to manipulate how others saw him by taking on another man's identity. Draper's self-appraisal is based on others seeing him as the successful advertising executive in his Coupe de Ville, rather than as the whore-child of his youth.

Usually, liars lie for financial gain. Draper lies for spiritual gain. Rand would argue that Draper's attempt to improve his self-esteem through deceit is futile for all the reasons dishonesty is a vice. In some respects, Draper is placing himself in a much more precarious position than the run-of-the-mill liar, as his self-esteem, rather than merely his financial position, depends on him maintaining his deception. In attempting to improve his self-esteem through manipulating how others see him, Draper has placed his self-esteem in opposition to reality. The facts that threaten the financial gains of a run-of-the-mill liar threaten Draper's self-esteem. Draper's constant battle with reality is not just to protect his secrets, but, more fundamentally, to protect his self-worth. It is little wonder that Draper oscillates between ruthlessness and drowning his consciousness in whiskey, as he engages in an ultimately futile attempt to maintain a self-esteem under constant threat from the ordinary events of everyday life.

The Universe Is *Not* Indifferent

Don Draper claims that "the universe is indifferent" ("The Hobo Code"). Rand disagrees. She argues that the universe is benevolent. Rand is not suggesting that there's a divine presence that intervenes in the workings of the universe so that everything turns out for the best.[20] Strictly speaking, concepts such as "indifferent" and "benevolent" do not apply to the universe. Rand's claim is that the universe is benevolent in the sense that the universe is intelligible, and so if we adhere to reality we will likely be successful in sustaining and nourishing our lives.[21] We are not doomed by our own nature to suffer. Rand does not deny that there are tragedies and disasters. Her point is that these are exceptions, not the normal state of human affairs.

Rand would not be surprised that Draper finds the universe indifferent. A benevolent universe is indifferent to those who attempt to act in defiance of the facts of reality. Cooper thinks that Draper is completely self-interested, but there's nothing self-interested in banging one's head against an immovable obstacle. What is, is, and Draper attempting to pursue his self-interest in defiance of the facts will only doom him to a series of tragedies and disasters of his own making. In "Marriage of Figaro," a guest tells Draper that Madison Avenue must treat him well, as this is as good as it gets. Several hours later, Draper is sitting in his car, alone, in front of a railway crossing, staring vacantly into the distance. Draper appears to have achieved everything society could offer. This success is illusory, though, as he's living a second-hand life built on a shoddy foundation of deceit.

NOTES

1. Michael Paxton, *Ayn Rand: A Sense of Life, The Companion Book* (Utah: Gibbs Smith Publisher, 1998), 163. See also Jennifer Burns, *Goddess of the Market: Ayn Rand and the American Right* (New York: Oxford University Press, 2009), 189–213.

2. Leonard Peikoff, *Objectivism: The Philosophy of Ayn Rand* (New York: Meridian, 1993), 17–23.

3. Ibid., 193–198.

4. Jerry Kirkpatrick, *In Defense of Advertising: Arguments from Reason, Ethical Egoism, and Laissez-Faire Capitalism* (Claremont, CA: TLJ Books, 2007), 22.

5. Peikoff, *Objectivism*, 207–220. See also Tara Smith, *Viable Values: A Study of Life as the Root and Reward of Morality* (Lanham, MD: Rowman & Littlefield, 2000).

6. Peikoff, *Objectivism*, 220–229, 250–324. See also Tara Smith, *Ayn Rand's Normative Ethics: The Virtuous Egoist* (New York: Cambridge University Press, 2006).

7. Jan Österberg, *Self and Others: A Study of Ethical Egoism* (Dordrecht, The Netherlands: Kluwer Academic Publishers, 1988), 14.

8. Peikoff, *Objectivism*, 229–241.

9. Ibid., 229.

10. Jesse McLean, *Kings of Madison Avenue: The Unofficial Guide to* Mad Men (Toronto: ECW Press, 2009), 85.

11. Peikoff, *Objectivism*, 235–236. Rand was sometimes asked why she used the word *selfishness* to denote virtuous qualities. Rand recognized that self-sacrifice and other-sacrifice entail each other. If there's someone making sacrifices, there must be someone collecting them. Selfish, Rand argued, is what conventional egoists call those who refuse to be altruistic and sacrifice to them. Rand was notorious for her opposition to altruism. Her position, however, is often misunderstood. Rand was opposed to the use of altruism by conventional egoists to morally disarm their victims. She was not opposed to helping others. Thus Rand wanted to reclaim the word *selfish*, much in the same way as homosexuals would later reclaim the words *gay* and *queer*.

12. Ibid., 286–288.

13. Ibid., 267–276.

14. Chris Matthew Sciabarra, *Ayn Rand: The Russian Radical* (University Park: Pennsylvania State University Press, 1995), 255. Nathaniel Branden originated the concept of psychological visibility.

15. McLean, *Kings of Madison Avenue*, 177.

16. Peikoff, *Objectivism*, 251–259.

17. *Journals of Ayn Rand*, edited by David Harriman (New York: Plume, 1999), 88.

18. Ayn Rand, *The Fountainhead* (London: HarperCollins, 1994), 591.

19. Peikoff, *Objectivism*, 305–310.

20. Douglas B. Rasmussen, "The Aristotelian Significance of the Section Titles of *Atlas Shrugged*: A Brief Consideration of Rand's View of Logic and Reality," in *Ayn Rand's* Atlas Shrugged: *A Philosophical and Literary Companion*, edited by Edward W. Younkins (Aldershot, England: Ashgate, 2007), 33.

21. Peikoff, *Objectivism*, 342–343.

AN EXISTENTIAL LOOK AT *MAD MEN:* DON DRAPER, ADVERTISING, AND THE PROMISE OF HAPPINESS

Ada S. Jaarsma

Today, we live in a world permeated by advertising. But branding messages about products and corporations have not always been so pervasive. A turning point in the development of sophisticated branding campaigns is dramatized in *Mad Men*. Set in the early 1960s, the series reminds us of a time when television was just beginning to expand the scope of advertising and when ad agencies were experiencing greater pressures and glimpsing broader possibilities for the nature of marketing.

In 1960, not everyone on Madison Avenue understood the value of innovative marketing for advertisers. In season one of *Mad Men*, upon glimpsing a new ad campaign for Volkswagen, the folks at Sterling Cooper mock what they perceive as a misunderstanding of what an ad is supposed to achieve. Rather than specifying the details of the product—the new VW bug—the advertisement shows an image of the car, with the word "Lemon" below it. Only one person comments softly, "I think it's funny."

As the storyline progresses, however, Don Draper, the leading ad man at Sterling Cooper, begins to demonstrate to his coworkers—and to the viewers—the wide-ranging power of effective branding campaigns. Draper explains, for example, that his skills as a consummate salesman involve the ability to construct objects of desire for others: "The reason you haven't felt [love] is because it doesn't exist. What you call love was invented by guys like me to sell nylons" ("Smoke Gets in Your Eyes," episode 101).

Draper seems to get something right here about advertising's ability to create the desires of consumers, but what does *Mad Men* itself, as a television show, demonstrate about the force of advertising to actually promote, shape, and sell us ourselves? Does the show provide hope that individuals might find ways to resist such power? Where would such resistance be found?

Branding the Self

It's tempting to write off Draper's comments as hopelessly cynical: love doesn't exist because Madison Avenue invented it to brand nylons. Rather than discarding his perspective as too disillusioned, however, let's take Draper at his word in order to think carefully about the power of advertising to shape our very sense of ourselves. If we can identify the precise nature of its capacity for influencing us, then we can begin to take responsibility for our own actions as consumers. When he comments that "guys like me" invented love to sell nylons, Draper is asserting an argument about our own susceptibility, as consumers, to the messages of brand managers.

A brand is a coherent set of values or ideals that convinces consumers about the desirability of a commodity or the trustworthiness of a corporation. Nylons, in Draper's example, are packaged under brand associations of "romance" or "falling in love." In the specific case of nylons, the world's first synthetic stockings, DuPont's invention brought together modern science with domestic, feminine ease. Its successful marketing, however, did not employ the brand name DuPont since it reminded the public of "chemistry."[1] Rather, the name of the product's material, "nylon," became synonymous with the general category of "stockings," the branding so successful as to be rendered invisible. A brand works when it achieves several goals: it resonates with prevailing ideals in society; it advances the sense that a product—or a corporation—is better than what already exists or what competitors can offer; and it gives rise to new values, consistent with the associations of the brand.

One plausible way to make sense of advertising's power is to consider whether our choices as consumers reflect well-reasoned responses to the facts found within ad campaigns. If this accurately describes how advertising affects us as consumers, then the best or most profitable branding messages would make good use of scientific reasoning and logical argumentation. Along these lines, we could equip ourselves with rigorous critical thinking skills in order to resist fallacies and false information in advertising; we could appeal to objective truth in order to find confidence in our own decision-making, refusing to remain susceptible to misleading commercial influences.

If advertising is, in fact, about validity and truth, then we can describe it philosophically in terms of "enlightenment." One of the most influential theorists of enlightenment, Immanuel Kant (1724–1804), explains that every individual, employing the courage of independent thought, can learn how to question authority. As thinking people, we need not stay at the mercy of those "guardians" who have more power or access to information; rather, we can and should participate in public debates, demanding truthful facts and holding government and corporate leaders accountable.[2] A magazine like *Consumer Reports* is a good example of this approach to consumption: the more empirical data to which consumers have access, the more enlightened their consumer choices will be.

The problem with this approach is that advertising rarely even pretends to make good arguments. By branding nylons in terms of "romantic love," ad men like Don Draper are mobilizing other forces besides truth or logic that drive consumer choices—forces such as the longing for meaning or authenticity. The school of philosophy called existentialism seems much more applicable to Draper's understanding of the power of advertising. Existentialism promotes deep skepticism toward enlightenment and reason. Instead of seeing the process of decision-making as reasonable, existentialism emphasizes the desires and anxieties that drive our choices. By shifting focus from objective reason to subjective passion, existentialism reveals the ways we, as individuals, actually strive to become selves—the ways in which our choices produce the very meaning of our existence.

On this account, rather than reflecting our agreement with the facts of an ad campaign, then, our consumer habits actually *give rise* to values—values that imbue our identities with meaning and direction. In the words of a contemporary marketing researcher, "Everything is a brand: Coca-Cola, FedEx, Porsche, New York City, the United States, Madonna, and you—yes, you! A brand is any label that carries meaning and associations."[3] This statement—you are a brand!—is a celebratory approach to the ways in which branding gives rise to meaning. A more existential understanding would call attention to the ways in which we do—and do not—accept responsibility for our meaning-making choices. When we allow an ad campaign to prescribe the values that we then express in our consumer choices, we are refraining from *choosing* to choose. In existential terms, we are then in "bad faith," rather than expressing authenticity or "transcendence."

Does advertising, as Draper seems to suggest, tend to lead to bad faith and an absence of authentic desire? Does the show's portrayal of advertising provoke awareness of bad faith? At its core, existentialism is about the hope that we can discover a meaningful and authentic existence. To describe *Mad Men's* understanding of advertising as "existential," we would have to find evidence not only of an understanding of the passion and anxiety of existence but also, perhaps more importantly, some sense of the hope that individuals can find in the very process of becoming an existing self.

"Freedom from Fear": What Advertising Promises

At the beginning of season one, we learn that growing public awareness of the toxicity of tobacco is making it difficult to sell cigarettes. Advertisers are no longer allowed to make claims about the relative safety of one brand of cigarettes over another. During a pitch for a new Lucky Strike campaign, Draper decides to move away from the logic of fear and safety altogether. He points out that "this is the greatest advertising opportunity since the invention of cereal"—referring to the opportunity to say anything he wants about the brand of Lucky Strike cigarettes: "Lucky Strikes—It's Toasted" ("Smoke Gets in Your Eyes"). In other words, the actual "specs" of the product don't matter at all—and in this case, they hurt rather than help a new ad campaign. What *does* matter here is the experience that we enjoy when we encounter effective branding: the creative and affective force of advertising.

Draper continues: "Advertising is based on one thing: happiness. And you know what happiness is? Happiness is the smell of a new car; it's freedom from fear; it's a billboard on the side of the road that screams with reassurance that whatever you are doing is okay. You are okay." According to Draper, advertising's power rests in its promise to intercede in an individual's choices: a promise to remove the fear and uncertainty that characterize real choices. To translate Don's definition into existential terms, whereas becoming an authentic self results from passion and anxiety, being a consumer involves no such risk.

The "freedom from fear" promised by advertising is how existentialists describe the symptoms of a person in bad faith. In the introduction to *The Second Sex*, the existentialist philosopher Simone de Beauvoir (1908–1986) explains that "those who are condemned to stagnation are often pronounced happy on the pretext that happiness consists in being at rest."[4] Whereas the consumer might seem liberated and self-actualized, de Beauvoir explains, the consumer's "happiness," predicted by Draper, is more accurately understood as stunted, meaningless, "a degradation of existence."[5] The only way to achieve authentic selfhood is to "expand into an indefinitely open future."[6] There is no other justification for one's existence. Don's summary of the billboard's branding message, then—"Whatever you are doing is okay. You are okay."—dramatizes the bad faith of consumption. By accepting the billboard's offer, I am identifying myself as an object that is passively determined by outside forces. As a result, I need not accept responsibility for my own freedom. In other words, I need not consider the ways in which my decisions, regardless of whether I acknowledge them, arise from and perpetuate fear.

Although my choices as a consumer may *seem* both free and responsible, from the perspective of the existentialists, I am likely relinquishing my freedom in order to rely on external guidance. According to the existentialist Jean-Paul Sartre (1905–1980), an individual is in bad faith when "she realizes herself as *not being* her own body, and she contemplates it as though from above as a passive object to which events can *happen* but which can neither provoke them nor avoid them because all its possibilities are outside of it."[7] If I see myself as an *object*, I need not stake myself on values that I have created nor risk everything for the meaning that I have generated. Rather, I deceive myself with the impression that the very direction of my life has been already decided, likely by the various aspects of the situation in which I find myself.

In Sartre's terminology, to take up my freedom authentically is to "transcend" my situation, but to be in bad faith is to reduce my existence to the "facticity" of my situation—to the objective facts of my body or to the specific aspects of my role in society. Probably more than any other character in *Mad Men*, Don's wife, Betty, shows us the passivity and self-deception of bad faith. Lying on the couch in her psychiatrist's office, Betty reflects on her neighbor, the divorcée Helen. "It must be so hard for her. I mean, seeing happy families all around. But I don't know what I can do. I mean, I can't just disappear—I live there" ("New Amsterdam," episode 104). By all accounts, Betty has achieved all of the goals of white middle-class femininity: suburban domesticity, motherhood, marriage to a successful man. If she measures the value of her life according to external social prescriptions, she should find the kind of "happiness" that Don locates in consumption: conformity granting her the sense that she is okay.

Betty, however, does not seem okay, and her interactions with Helen seem to be awakening a sense that her life could be more meaningful. Helen is an independent, politically savvy woman who has chosen divorce over staying with an unfaithful husband. In contrast, Betty remains with her own unfaithful husband, but not because she is adopting an open-minded approach to nonmonogamy. Betty is staying with Don because she seems content with deceiving herself about his evident infidelity, maintaining an illusion of comfort and success. Continuing her reflections, she declares, "Of course, my real concern is those children. That poor little boy. The person taking care of him isn't giving him what he needs."

The little boy, Helen's son, has recently told Betty that she looks like a princess, an accolade that seems familiar and gratifying to Betty. Although she seems to be empathizing with Helen's son, it's likely that Betty is inadvertently confessing her own longings—for the approval that she feels she deserves. If this interpretation lines up, then she is actually saying, "The person taking care of me isn't giving me what I need." In this statement, we can see how she is positioning herself as a passive recipient, even a child, waiting for her husband's attention.

De Beauvoir tells us why some women would rather remain in bad faith than become attuned to their own passions: namely, because they are very well rewarded for their position as the "other." Betty Draper's life at the beginning of season one closely resembles the housewife that de Beauvoir condemns. By failing to *choose* to choose, Betty rests in the stagnant position of the socially well-regarded woman, an object rather than an active subject. However, in 1960, the women's movement spurred by second-wave feminism is just around the corner, and we get the sense from Betty's fascination with Helen that her willingness to remain stagnant is slowly dissipating. Indeed, in seasons two and three, Betty's decisions seem to indicate a deepening sense of self-responsibility, especially in relation to her husband and to other men. This existential movement culminates, perhaps, in her choice at the end of season three to leave Don. She fails, however, to demonstrate the kind of freedom that de Beauvoir is hoping that women will embrace: namely, the freedom of becoming a woman without the safety of a man's patronage. Betty replaces Don with Henry Francis, an equally successful and potentially more attention-granting man. At the same time, Betty's character does seem to be inspired by Betty Friedan's second-wave book *The Feminine Mystique*, which challenged America's middle-class housewives to awaken from their 1960s domesticity. If this is so, then perhaps season four's narrative arc will include Betty's continued movement away from conventionality toward existential passion and authenticity.

Objectification and Underwear

In his description of advertising in 1960s America, the philosopher Herbert Marcuse (1898–1979) explains that consumption perpetuates itself because "the established values become the people's own values."[8] The established values, according to Marcuse, line up exactly with prevailing capitalist ideals of profit, efficiency, aggression, and competition. As our analysis of Betty reveals, they also encourage individuals to find meaning in complying with these dictates.

By internalizing the values found in ad campaigns, consumers not only relinquish responsibility for decision-making, they begin to express their very identities as individuals through consumption; it becomes almost impossible to contemplate resisting capitalist values. We can read Marcuse's words as a warning about the powers of advertising: if we fail to take responsibility for *choosing* to choose, we will likely internalize the ideologies of the dominant culture by consuming along the prescribed lines of ad campaigns.

While consumption might promise a release from anxiety, it only leads to more anxiety, however, and *Mad Men* supplies numerous examples of characters whose conformity to the prevailing ideologies of 1960 America highlights a lack of authenticity and lingering dissatisfaction. For example, Salvatore Romano, the artist at Sterling Cooper, reminds us time and again that the dominant social prescriptions forbid any expression of open homosexuality. Upon proudly showing Don a drawing of a man that, from Sal's perspective, demonstrates sexuality and attractiveness, Salvatore is told, "It needs sex appeal," and he is advised to "add a woman in a bathing suit, put her next to your guy." The only version of sexuality deemed legitimate by the ad world is one that objectifies women from a heterosexual male position ("Smoke Gets in Your Eyes"). And it's not only ad campaigns that need to comply with this stricture. Although he gives off the signals of a gay man, in the same episode Sal himself protests at one point, "So we're supposed to believe that people are living one way, and secretly wishing the opposite? That's ridiculous." It's not until season three that Sal's wife, Kitty, seems to glimpse the truth about her husband's sexual identity ("The Arrangements," episode 304). Beyond committing himself to a life of deception, Sal has consigned his wife to a kind of marriage that she clearly did not sign up for.

But is it fair to condemn Sal, a closeted gay man, as someone in bad faith, especially given the rampant homophobia that he faces every day? According to de Beauvoir, the "drama" of existentialism for women—and others, like Sal, who confront an objectifying gaze—consists of struggling for authenticity and freedom *while also* refusing to comply with disempowering social standards. In contrast, the drama of individuals like Don Draper consists of resisting the temptations of privilege: refusing to objectify others *while also* acknowledging the highly subjective and contingent aspects of the power that they enjoy.

While the bad faith of privilege is perhaps easily understood, given how it enables individuals to lay false claims to rightness and deservingness, it may be harder to make sense of the bad faith of conformity: Why would individuals be complicit with their own oppression? Marcuse's analysis of consumption, just described, provides one explanation: when I internalize the dominant values of society, I am rewarded for my obedience and thus have a stake in the perpetuation of those very values.

We can see this cycle at work in the ways in which undergarments are discussed and advertised in *Mad Men*. On her first day at the office, Peggy Olson is told repeatedly that her success at Sterling Cooper depends upon her conformity to highly specific standards of femininity. Upon meeting her, for example, Pete Campbell suggests, "Wouldn't be a sin for us to see your legs. Draw your waist in, you might look like a woman." Similarly, Joan, the office manager, tells Peggy, "Go home, take a paper bag, and cut some eyeholes out of it. Put it over your head, and get undressed and look at yourself in the mirror. Really evaluate where your strengths and weaknesses are. And be honest" ("Smoke Gets in Your Eyes").

In order to achieve this "honesty," Peggy needs to examine herself from a man's perspective. "Bras are for men. Women want to see themselves the way men see them" ("Maidenform," 206). This comment, made by Paul Kinsey while brainstorming a new Playtex bra ad, lays bare the heterosexual dynamics of social norms. According to her coworkers, Peggy must literally reshape her body into proper contours—by donning highly constraining undergarments. It's clear from Joan's advice to Peggy that the virtues of "honesty" have to do with the overarching goal of the job: "If you make the really right moves, you'll be out in the country and you won't be going to work at all" ("Smoke Gets in Your Eyes"). In other words, Peggy will know when she has achieved the highest success possible, only attainable via a man's patronage: namely, suburban wifehood.

In a radio interview with *Mad Men*'s creator, Matthew Weiner, the National Public Radio host Terry Gross points out that bras are actually an invisible star of the show, since a striking feature of each episode is the pointy "bullet bra" sported by the lead actresses. Explaining the importance of this aesthetic aspect of *Mad Men*, Weiner responds that the silhouette of a woman's body could change every year, in accordance with changing styles, just by altering her underwear. A function of the ad men's bra campaigns, then, is to illustrate the current proper female shape, attainable through undergarments.[9]

This reliance on underwear may strike us as hopelessly outdated. While in 1960 girdles were worn by most women because they "control jiggling" and hold up stockings, the girdle was replaced by the 1970s with a new prescription: women should reshape their own bodies through exercise and dieting.[10] Rather than writing off the pressures of objectification as historical and therefore no longer relevant to ourselves, however, existentialism challenges us to see how there is some-thing *subjective* about our willingness to conform to social pressures. We are internalizing desires and values that in turn shape who we become.

Existentialism and Authenticity

At the end of the very first episode, Pete Campbell shows up at Peggy Olson's door, stating, "For the first time today, I'm not selling anything" ("Smoke Gets in your Eyes"). Campbell's comment gestures toward the hope that advertising doesn't need to encompass all aspects of everyday life. But how *is* authenticity possible in an overly commercial world? Given the many examples of bad faith, do we also find existential hope in *Mad Men*'s depictions of 1960s Madison Avenue?

One approach to answering these questions is to consider the show as a feminist production, one that takes women's perspectives seriously and, more importantly, provokes criti-cal attention to gendered inequalities. It seems relevant, for example, that while nearly 80 percent of television programs in the 2007–2008 prime-time season had no women writers,[11] seven of the nine writers of *Mad Men* at the start of season three were women.[12] It also seems noteworthy that the show's creator, Matthew Weiner, is attuned to the gendered dynamics of objectification. In a radio interview, he states, "I'm always interested in where is the boundary, at which point where men can stop speaking for women."[13]

That same boundary, of course, marks the point at which women can start speaking for women—a point that, accord-ing to de Beauvoir, needs to be achieved in order for men to "stop speaking for women" and for women to adopt compelling voices. We all need to confront the actual embodied situations in which we find ourselves. For example, de Beauvoir explains that whereas a man thinks of his body as a "direct and normal connection with the world," a woman experiences her body as a prison.[14] These different embodied experiences extend directly into how men and women speak to each other. If a man and a woman are arguing, de Beauvoir claims, the man, by virtue of his privileged sense of normalcy, always has recourse to the statement "You think thus and so because you are a woman."[15]

And a woman cannot say the same thing in response. The statement "You think that because you are a man" would sound almost silly because it is naming the most normal form of gendered reality: being a man. As an existential thinker, de Beauvoir is challenging both men and women to become authentic. For a man, in this case, authenticity includes affirming the freedom of others, relinquishing the temptation to ground his own sense of self in the objectification of women. For women, authenticity includes taking up the responsibility to "become" a woman rather than accepting the temptations of bad faith.[16]

In *Mad Men*'s first season, one character stands out as an example of authenticity, at least when it comes to gendered embodiment: Rachel Menken, the owner of a large department store. Upon approaching Sterling Cooper for an innovative new ad campaign, Menken's first words to Draper are, "You were expecting me to be a man. My father was, too" ("Smoke Gets in Your Eyes").

This greeting sets the tone for Menken's impassioned refusal of the objectifying pressures that she faces. Just a second earlier, Draper stretches out his hand to greet the client that *he* is expecting—a man who turns out to be an employee at Sterling Cooper, hurried up from the mailroom to be the token Jewish representative at the meeting with Menken. Aware of the confusion that her body elicits, Menken meets Draper head-on, not apologizing for being either Jewish or a woman. After she dismisses Draper's marketing suggestions as stereotypical and unimaginative, the meeting ends badly, with Don walking out, declaring, "I'm not going to let a woman talk to me like that."

Their second encounter exemplifies the gendered predicament described by de Beauvoir. To Don's pointed question— "Why aren't you married?"—Rachel responds, "If I weren't a woman, I would be allowed to ask you the same question. And if I weren't a woman, I wouldn't be asked to choose between putting on an apron and the thrill of making my father's store what I always thought it should be" ("Marriage of Figaro," episode 103). Rachel resists occupying the position of "woman," as signaled to her by Don, since this would simply validate the unequal dynamic that he is taking for granted. Rather, she calls out the situation for what it is—a contingent yet influential set of circumstances that highlights her own female body while rendering his body invisible.

According to existential thought, there is no objective set of values to which we can reliably appeal for making authentic decisions. Rather, we each need to *choose* to choose our own subjective truths. In other words, I accept that I am the source of the values in my world, and I *cause* there to be a world because I project myself beyond the world toward my own possibilities. In this way, the future opens up as a horizon full of meaning and passion. Resistance to advertising, then, is possible, but only if I take up my own freedom to become authentic. If I fixate on acquiring consumer goods in accordance with branding messages, I mistake my consumer self for my existential self, and so give up, somehow, the hope for a meaningful and unpredictable future.

Television and Existential Awakening

In the same conversation, Don tells Rachel, "You are born alone, and you die alone, and this world just drops a bunch of rules on top of you to make you forget those facts, but I never forget. I'm living like there's no tomorrow because there isn't one." The consummate ad man, Don has lost his sense of a meaningful tomorrow. He knows first-hand that the power of branding deludes us about how to become passionate selves, and yet he isn't able to stake his own claims to authentic existence. The hope of *Mad Men*, however, might be that we, as viewers, are prompted to see through Don's bleak worldview, with television perhaps being an occasion for our own existential awakening.

NOTES

1. Regina Lee Blaszczyk, "Designing Synthetics, Promoting Brands: Dorothy Liebes, DuPont Fibres and Post-war American Interiors," *Journal of Design History* 12(1), 2008, 85.

2. Immanuel Kant, "An Answer to the Question: What Is Enlightenment?" In *What Is Enlightenment: 18th Century Answers and 20th Century Questions*, edited by James Schmidt (Berkeley: University of California Press, 1996), 58–64.

3. Philip Kotler, "Brands," *Marketing Insights from A to Z* (Hoboken, NJ: John Wiley, 2003), 8.

4. Simone de Beauvoir, "Introduction," *The Second Sex* (New York: Vintage, 1989), xxxiv.

5. Ibid., xxxv.

6. Ibid., xxxxv.

7. Jean-Paul Sartre, "Bad Faith," *Basic Writings*, edited by Stephen Priest (New York: Routledge, 2001), 215.

8. Herbert Marcuse, *An Essay on Liberation* (Boston: Beacon Press, 1969), 13.

9. "The Men behind AMC's Hit 'Mad Men,'" *Fresh Air*, National Public Radio, aired Sept. 25, 2009. Available online: www.npr.org/templates/story/story.php?storyId5113180227.

10. Wendy Burns-Ardolino, *Jiggle: (Re)Shaping American Women.* (Plymouth, UK: Lexington Books, 2007), 24, 88.

11. Martha M. Lauzen and Douglas M. Deiss, "Breaking the Fourth Wall and Sex Role Stereotypes: An Examination of the 2006–2007 Prime-Time Season," *Sex Roles: Journal of Research* 60(5–6), 2009, 379–86.

12. Amy Chozick, "The Women behind 'Mad Men,'" *Wall Street Journal*, August 7, 2009.

13. "The Men behind AMC's Hit 'Mad Men.'"

14. De Beauvoir, xxi–xxii.

15. Ibid., xxi.

16. Ibid., xxx.

PART THREE

"AND YOU KNOW WHAT HAPPINESS IS?": *MAD MEN* AND ETHICS

"IN ON IT": HONESTY, RESPECT, AND THE ETHICS OF ADVERTISING

Andreja Novakovic and Tyler Whitney

In "A Night to Remember" (episode 208), Betty has been preparing a dinner party all week and is proud to present the international foods and beverages she has selected for the occasion. When she draws her guests' attention to the Heineken beer from Holland, Herman "Duck" Phillips, head of accounts at Sterling Cooper, is stunned. He explains that Don, Betty's husband, had proposed a marketing strategy for Heineken to target women like Betty. "He said you were the market, and you are." Betty waits until her guests have left before she confronts Don about the incident and accuses him repeatedly of embarrassing her. She points out, "And then you laughed. . . . Must be so funny, being in on it." This confrontation eventually leads to a crisis in Betty and Don's marriage and provokes Betty to banish Don from their home. It is also the first time—and so far the only time—in *Mad Men* that we witness a confrontation between the ad man and the consumer he has allegedly "duped."

At first glance, it may look like the Heineken incident is merely an excuse for Betty to confront Don about an even greater source of embarrassment, namely, his affair with Bobbie Barrett. In the previous episode ("The Gold Violin," episode 207) Don and Betty attended a gala during which Betty found out about Don's infidelity. She was seated next to Jimmy Barrett, watching Don and Bobbie talking business at the bar, when Jimmy first broke the news to her. What Betty realized was not just that Don is cheating on her, but that he is cheating on her with someone he clearly respects more than her. As Jimmy put it, "Look at us, over here at the kids' table," while their spouses are conversing like adults. It seems that the real issue in both situations—Don's overt affair with Bobbie as well as Betty's sense of being duped by Don's advertising scheme—is respect. This suggests that the Heineken incident is more than an excuse for Betty. It reveals the basic structure of their marriage, in which Don lies to her and treats her like a gullible child.

This structure becomes most explicit when they confront each other in the roles of advertiser and consumer. According to Betty, Don and his colleagues are all "in on it," and they laugh at her because she is not. But the Heineken incident does more than expose the lack of honesty and respect in their personal relationship. It also raises questions about the ethics of advertising and the possibility of honesty and respect in the relationship between ad man and consumer.

Advertising poses at least two central ethical concerns. On the one hand, its methods seem to involve forms of manipulation that undermine the status of the consumer as agent. In other words, the consumer is subject to influences that remain opaque to her and so is not in a position to make her decisions on the basis of reasons. On the other hand, advertising involves an asymmetry in knowledge, because the advertiser is said to know the consumer's desires better than she knows them herself. Inspired by *Mad Men*'s treatment of these concerns, we want to explore the extent to which advertising is in tension with honesty and respect and ultimately raise the question of what an honest and respectful form of advertising might look like.

Respect and Honesty in Kant's Ethics

Before examining the ethical debates surrounding advertising, let's consider an argument for the codependence of honesty and respect. The German Enlightenment philosopher Immanuel Kant (1724–1804) identifies respect as the most basic ethical attitude owed to persons irrespective of their individual achievements. According to Kant, "Every human being has a legitimate claim to respect from his fellow human beings and is *in turn* bound to respect every other."[1] In this way he challenges our ordinary notion of respect as something that must be earned. For Kant, to respect someone is to treat that individual as an agent capable of acting rationally, while disrespecting her is in effect to deny her personhood—that is, to deny that she is a person.

Kant also gives us reasons to think that respect in this sense is incompatible with dishonesty toward others. In his "categorical imperative," specifically his formula of humanity, Kant argues that we ought never to treat another person merely as a means, but always also as an end.[2] Although this claim has a range of implications, his examples suggest that one of his targets is a certain kind of deception. Kant describes someone who sets out to make a lying promise, acting on the principle that when in need, it is permissible to borrow money without the intention of repaying it. Such an action fails the categorical imperative because I can only attain my goal—getting the other person to lend me money—as long as I withhold my true intentions from her. In other words, I cannot in principle communicate my principle of action without undermining that very action. So one aspect of treating others as ends, and not merely as means, is to act in such a way that I am able to disclose my own ends to them. Kant takes the codependence of honesty and respect very seriously. In his essay "On a Supposed Right to Lie from Philanthropy,"[3] he argues that it is never morally permissible to lie to another, even when one's intentions are supposedly philanthropic, though we do have a duty to make the happiness of others our end.

The Kantian model suggests that the appropriate attitude toward agents—beings who have reasons for doing what they do and are not merely determined by impulses and desires—is one of respect. We can see this distinction clearly by contrasting it with our attitudes toward children. While we should respect children in a certain sense—since they are potentially rational creatures, we have a negative duty not to harm them and a positive duty to make their happiness our end—we also treat children as unprepared to make their own decisions, for children are not yet capable of understanding what they are doing and why they are doing it. This is why we don't have a duty to be honest with them in the way we ought to be with adults. So Betty's realization that she is seated at the "kids' table" while her husband is engaging in a serious conversation with another woman only emphasizes Don's pervasive lack of respect for her, for this is not the first time that she finds herself reduced to the position of a child.

Brainwashing on Madison Avenue

In the context of advertising, the problem of agency arises most prominently in discussions about the methods advertisers employ in order to persuade consumers to buy a particular product. Cultural critics writing during the time in which *Mad Men* takes place frequently described advertising strategies as ensnaring consumers in a "helpless state" of vulnerable suggestibility.[4] In addition to the focus groups, two-way mirrors, and statistical models employed by Sterling Cooper, ad men at the time applied psychological research on visual perception and on the nature of human desires to devise elaborate campaigns that sought to infiltrate the realm of the unconscious and manipulate the individual's actions without her knowledge.

While advertisers had in their possession a map of the human psyche—a seemingly endless reservoir of information regarding the influence of packaging art, commercial slogans, and product placement—the consumer was denied access to the factors motivating her decisions and was instead guided by invisible forces beyond her control. The consumer could no longer be conceived of as a self-conscious agent, but rather as a passive recipient of subliminal messages and advertising tricks that compelled her to blindly choose products for reasons of which she was not conscious and so could not retrospectively retrieve.

It is therefore not surprising that public anxieties surrounding the supposedly devious methods employed by advertisers were often articulated in terms of "brainwashing" and "hypnotic suggestion." First introduced by Edward Hunter in his 1951 book, *Brainwashing in Red China: The Calculated Destruction of Men's Minds*, the term *brainwashing* was originally used to describe an updated form of hypnotism, a kind of psychological warfare waged by Soviet and Chinese communists against both their own populations as well as captured American soldiers during the Korean War (1950–1953). Ironically, in Hunter's explicitly pro-Western account of the evils of Soviet brainwashing, he uses American ads and commercials to explain brainwashing to his readers. In doing so, he unintentionally suggests a disturbing overlap between communist strategies of indoctrination and the psychological underpinnings of Western advertising. Developers of the cutting-edge subliminal advertising technology "Precon" (short for "pre-consciousness")—which allowed companies to flash imperceptible images of various products for only a split second at a time during movies and television shows—would soon have to deny accusations by enraged citizens and governmental officials that they were "brainwashing" viewers without their knowledge.[5]

The ambiguous line separating communist propaganda and advertising in the United States was not only limited to the particularly objectionable use of subliminal images, but also encompassed more common tactics like product placement, slogans, and packaging art. In his 1957 bestselling study of advertising, *The Hidden Persuaders*, Vance Packard argued that American advertising and the broader culture of the West created passive citizens who were unable to resist the conformist trends of mass culture and helplessly surrendered to the marketing techniques cooked up on Madison Avenue. According to Packard, "Many of us are being influenced and manipulated, far more than we realize, in the patterns of our everyday lives."[6] He goes on to emphasize the ways in which products strategically arranged on the shelves of the supermarket are intended to "hypnotize" female customers "like a flashlight waved in front of [their] eyes."[7] We can imagine Betty Draper as fitting this description, although we never witness her behavior in the supermarket when she decides to purchase the Heineken beer.

Such manipulative techniques ultimately gave rise to heated debates regarding the ethics of advertising. One central question concerned whether these techniques were inherently pernicious or whether it was possible to employ them for good ends. The public, however, was not convinced by this distinction. First, people were suspicious about the supposedly good ends that motivated advertisers. Advertising did not look to be in the service of merely satisfying consumers' preexisting desires. In order to continue to sell products, advertisers quickly realized that their task also involved generating new desires and convincing consumers that they in fact needed these products. This made many critics skeptical that advertisers could ever have the consumer's best interests in mind. We can find such a critic in Roy, Midge Daniel's beatnik friend, who in "The Hobo Code" (episode 108) attacks a stoned Don Draper for being in the business of creating false needs: "You make the lie. You invent want. You're for them, not us."

Second, consumers worried about the loss of control in the face of manipulative methods that circumvented their conscious awareness. There seemed to be something inherently problematic about such forms of persuasion, regardless of the ends for which they were used. It did not look to be possible to retain one's agency when confronted with subliminal influences—including product placement and the color of the packaging—which elicited predictable responses and created a sense of compulsion to buy. As Vance Packard put it, advertisers invest products with a hypnotic quality "so that the housewife will stick out her hand for it rather than one of many rivals."[8] It is not clear that these compelled responses can even be considered actions in the proper sense, since the consumer is not fully aware of what she is doing and is certainly not aware of why she is doing it. According to the Kantian model, such behavior would not count as an expression of agency precisely because the consumer is here not acting on reasons at all, but on mere drives or impulses and is in this respect no different from an animal. The problem is not only that she is not being regarded as an agent, but that she in fact ceases to be an agent altogether, as her hand reaches blindly for the product calculated to draw her in.

Marketing and Marriage

In many ways Don Draper does not conform to this picture of advertising. In the very first episode of the series ("Smoke Gets in Your Eyes"), he dramatically discards the psychological research intended to appeal to the subconscious desires of the consumer—in this case, the Freudian death drive. It looks as if Don rejects scientific calculations of consumer responses in favor of an intuitive grasp of the psyche, which he takes himself to possess. Don believes that he has privileged knowledge of important facets of the human being that often fall through the cracks of statistical research on desire and motivation. We see him turning to film and poetry rather than to psychological reports employed by many of his contemporaries.

At the same time, the Heineken incident provides us with one of the only glimpses into Don's attitude toward the consumer. Most of the show takes place within the office, where we see Don interact with clients and other executives but not with the consumer to whom he is tailoring his ads. Don's strategic placement of the beer amidst elaborate end-aisle displays and his attempt to target a particular demographic—in this case, the wealthy, educated suburban housewife—are both very much in line with the kinds of tactics dominant at the time, as we have already seen in Vance Packard's account. It is interesting that the only concrete example of a persuaded consumer turns out to be Betty, Don's wife.

In fact, Don admits that he frequently uses personal knowledge for advertising purposes. When Betty confronts him about the Heineken incident, he replies, "I use our life in my work all the time. They pay me for that." This privileging of personal knowledge over mass-market research becomes most explicit in his subsequent conversation with a representative of Heineken. The latter, impressed by the success of the proposed campaign in the context of Don and Betty's dinner party, remarks, "Not exactly scientific, although it sounds like you do know your wife." But Don's knowledge of Betty is not of her particular or idiosyncratic qualities. Rather, he knows her as a type—in particular, as a wealthy, educated, suburban housewife. This seems to be the reason why his personal knowledge is even relevant to his work, why he gets paid to use his life for advertising.

Betty clearly feels threatened by his knowledge of her. She seems uncomfortable with the fact that she can be reduced to a social category and that her responses can be so easily predicted. She ultimately retaliates by insisting that she does have the same kind of knowledge of him that he has of her. "You think you know me?" she retorts during the argument after the notorious dinner party. "Well, I know what kind of a man you are!" There she tries to assert that Don can also be reduced to a type and that she knows his "kind." But it is ultimately more an expression of a desire, motivated by her sense of powerlessness, for she in fact has very little knowledge of him. At the time, she knows nothing about Don's past, or even about his current activities. For example, when she searches his papers for evidence of his infidelity, she finds nothing but advertising slogans written on napkins and scorecards. Excluded from Don's professional life, to which she is little more than a glamorous accessory, she is limited to her perspective from the "kids' table." Moreover, when she does attempt to enter the world of advertising by modeling in a Coke commercial, Don ultimately thwarts her effort to cross over from consumer to advertiser. He does so indirectly, by turning down another job offer knowing that Betty will thereby be fired. While this incident contains certain ambiguities concerning Don's motivation for terminating her modeling career, he is clearly displeased by the prospect that she would enter this world.

Just as cultural critics and the public at large articulated fears concerning an asymmetry of knowledge between consumer and advertiser, Betty is repeatedly placed on the other side of this divide, a perspective that excludes her from becoming privy to Don's activities as an ad man as well as to his extramarital affairs. The Heineken incident therefore exposes the frightening similarities between her ignorance of the marketing strategies at play in the supermarket and her lack of knowledge of the lies Don feeds her. When in "Six Month Leave" she remarks, "I thought you could talk anyone into anything," she is alluding to both Don's professional as well as his personal demeanor. She frames the Heineken incident as an issue of respect, asking Don why he "insists on humiliating" her, and Don eventually admits in the season two finale ("Meditations in an Emergency") that he was "not respectful" to her. This conflict points to the slippage between Don's attitude toward Betty as a consumer and his treatment of her as a wife.

Don claims that advertising should be aimed at selling happiness. In the first episode ("Smoke Gets in Your Eyes"), he announces that "advertising is based on one thing: happiness. And you know what happiness is? Happiness is the smell of a new car; it's freedom from fear; it's a billboard on the side of the road that screams with reassurance that whatever you're doing, it's okay. You are okay." This is the good end for which he employs deceptive measures, presenting a product in the most favorable light, even if that means neglecting its negative qualities. When Don discards the psychological research on the Freudian death drive, he is not merely rejecting the use of science in advertising; he is arguing that people do not want to know the harmful effects of cigarettes, but want to believe that smoking will make them happy. According to Don, happiness is what justifies his use of manipulative methods, since people want to be sold happiness even at the expense of truth.

He extends this conception of advertising to his marriage, telling Betty that she does not need to know about his premarital and extramarital life, as long as her needs are met and her desires satisfied. Kant would agree that we ought to make other people's happiness our end, and he considers this an integral aspect of respect. At the same time, Kant objects that it is ever morally permissible to pursue this goal at the cost of honesty. So Don's attitude toward the consumer as well as toward his wife is in tension with the Kantian requirement that we must treat others never merely as means, but also always as ends.

The Question of Ethical Advertising

In accusing Don of thinking that he can talk anyone into anything, Betty indicates that ad men presuppose a certain conception of others, which is problematic as such and becomes even more so when it infects interpersonal relationships. In "The Question of Morality," the last chapter of *The Hidden Persuaders*, Vance Packard had already raised questions about the compatibility of advertising and ethics, focusing on what he took to be advertisers' basic attitude toward the human being. He writes,

> What are the implications of all this persuasion in terms of our existing morality? What does it mean for the national morality to have so many powerfully influential people taking a manipulative attitude toward our society? Some of these persuaders, in their energetic endeavors to sway our actions, seem to fall unwittingly into the attitude that man exists to be manipulated.[9]

Although this observation does not imply that advertisers must adopt this picture of man, it suggests a general tendency in this business of persuasion, which has particular bearing on the problem of respect. Packard goes on to cite a comment by a public relations man in 1954 who claimed that manipulation of the human being "inherently involves a disrespect for the individual personality."[10] It is worth recalling that Kant considers respect to be incompatible with an attitude toward people as mere means to be used, manipulated, and deceived. Given Kant's argument, is it possible to honor the ethical standard of respect in the context of advertising?

We can begin to address this question by considering what it would mean to influence people in an honest manner. According to Kant, persuasion is unethical if you cannot reveal what you are doing to the person affected by your action because she would not agree to it. This is most explicit in the example of the lying promise, since the individual you are deceiving would never lend you money were she aware of your true ends. In the case of advertising, the question would have to be posed in the following terms: Would a consumer buy the product were she aware of why she is buying it, or do these influences on her decision have to remain opaque to her for advertising to achieve its aim? In fact, Vance Packard understood his own book as contributing to an ethics of advertising because it revealed the methods being used behind the scenes. For Packard, the possibility of ethical advertising came down to the question of knowledge. "In virtually all situations," he claims, "we still have the choice, and we cannot be too seriously manipulated if we know what is going on."[11] Although there is no reason to conclude that advertising must in principle keep its own methods concealed, the worry is that knowing these methods would detract from their commercial efficacy, given that our responses to ads would no longer be immediate and passive.

Interestingly enough, *Mad Men* seems to have provoked sponsors like Canada Dry and BMW to present themselves as companies that subscribe to more transparent forms of advertising. As a television show that continues to rely heavily on commercial support, its exposure of the means of manipulation employed by advertisers might look to be at odds with the necessary conditions for its continued existence. Commercial advertisers have instead attempted to set themselves apart from the underhanded tricks of the trade and incorporate this critique into their own methods. First, commercials aired during the show are often preceded by a list of facts about the history of each company set against the backdrop of images from the show's opening credits. Second, the commercials themselves present a more straightforward description of the product, whose quality they claim has stood the test of time without the need for slogans and gimmicks. *Mad Men*'s fictional picture of the world of advertising seems to have had an effect on this world by inspiring ads stripped to the bare minimum in which the products supposedly speak for themselves. Such efforts can be described as ways of staging more transparent forms of persuasion. In short, it looks like a television program that explores the ethics of advertising has given rise to the advertising of ethics, suggesting that, unlike Betty Draper, contemporary viewers can become "in on it."

NOTES

1. Immanuel Kant, "The Metaphysics of Morals" [1797]. In *Practical Philosophy*, edited by Mary J. Gregor (Cambridge: Cambridge University Press, 1996), 579 [6:462].

2. Immanuel Kant, "The Groundwork of the Metaphysics of Morals" [1785]. In *Practical Philosophy*, edited by Mary J. Gregor (Cambridge: Cambridge University Press, 1996), 80 [4:429].

3. Immanuel Kant, "On a Supposed Right to Lie from Philanthropy" [1797]. In *Practical Philosophy*, edited by Mary J. Gregor (Cambridge: Cambridge University Press, 1996), 605–615.

4. Marshall McLuhan, *The Mechanical Bride: Folklore of Industrial Man* (New York: Vanguard Press, 1951), v.

5. "Subliminal Ads Wash No Brains, Declare Moore, Becker, Developers of Precon Device," *Advertising Age*, 28(48), December 2, 1957, 81.

6. Vance Packard, *The Hidden Persuaders* (New York: David McKay Company, 1957), 3.

7. Ibid., 108.

8. Ibid.

9. Ibid., 255.

10. Ibid., 259.

11. Ibid., 265.

CREATING THE NEED FOR THE NEW: "IT'S NOT THE WHEEL. IT'S THE CAROUSEL."

George Teschner and Gabrielle Teschner

Advertising turns the strange and new into the familiar and necessary. We are led to believe that the products of industrialized society were needed before they were invented. It is difficult to accept that advertising crafted your needs for the toothbrush, the cell phone, and cruise control, but society collectively goes about approving and rejecting so-called necessities subconsciously on a daily basis. Our habits and expectations adjust accordingly. Think of the scene in which Sally Draper walks into her mother's room with a plastic dry-cleaning bag over her head ("Ladies Room," episode 102). We know instantly that this means danger, but Betty merely scolds her for emptying the bag's contents. Someone at some time campaigned to plant the warning of choking squarely in our memory, just as ad agencies were instrumental in convincing us of the value of the family car over public transportation.

Advertising may be many things—communication, information, entertainment—but most of all, it is creative persuasion. In vitro fertilization, surrogate motherhood, smart bombs, and cell phones all have associated meanings that challenge our values. In *Mad Men*, we watch how advertising in technological society plays out in the lives of characters who are instrumental in creating it. During the late 1950s and early 1960s, technological innovations like diet soda, the Pill, Liquid Paper, and the Rolodex all had to be seen through the lens of a new system of values to be commercially viable. They had to be transformed from novelties into necessities.

In the absence of technology, humans would be fewer in number, would occupy much less of the surface of Earth, and would be confined to areas where there was a natural abundance of food. But humans *could* live without technology. It is not humans who need technology; it is technology that needs technology. Instead of drinking water from a forest stream, our need is met by turning on a faucet. The faucet, however, needs water to be collected in reservoirs. Engines and electric motors need to pump water through pipes that have been made from steel and plastic, which in turn need to be made at foundries and chemical plants. The needs spread across the entire web of technological society. One thing needs another, but are these our needs? Advertising convinces us that they are.

Manufacturing Truth "on a Bed Made of Money"

Advertising, like technology, aims at prediction and control. When Don is working on the Heineken account, he suggests that the target market should be housewives. Indeed, he appears to foresee that his own wife will buy Heineken for her dinner party. Believing that Don arranged the whole thing to prove his point, Betty accuses Don of embarrassing and humiliating her ("A Night to Remember," episode 208). As Betty bears witness, advertising offends the humanistic ideal that human beings are free and autonomous agents of their actions. While Betty seems to take offense at just this one instance of advertising, others find the whole advertising industry problematic. When Midge, Don's Greenwich Village lover, takes Don and her friend Roy to a bohemian nightclub, Don defends his job in advertising, saying to Roy, "People want to be told what to do so badly that they will listen to anyone" ("Babylon," episode 106). Roy had complained that Madison Avenue created the religion of mass consumption, and he was right to a certain extent. It is a religion in the sense that advertising has made commodities into totems and fetishes. Roy is mistaken, however, when he says that advertising is "perpetuating lies." In actuality, advertising is creating truths, albeit ones that are relative and impermanent.

Traditionally, philosophers have defined knowledge as "justified true belief." Today it is advertising that creates the standards for what is counted as "justifiable," "truthful," and "believable." This is no different from the role that other institutions have had in society. During a sales meeting for an ad for Popsicles, Peggy compares breaking a Popsicle in half with the ritual of giving Holy Communion and says, "Let me tell you something, the Catholic Church knows how to sell things" ("The Mountain King," episode 212).

Roy asks Don how he sleeps at night. Roy is assuming that there is some independent moral standard, a conscience, or a universal moral nature against which the values of consumerism can be judged. As he pays for the round of drinks, Don replies that he sleeps on "a bed made of money" ("Babylon"). Instead of moral sensibility, Don is talking about power. Money can be exchanged not only for material comforts, but also for respectability, for freedom, for influence, and for a person's identity.

Technology is all about power and efficiency. Karl Marx (1818–1883) criticizes money for the "distorting and confounding of all human and natural qualities," but acknowledges that money "converts my wishes . . . into their sensuous, actual existence—from imagination to life, . . . from imagined being into real being . . . [money] is the truly creative power."[1] Advertising creates values, but it also creates the power necessary to realize those values in what is tangible and real. Roy's criticism of Madison Avenue can end only in resentment. Its passion can live only in relation to, and in repeatedly recalling, that which it despises. In resentfully pointing the finger at those more powerful than him, Roy exemplifies what Friedrich Nietzsche (1844–1900) calls the "slave mentality."

Don understands something about Roy that Roy doesn't understand about himself. Roy's values are no different from that of the "middle class" that he rejects. Don says to Roy, "And I have a feeling that you spent more time on your hair than she did," referring to Midge. Despite Roy's ideology, his values are middle-class—the values of the average consumer. If he and Midge both spent time on their hair, it is because advertising made it important. Roy complains that Broadway is the birthplace of mediocrity. Don replies coolly that if Broadway is its birthplace, then their nightclub is where it is conceived. The tiff between Roy and Don takes place against the background of performances of the reading of a matrimonial section out of a local newspaper and the recitation of kitsch political poetry by a woman who exposes her breasts at calls from the audience. Don says, sarcastically, "I should go . . . too much art for me." If the art of Broadway is mediocrity, then Don, who is free of the rigid ideology of Roy, perceives that the performance "art" that they witness in the bohemian nightclub is no different.

Draperian Nihilism

For Nietzsche, the role of creating value in society was in the hands of what he called the *Übermensch*, the "overman," aka the "superman," who out of a tragic and nihilistic consciousness affirmed life and human existence by creating values where none had existed before. These values eventually are experienced by culture as integral and necessary to its existence, defining what it means to be human, setting the standards for what is morally good, aesthetically beautiful, and epistemically true. Don Draper asks Rachel Menken, the wealthy Fifth Avenue department store proprietor, why she is not married. Her reply is that she has never been in love. Draper retorts, "What you call love was invented by guys like me to sell nylons" ("Smoke Gets in Your Eyes," episode 101). If what Draper says is true, love, which many regard as the deepest and most real of human emotions, turns out to be a construct invented by the advertising industry to sell clothing. Rachel maintains that love is not just a slogan. She means that it is not just a word, but that there is a thing, an objective reality, to which the word corresponds. Rachel believes that if there were no word *love*, the thing, love, would nevertheless be something that people would feel; it would still exist without the word. Draper, though, says that the reason she has not felt it is because it does not exist.

The common belief is that love unites people, creates community, and binds together lovers, families, and marriages. Instead, Draper says that we are "born alone and die alone." The rules of society, that is, its customs, taboos, and values, are designed, according to Draper, to make us forget our solitary existence. He, on the other hand, "never forgets it, and lives as if there is no tomorrow . . . since," as he claims, "there is not one" ("Smoke Gets in Your Eyes").

For Nietzsche, creativity is only possible within Draper's style of nihilism. It is out of the absence of all and any value that the Nietzschian *Übermensch* creates new value. Unlike the "herd," who believe that these values are universal, objective, and real, the Nietzschian overman sees the values against the background of nihilism and knows them to be human inventions.

Anti-foundationalism is the position that there is no unchanging and universal basis of value. Draper's life embodies anti-foundationalism, in which stable social institutions like marriage and family are fleeting and evanescent. Suzanne Farrell, the critical but seducible grade-school teacher, tells Don about a student who asks whether everyone sees the color blue the same way ("The Color Blue," episode 310). Don explains that "people may see things differently but they don't really want to." It is not only the color blue that is experienced differently, but every sensation, emotion, and thought. Don says his "job is about boiling down communication to its essentials." It is social convention that creates the illusion that the same word means the same thing to different people. The belief that we share a common world is a construct of language. A person who sees only shades of gray can effectively use a color vocabulary with someone who sees color, although unknown to each, their perceptions are very different. Don's reply gives a further level of depth to his remark to Rachel that we are "born alone and die alone." No matter how intimate we feel with another person, we may live in totally different worlds. Linguistic convention just makes it appear otherwise.

The Camel, the Lion, and the Child

How necessary is such a nihilism for the creativity required to advance culture-transforming technologies? Nietzsche, in "The Metamorphoses of the Spirit,"[2] a chapter from *Thus Spake Zarathustra*, describes the genesis of the creative spirit in three stages—the camel, the lion, and the child. The first (the camel) is the load-bearing spirit that bears the weight of the taboos of society. The lion represents the power that kills the dragon of the sacred Thou Shalts and Thou Shalt Nots—the permission and prohibition of society. The third stage of the spirit is the child, which Nietzsche calls "a new beginning" and a "self-propelled wheel," where human consciousness is no longer burdened by the norms of society. It is able to create out of forgetting, innocence, and spontaneity. Creation and destruction are never far apart.

Don Draper embodies what for Nietzsche are the destructive and creative dimensions of the spirit. At the end of the third season, Don confronts Roger and Bert with the proposal to form a new company after hearing that Sterling Cooper is to be once again bought and sold. The consequence of the creation of Sterling Cooper Draper Pryce likely will be the destruction of the livelihood of everyone else who worked at the old firm. The destruction of the old constitutes a forgetting and a sinking into the unconscious that is often associated with dreams.

While developing the ad campaign for a cigarette company threatened by reports that smoking causes cancer, Don falls asleep. Describing the essence of the creative process, Draper once advised Peggy, "Just think about it deeply, and forget it, and an idea will jump in your face" ("Indian Summer," episode 111). He comes to the meeting with the Lucky Strike executives empty-handed. After an embarrassing silence, the executives begin to leave. Suddenly Draper, appearing inspired, comes up with the slogan "It's toasted." He does not challenge or debate the report that cigarettes are poisonous, which he earlier drops in the trash and calls "perverse." He diverts attention toward what sounds completely affirmative. His slogan addresses the subliminal associations that surround the connotations of words. Advertising is designed, he claims, to make people feel good about themselves. It gives them the reassurance that "Whatever you are doing is okay. You are okay" ("Smoke Gets in Your Eyes"). This is not deception, not lying, but the power of words to create reality. For Draper it is a reality without a past and without a future. As he says, he lives as if there is no future because there is none, nor is there any reality other than the ones posited and shaped by language.

An Indifferent Universe

The absence of values, other than the ones that we create, is the nihilism of Nietzsche. This is, of course, hard to accept for those who believe in truth. Roy again critiques Don: "You make the lie . . . you invent want." Roy is assuming that there is a difference between truth and "the lie," between natural wants and those that are artificial. Don responds by saying, "There is no big lie. There is no system. The universe is indifferent" ("The Hobo Code," episode 108).

In Don's life, this indifference negates a myriad of values such as loyalty, honesty, reliability, and, in this case, truth. There is nothing in the nature of things that would serve as a way of differentiating true from false, right from wrong, honest from dishonest. Don does not show the slightest qualm in telling Betty that he is leaving for work when he is on his way to spend the night with his daughter's elementary school teacher. He lies to Betty without the apparent sense that he is violating her trust. He tells her, "Betts, I have no choice," to which she replies dutifully, "I see how hard you're working" ("The Color Blue"). Betty is assuming the role of the supportive wife, and clearly Don often does not have values beyond the utility of the moment.

Efficiency Is the Highest Value

The supreme and absolute value in technological culture is efficiency—efficiency as an end in itself. Means trump ends. An exclusively instrumental system of values does not ask what is it all for, what end or ultimate goal is being served. Without something that has intrinsic value (that is, something valuable in itself and not as a means to an end), there is no foundation to provide a lasting support for value judgments. As Joan says to

Peggy, "If you are even thinking of passing judgment, you are in the wrong business" ("5G," episode 105). This is the ethical mantra of exclusively technological consciousness.

Don's responsibility is to create an advertising campaign that will sell cigarettes. To consider consequences is, in Don's words, "perverse" ("Smoke Gets in Your Eyes"). The concern for final ends and foundations is ignored, provided that a means is found to solve the problem at hand. Roger Sterling praises Don for his moment of inspiration. Peter Campbell says, "I was telling them how amazing you were. I am still tingling" ("Shoot," episode 109). Neither middle nor upper management at Sterling Cooper ever considers the morality of their actions. Why should they? The universe is indifferent and you are part of the universe.

When Peter tells Bert Cooper that Don Draper is really Dick Whitman and accuses Draper of being a "fraud, a liar, and a criminal even," Cooper replies, like someone speaking to the moral innocence of a child, "Who cares?" Cooper draws attention back to the immediacy of the moment, telling Campbell, "A man is whatever room he is in," adding "At this moment, Donald Draper is in this room" ("Nixon vs. Kennedy," episode 112). So Donald Draper is no other than Donald Draper at this point in time and space. He may have been Dick Whitman in the past, and he may become someone else in the future, but he is Donald Draper here and now. Appearance is reality. Saying so makes it so. There are no meanings other than the ones we construct. This is the positive side of the claim "the universe is indifferent." It gives us the freedom to create—even our own identities.

The *Principium Individuationis*

For Nietzsche, a precondition for great art is the collapse of what he calls the *principium individuationis*,[3] the principle of individuation, or the personal ego. The disintegration of the ego results from the insight that the universe is indifferent—the "abyss of being." True artistic achievement becomes possible, according to Nietzsche, by the artist overcoming the purely personal and subjective and attaining the objectivity and the universality of detached contemplation.

Don Draper's identity is fluid and mercurial. Dick Whitman became Don Draper. Recalling his troubled past, he looks out of the train at his family standing before the coffin of Dick Whitman (containing the body of Don Draper) and sees, as the train pulls away, the person who he was disappear. He severs the one remaining connection with the life of Dick Whitman by refusing reunion with his half-brother, explaining to him that he has a life "that goes only in one direction—forward" ("5G"). He coldly tells Adam, "I don't want to see or hear from you ever again. . . . You thought that I was dead, just go back to thinking that."

When Peter Campbell threatens to reveal his identity, Don rushes to Rachel Menken ready to leave everything behind. "We'll start over again like Adam and Eve," he says. Rachel's life and identity are securely rooted in running her father's department store. She asks Don what kind of man he is that he can leave his wife and children. Even his relationship to advertising is tenuous. He says to Roger, after an offer to go with the much larger firm of McCann Erikson, "If I leave this place one day it will not be for more advertising." On his trip to California he disappears and takes up with Joy and her family, whose sexual liberty, financial freedom, and degree of leisure shock even Don ("The Jet Set," episode 211). Don's suitcase is delivered to his home in Ossining and left at the front door, while his team back at Sterling Cooper wonders what has happened to him. Joy's family represents a level of wealth that is orders of magnitude removed from the lifestyle Don has known. When he is abruptly introduced to their world, he becomes disoriented and faints. This fainting spell and the periods of sleep that often precede his artistic insights represent moments of inspiration resulting from a discontinuity in his identity and his world.

The Carousel

Martin Heidegger (1889–1976), the first Western philosopher to think deeply about technology, contrasted the technology of ancient Greece with the technology of contemporary Western culture. He argued that in ancient Greece what was useful (*techné*) was not separate from what was true (*epistemé*), the making beautiful (*poésis*), and holy (*promos*).[4] Art was a single manifold. An instrumental object that was not at the same time a revealer of truth, that did not possess elements of the beautiful and the sublime, was a thing of diminished value, something that at some level was offensive. A simple tool or artifact revealed or opened up a way of interpreting the world. Truth for Heidegger is a bringing-to-light of something that was not seen previously. The kind of making that in ancient Greece was called *techné* brought to light something that was simultaneously beautiful and sublime. A humble kitchen utensil can make a statement about the relation between man and Earth and the meaning of food that is implied in the instrument's design. When art is not at the same time a revealer—an interpretation that opens up features of the world that otherwise would be concealed—then art is merely a science of taste reduced to the level of ornamentation. Heidegger is not talking about art typically displayed in museums, but art that is at the same time useful and true in the sense that it reveals an interpretation of what is that did not exist before. Advertising is such a form of art.

Don Draper creates an advertisement for Kodak's new slide projector that uses a circular tray that stores and loads slides automatically. Kodak's technical staff prosaically calls it the Wheel and the Donut. Duck Phillips, impressed, says it is "actually a hell of a gadget, continuous, and doesn't jam."

He asks Don to "find some way of putting the Wheel into the future with some legs" ("The Wheel," episode 113). The Wheel is not going to have a future unless it is reinterpreted in a way that integrates it seamlessly into people's lives and opens up a world that they never lived in before. Pointing to the projector on his office desk, Don asks Harry Crane what its purpose is, but Harry, not seeing anything beyond the commercial value, cynically says, "To sell projectors to people that already have them." Harry tells Don about how he once took "artsy" black-and-white pictures of handprints on glass that reminded him of the Lascaux cave paintings. The hands, he said, looked like they were reaching through the stone and saying "I was here." Harry leaves Don in silence, and Don then falls back to sleep.

Don frequently emerges from sleep with subliminal insights, and in this case with pieces of the conversation he had with Harry. In the presentation, Don transfigures the Wheel into the Carousel, comparing it to a merry-go-round and associating it for his audience of Kodak executives with memories of childhood and important milestones in the life of a family—his family. Don speaks of the Carousel as reaching back into the past, as a time machine that takes us back to a place where we know we were loved. Harry Crane, whose marriage is in trouble, is so moved by the presentation that he is compelled to leave the room. It is noteworthy how this form of art that is advertising is able to produce wealth when properly positioned between buyers and sellers in the economy of exchange.

The Carousel is art, which in Heidegger's thought redefines objects by revealing the world in a new light. It reclassifies and reinterprets objects so that they take on additional values besides usefulness, such as monetary values. But it is other values as well that give us what, in Don's words, is a "sentimental bond with the object." It adds to what is exclusively utilitarian the other elements of Heidegger's single manifold.

It moves the object from what Duck called "a hell of a gadget" into a focal point of community and meaning.

Creator versus Consumer

We ask what kind of consciousness is able to bring about this redefining of the present into a new and different future. It is the difference between the creator of value and the consumer of value. Don Draper creates from a consciousness that is outside community. He says, "You are born alone and die alone, and the world just drops a bunch of rules on you to forget those facts . . . but I never forget" ("Smoke Gets in Your Eyes"). It is living outside those rules that enables Don Draper to be a creator of culture and not merely a consumer.

Draper rejects the Right Guard deodorant advertisement that compares the aerosol can to a rocket. Paul Kinsey says, "It is space age, it's steel, it is even shaped like a rocket, it's shiny, it's explosive; it's from the future" ("Ladies Room"). The art that accompanies the copy depicts an astronaut suspended in space. To see the aerosol can as a rocket does not redefine the aerosol can in a way that inserts it as a necessity into the lives of people. "Who buys this? . . . Some woman," Draper says "Bring it down to earth."

To integrate the object into human existence requires redefining how it is perceived—not as a rocket, a machine, or a tool, but instead in terms of the intimacy between a man and a woman. Draper asks, "What would make a woman look at a man's deodorant and say 'I want that'?" He later muses, as he lies in bed beside his lover Midge, "What does a woman want? . . . Any excuse to get closer." Midge observes, "There is the ego that people pay to see." However, this slogan does not come from the ego but from a place beneath and behind the ego. Don's answer carries with it all the gender issues of the time, but he turns the aerosol can from a masculine image into a feminine icon—something that brings a man and a woman together.

A Tragic Hero

Don Draper is a tragic hero. He is heroic because he is at the front line where technological innovation, which produces the new, confronts the status quo and well-entrenched value systems that desire to see and do things the old way. Technological innovation shakes up infrastructure. The failure to introduce the metric system into American culture is an example. Few Americans think of distances in kilometers despite daily being face to face with the metric scale on the speedometer. Don must place himself outside the norms of culture in order to create values that embrace innovation. The tragic side of this results in destructive behavior that damages his relationship with his family and distances him from his coworkers. He lives a secret and solitary life. As Harry says about Don, "No one ever lifted that rock" ("Ladies Room").

Don Draper's work requires him to appeal to impulses in people that they are unaware of in themselves. Most women would not admit that they want to be Jackie Kennedy by day and Marilyn Monroe by night. But to sell undergarments, Don must remain in touch with these impulses, which are unconscious and repressed. As Don says, in contrasting himself with Duck, "I sell products, not advertising." Duck is a businessman. His thinking is calculative. Don is an artist, and, despite his tailored suit and suave civility, he must periodically descend into the subliminal side of culture to move its values into the future.

Each of Us Would See Ourselves

The animation that accompanies the opening credits shows a man falling past skyscrapers, cathedrals of commerce, and floating advertising slogans. He falls because his life is tragic. If the well-tailored figure were to turn around, we would each see ourselves. We are all moved by an unrelenting pressure to incorporate technological innovation into our lives. Even the wisdom and ideals of our leaders and pundits are no greater than the advertising slogans that make us aware of needs that did not before exist.

NOTES

1. Karl Marx, *Economic and Philosophic Manuscripts of 1844*, "The Power of Money" (Moscow: Progress Publishers, 1959), 61.

2. Friedrich Nietzsche, *Thus Spake Zarathustra* (New York: Penguin, 1969), 54.

3. Friedrich, Nietzsche, *Philosophy of Nietzsche, Birth of Tragedy* (New York: Modern Library, 1954), 959.

4. Martin Heidegger, *The Question Concerning Technology* (New York: Harper Torchbooks), 34.

"YOU'RE LOOKING IN THE WRONG DIRECTION": *MAD MEN* AND THE ETHICS OF ADVERTISING

Adam Barkman

In the very first episode of *Mad Men* ("Smoke Gets in Your Eyes), we are dazzled by Don Draper's advertising skills. Lucky Strike cigarettes is feeling the heat in regard to government regulations on smoking, and it's up to Sterling Cooper to give them new ideas about how to promote their product. In a moment of inspiration, Don suggests they simply focus on one positive thing related to their cigarettes: the tobacco is "toasted." Don's point is that advertising is "based on one thing: happiness," and Lucky Strike needs to keep this—that is, the positive—in mind with their ad campaign. After a successful pitch, Don and his boss Roger Sterling retire to Don's office, where Don looks heavenward and says, "Thank you up there," to which Roger replies, "You're looking in the wrong direction."

And this raises an important question: just what are the ethics of advertising? While Roy Hazelitt sees advertising as a "big lie" and Don's father thinks that creating ads is equivalent to "grow[ing] bullshit," most people don't think advertising in itself is immoral.[1] After all, producers need a means by which they can make the public aware of their products. Still, there are abuses in advertising. Typically, such abuses manifest themselves in four ways: (1) through producers and ad agencies creating advertisements that lie; (2) through producers and ad agencies manipulating and coercing the public; (3) through government action or inaction; and (4) through insufficiently allocating moral responsibility with respect to advertising.[2]

Truth, Lies, and Advertising

Ads aim to not only inform but persuade, and both activities can be done either morally (through appropriate truth-telling) or immorally (by lying). In order to understand the nature of an immoral or lying ad, we first need to be clear about the nature of truth and of true ads.

Truth has to do with both the rational person's intellect and his will. As for the intellect, truth is usually understood to be a kind of equality, rightness, or correspondence between an idea or a sign and the thing itself or signifier. For example, if Don were to think of an ad expressing the proposition "Heineken is a famous international beer," this would be an ad expressing a true proposition, since there is an equality, rightness, or correspondence between these words or signs ("Heineken is a famous international beer") and the things understood or signified (the beer, its country of origin, and its fame). Yet that's not the full extent of truth. The equality or rightness between a sign and its signifier isn't limited to literal statements as in the Heineken case. For example, if an ad for Father Gill's church were to say something like "Come Meet Your Shepherd," these words would literally be false (since God isn't literally a shepherd) but would (if you believe in God) still be true since there is an equality, rightness, or correspondence between the metaphor "shepherd" and God. Additionally, this ad might be superior aesthetically and more informative than an ad that read "Come Meet Your Benevolent Superintendent."

As for the will, truth can be expressed by it through words and actions. Thus, it's one thing to know the truth in one's intellect and another to express the truth through one's will. Moreover, the truth as a manifestation of the will can be both inward insofar as the will embraces or loves the truth it knows and outward insofar as the will expresses the truth external to itself to another. The will that loves truth and expresses it to others is the will associated with virtuous character and hence is, as Peggy Olson tells Pete Campbell, something that "people respect."[3]

So that's truth, but what about lies? Like truth, lies are not easy to define; rational, well-meaning people can disagree about what exactly lying is. I would define *lying* as a person communicating something that that person believes to be false, trying to hide this so that another will believe it to be true, and doing so all with the intent to hurt or at the very least implicitly disrespect the other person. For example, if ads for the Electrosizer were to promote it as a weight-loss machine when in fact Sterling Cooper knew that it didn't help with this, then this would be lying and immoral.[4] Or again, if Caldecott Farms were to deny (rather than just not mention) that it uses horse meat in its dog food, this would again be a lie.[5] However, if Sterling Cooper were unaware, and had no reasonable way of knowing, that the Electrosizer didn't help with weight loss, then this wouldn't be lying—at least not on the part of Sterling Cooper, though the company that made the Electrosizer would still be culpable for failing to tell Sterling Cooper what their product does and doesn't do. Ditto, of course, for Caldecott Farms.

Moreover, an important qualification built into my definition of lying is that, despite what some philosophers like Thomas Aquinas (1225–1274) have said, not all deception is lying or immoral.[6] For instance, let's imagine that Helen Bishop were to come to the Draper residence to escape from her drunk, abusive ex-husband, and let's imagine that her ex asked Betty Draper if Helen were in the Draper home. In this case, it might be acceptable for Betty to deceive or mislead the ex provided that she not do so out of a desire to hurt or even implicitly disrespect him, but rather out of a desire to protect Helen. (Let's suppose Betty had good reason to think Helen would be beaten if she were handed over to the ex.) This, then, is deception, but not lying. Or again, if Don were playing tennis and he happened to look one way to fake out his opponent and then hit the ball the other way, this would be deception, but it would hardly, on my account, be considered a lie or immoral (and here we must remember that actions, just as much as words, can communicate deceit).

Nevertheless, I do think that "white lies" *are* immoral, since although the person who tells the white lie often appears to be deceiving the other person for the sake of that person, what he is actually doing is disrespecting the other person since he believes, on one level, that the other person, though an equal in terms of being a rational soul, is unworthy of being treated so. To tell a person a white lie, in short, is to dehumanize that person. Thus, when Don and Betty tell their children white lies concerning the couple's marital breakup, they act immorally. Children, just as much as adults, have rational souls and thus deserve to be treated accordingly—though of course the truth should always be communicated tactfully and sensitively, and not everything that is true needs to be said at every moment and on every occasion.[7] As a result, Don and Betty should tell their children that they are getting divorced, but they don't need to reveal all the details that led to that decision.

The definitions I've just given for truth and lies afford us reasonable standards with which we can investigate five particularly interesting advertising concerns. The first concern is that an ad can be a lie simply by making claims such that a normal person reading or watching it quickly and without great attention could make false inferences and draw false conclusions. In other words, no false claim has to be made in order for an ad or a label on a product to be a lie. For example, if two bags of chips, each by a rival producer, were to have the same quantity but one bag—the Utz potato chips—is larger than the other, Utz might be trying to deceive the customer into thinking he will get more chips by buying the larger bag. Of course, *legally*, Utz isn't at fault since the weight of the contents is written on the bag, but *morally* the company is probably culpable.

The second concern, this time in defense of advertisers and producers, is that although on one level some products, such as cosmetics, appear to make false promises—for instance, that if you use this Belle Jolie lipstick you will look like the model advertising it—this isn't necessarily so. Most women *know* that even when they use a particular cosmetic, they won't necessarily look like the model who promotes that product.[8] In other words, since the apparent "promise" isn't understood by anyone to be a promise, no deception, and certainly no lie, has occurred. Indeed, most of the time the cosmetic product delivers on its actual promises—namely, to help make its user, like the model who promotes it, look better and feel more self-confident.

The third concern, flowing from the second one, is that product association isn't necessarily wrong. For instance, it isn't immoral for Don to associate Bethlehem Steel with major American cities ("New York City—Brought to you by Bethlehem Steel") nor is it necessarily a lie for Banana Republic to use Jon Hamm look-alikes to promote its new suits, since the goal in both cases is not to lie, but to assert positive associations: the strength of steel with the strength of New York, and the elegance and style of Don Draper with Banana Republic's suits.[9]

The fourth concern, again in defense of the advertiser, is that advertising a product simply for the sake of name recognition isn't necessarily dishonest or immoral. For example, if Volkswagen were to do a marketing blitz with images of Beetles in every major magazine and on every major television network, this wouldn't necessarily be wrong. Let's assume Volkswagen's goal isn't to assert anything untrue about the Beetle but rather to get people thinking about the car. Of course, it probably *was* immoral for Sterling Cooper to buy out all the advertising time on a particular network in a particular state to promote Secor laxatives (while at the same time leaving room only for the occasional Nixon ad), since by doing so they prevented other ads (in this case, for Kennedy), from being aired.[10] Choice, here, was eliminated, not expanded.

The fifth and final concern is that an ad may be considered a lie and immoral if the product in question is potentially dangerous but the ad doesn't indicate the dangers. For instance, if the ads Sterling Cooper prepared for the Israeli Tourism Bureau were to present the ever-warring state of Israel as a completely safe and relaxing vacation spot, this might be immoral, since although Israel is well-worth visiting, it's not a purely safe and relaxing place to be.[11] An ad for John Deere tractors, however, need not promote the fact that its product can cut off feet, since this happens only when the product is misused—and misused in a stupid way.[12]

Public Manipulation and Coercion

Following from our discussion of immoral, persuasive advertisements come two intimately related issues: public manipulation and public coercion. If, as Aristotle (384–322 BCE) and others have argued, justice means treating each person or thing as he or it ought to be treated, and if all people are equal at least in terms of possessing rational souls, then every person—at least on the level of possessing a rational soul—should be treated as an end in itself, and not as a means to an end.[13] For instance, although in respect to age and position in their company, there is a legitimate inequality between Don and Pete, in respect to being endowed with rational souls, Don and Pete are equals and equally deserve to be respected with the truth. Consequently, it's legitimate for a company like Admiral (which is made up of rational souls) to try to *persuade* the black community (also made up of rational souls) to buy its televisions, provided that such persuasion isn't done immorally, that the ad itself doesn't feature any immoral content, and that what the company is trying to sell—in this case, televisions—isn't itself immoral.[14] Persuasive ads, in short, ought to treat people as *ends* in themselves even while trying *ethically*, both in terms of presentation and content, to convince people of the value of the *ethical* product being advertised.

It follows, then, that persuasion is not the same as manipulation and coercion, since these—manipulation, through subtle trickery, and coercion, through psychological or physical threats—treat the public as a means to an end (that is, a means to profit). Since manipulation is more common, let's start with that.

Bypassing the most clear-cut case of advertising manipulation—subliminal or subconscious advertising—let's consider ads aimed at children, especially preschool children or children whose cognitive faculties are not well developed. Since these children find it hard to distinguish clearly between fact and fancy, they are highly susceptible to ads. If these children see something often enough, they will want it: no ifs, ands, or buts. For instance, if, during *Sesame Street* (say, its *Mad Men*-centric episode, which aired during its fortieth season), McDonald's were to advertise its generally unhealthy Happy Meals, young children would probably crave them. Setting aside the question of whether or not it's immoral for McDonald's to advertise its food, period (that is, is it immoral to promote unhealthy food?), it probably is unethical for McDonald's *or any company in general* to advertise to such young children. The reason for this is that since advertisements should aim at the person who will buy the product, and since it's the parents, and not the preschool children, who will buy the product, products for preschool children should be advertised to parents and not to children. Producers and ad agencies that aim their ads at preschool children often reply to this kind of reasoning by pointing out that it's still the parents, and not the children, who have the final word about whether the product is purchased or not. In other words, products can be aimed at young children, but parents can still say no to their children's request for that product. This line of argument fails, however, since ads aimed at children are, in fact, intended to *use* children as a means to pressure their parents into purchasing a given product. Thus, even if the product itself isn't immoral and the ad neither contains immoral content nor is a lie, this kind of advertising is wrong because it dehumanizes children.

Now let's consider coercion, particularly, the question of a company preying on a particular group of people's fears. For instance, it's not immoral for Right Guard ads to state the simple truth that if a man uses deodorant, he will smell better than if he doesn't, and if he smells better, then he will make himself more attractive to members of the opposite sex. Or again, it's not wrong for Pepsi to imply that by drinking its new diet soda, Patio Cola, women will be thinner than if they drank regular Pepsi, and thus will make themselves more attractive to men.[15] It would, however, be immoral for Clearasil to produce an ad aimed at emotionally insecure teenagers that callously showed a boy with clear skin getting all the girls and a boy with some acne living as a social outcast. Or again, if a nylon company were to use an ad that preyed on the fears of unmarried women in their thirties—that is, fears that without these nylons they will never get married—such ads *might* be immoral, since although these women in general are rational enough to process the difference between true and false advertising, sometimes emotionally weakened women (or men) can be inappropriate targets of certain ad campaigns. Consequently, when Don tells Rachel Menken, an unmarried woman in her early thirties, "What you call love was invented by guys like me to sell nylons," Don reveals an ignoble and immoral aspect of men like himself.[16]

Government

Producers and ad agencies aren't the only ones who can act immorally in respect to advertising. The government can misstep, as well.

The ethics of advertising isn't concerned with whether the government can prevent advertisements that promote products that the government has declared illegal, such as cocaine in the United States or the Bible in the former Soviet Union. If it's illegal, it can't be advertised, even if the product itself isn't immoral. (The question of whether a product *should* be illegal is not something covered by advertising ethics, though, of course, it's an important question in itself.) The ethics of advertising also is not concerned with the question of whether the government *should* make a product that is largely seen as immoral, such as pornography, illegal (and thus something that can't be advertised isn't something discussed here). Instead, the ethics of advertising is concerned with government action and inaction in terms of imposing reasonable restrictions on products that it deems legal.

In the United States, the Food and Drug Administration (FDA), for instance, imposes certain restrictions such as requiring producers to list the ingredients of food products on their packaging, restricting the sale of certain medications, and limiting when certain products can be advertised. Most of the time the FDA's restrictions are reasonable, although certain producers such as Lucky Strike cigarettes thought it unreasonable for the FDA to force them to put warning labels on their products. The question was: Do rational adults need this extra information, or is the government going too far?

I would say that the government would only have gone too far if they had forced Lucky Strike to put a label on their product saying something like "Smoking reduces your happiness" instead of merely stating something that essentially means "Smoking kills." The reason is that "Smoking kills" is a factual statement that perhaps not a lot of people in the 1960s were aware of, and so this information was, and probably still is, helpful. However, "Smoking kills" isn't necessarily the same as "Smoking reduces your happiness," since some people might think that losing five or ten years of their lives is worth the happiness they derive from smoking. In addition, it would be beside the point if I were to argue that, although I believe that smoking on a regular basis is immoral (since to do so is to knowingly shorten our lives and neglect the duties I believe we all have toward others), I agree with the FDA that cigarette producers have the right to advertise their generally harmful products (though not on TV or radio).

Sometimes, of course, governments fail in the other direction, by not imposing restrictions on advertising when they should. Personally, I think ads that use immoral content to promote products that aren't themselves immoral should be considered immoral ads and should be subject to legal restrictions. For example, I think Clorox bleach's *Mad Men*-inspired ad, which shows a man's white shirt with lipstick on its collar and reads "Getting ad guys out of hot water for generations," is an immoral ad because it uses adultery (jokingly or otherwise) to promote its product. However, it's hard to imagine the government asking Clorox to pull this ad. Or again, I think Sterling Cooper's Liberty Capitol Savings ad, which tries to sell "Executive Accounts"—accounts intended to help husbands hide money from their wives—is an immoral ad because although savings accounts aren't immoral, infidelity and dishonesty are.[17] And although I'm mindful of the slippery slope here, I think this kind of ad should be restricted, since any ad that openly promotes clear immorality should be considered harmful to the state.

Sharing Moral Responsibility

Throughout our discussion, we have looked at five major parties involved in questions of advertising ethics: (1) the producer or manufacturer, (2) the advertising agency, (3) the media in which or through which the advertisement appears, (4) the general public, and (5) government and governmental agencies.

The moral responsibility for advertisements lies chiefly with the producer of the product in question. The producer tells the ad agency what they want, and the agency caters to their wishes. Thus, in "Wee Small Hours" (episode 309), Conrad Hilton lambasts Don for failing to incorporate his vision of a Hilton on the moon ("When I say I want the moon, I expect the moon.") and Lucky Strike demands that Salvatore Romano be fired, supposedly because of his shoddy work on their ad campaign. Or again, Belle Jolie lipstick didn't want their ads to be aired during an episode of *The Defenders* in which abortion is discussed, and Sterling Cooper had to comply.[18] Clearly, the producer has more power and, hence, more moral responsibility in regard to advertising than the ad agency does.

Nevertheless, occasionally the tables are turned. For instance, though Horace Cook Jr. is the one with the money, he is a weak man and relies completely on *any* and *all* ads that Sterling Cooper can come up with to promote jai alai in America. Cook Jr. is "a fatted calf," and because of his weakness and stupidity, he could easily—unlikely though it may be—end up financing an ad campaign that is immoral and largely controlled by the ad agency.[19] Or again, when an ad agency doesn't particularly care about whether they have a certain producer's business or not, that agency might have more freedom and power, and hence more moral responsibility, in respect to the ads produced and aired. Perhaps if Sterling Cooper hadn't (immorally?) cut loose Mohawk Airlines, Mohawk would have given Sterling Cooper this kind of power.[20]

Media companies that run ads share some, though less, of the moral responsibility for running immoral ads, since even though they themselves didn't create the product or think of a way to sell it, they still have the freedom to refuse to propagate it. CBS, for example, didn't have to run *The Defenders* episode dealing with abortion nor would they have to allow, if it were the case, an immoral lipstick ad.

The public, too, shares some responsibility for the existence of immoral ads. If the public refused to watch or read immoral ads, and, indeed, if they blacklisted producers and media companies associated with such products, business for those companies wouldn't last long. For instance, if Betty were to see an immoral Heineken ad, she could write letters to both the media company that showed the ad and Heineken breweries, indicating that if such ads continue, she would boycott both companies.

Finally, governments and government-related agencies also share some of the moral responsibility for immoral ads because although the purpose of the government is to protect its citizens' freedom, often such protection occurs through restricting immoral things, such as unethical ads. For instance, the American government is right to demand warning labels be put on Lucky Strike cigarettes, since not to make such a demand would be to put the public in needless danger and hence would be immoral.

"The Wrong Direction"?

So, was Don "looking in the wrong direction" when he sold his idea to Lucky Strike? Yes and no. As we've seen, the ethics of advertising can be nuanced and tricky. There are numerous things and parties to consider with each ad requested, created, aired, viewed, and allowed. Don may be able to "talk anyone into anything," but should he do so?[21] Clearly, the answer to this question, at least, is no.

NOTES

1. "Babylon" (episode 106) and "Seven Twenty Three" (episode 307), respectively.

2. Richard De George, *Business Ethics*, 6th ed. (Upper Saddle River, NJ: Pearson, 2006), 337.

3. "Meditations in an Emergency" (episode 213).

4. "Indian Summer" (episode 111).

5. "The Gypsy and the Hobo" (episode 311).

6. See Thomas Aquinas, *Summa Theologica*, translated by The Fathers of the English Dominican (London: Christian Classics, 1911), pt. II–II, qq. 109–110.

7. "Shut the Door. Have a Seat." (episode 313).

8. "The Hobo Code" (episode 108).

9. "New Amsterdam" (episode 104).

10. "Shoot" (episode 109).

11. "Babylon" (episode 106).

12. "Guy Walks into an Advertising Agency" (episode 306).

13. Aristotle, *Ethics*, translated by Hugh Tredennick (Toronto: Penguin, 2004), 1129a17–1131a9.

14. "The Fog" (episode 305).

15. "Love among the Ruins" (episode 302).

16. "Smoke Gets in Your Eyes" (episode 101).

17. "5G" (episode 105).

18. "The Benefactor" (episode 203).

19. "The Arrangements" (episode 304).

20. "Flight 1" (episode 202).

21. "Six Month Leave" (episode 209).

IS DON DRAPER A
GOOD MAN?

Andrew Terjesen

When we are introduced to Don Draper in *Mad Men* ("Smoke Gets in Your Eyes," episode 101), he appears to be a character who is very progressive. He talks to an African American waiter in order to see why that waiter buys a particular brand of cigarettes. We're reminded of how unusual this is when a white employee comes over and asks Don if the waiter is "bothering him." Later we see that Don is involved with a bohemian artist and values her opinion as he tries to run some ad ideas by her. His enlightened attitudes toward women seem further evidenced by the way he dresses down Pete Campbell for harassing Peggy Olson and the fact that he politely refuses Peggy's advances. His only shortcoming seems to be that he is trying to sell cigarettes despite medical testimony highlighting their dangers. It isn't until the last scene that we see Don in a very different light, when he returns home to the suburbs to find his wife and two kids sound asleep. Of course, a few episodes later, we see hints that he has an even deeper secret.

In asking whether Don Draper is a good man, it might be tempting to simply weigh his positive qualities against his negative qualities and see which are greater. The problem with that approach is that it gives each quality equal weight. Does an enlightened attitude toward race relations counterbalance a lack of respect for one's marital vows? It would seem that in order to determine whether Don is a good person, we need to have a theory about what qualities count as good and how they rank against one another. That's what moral philosophers have been trying to do for millennia.

The Good in Don Draper

When it comes to judging whether someone is a good person, we can't just rely on individual instances of good actions. It would be hard to call Don Draper a good person just because he sometimes helped people in need. What really makes someone good is that they have a consistent response to people in need. The idea that a good person is someone who regularly does the right thing can be traced back to Aristotle (384–322 BCE). According to Aristotle, "Virtues arise in us neither by nature nor against nature. Rather, we are by nature able to acquire them, and we are completed through habit."[1] His point is that there is a big difference between *being* an honest person and *doing the same thing as* an honest person. When Don is confronted about his past, he almost always tells the truth (as an honest person would), but only after being dishonest or trying to evade the question.

If Don is a good person, then he has to display character traits that would be regarded as virtuous. Aristotle had a short list of ten virtues, but we don't need to abide by them. It would be enough if we could find character traits that would be labeled virtuous. One such trait has already been referenced. Don consistently exhibits very tolerant attitudes toward minorities and women.[2] Not only does Don talk to African Americans in a respectful manner, he seems to genuinely disapprove of racist stereotypes. When Roger Sterling serenades his new wife in blackface, Don appears to be the only person (other than Pete Campbell) who does not laugh at the routine; in fact he seems pained and disgusted ("My Old Kentucky Home," episode 303). And unlike Pete, he eventually walks away from the display.

In addition to his egalitarian attitude, Don also exhibits a consistent ethical streak when dealing with clients. It's a kind of honorableness that most of his coworkers seem to lack. When Don is told that he has to drop Mohawk Airlines as a client so that Duck Phillips can pursue an opportunity with American Airlines, Don balks. "I can't believe I look like an idiot for wanting to be loyal to these people" ("Flight 1," episode 202). In his attempts to dissuade Sterling and Cooper from dropping the airline, he appeals to the trust he's built and that no client deserves to be "thrown out the door for a wink from American." As Don sees it, dropping Mohawk makes Sterling Cooper a different kind of company than he thought he was working for.

Don also demonstrates an unusual amount of concern for the well-being of potential clients. When Pete brings in a client who wants to drop a ton of money on a campaign to increase public interest in jai alai, Don thinks that this is taking unfair advantage of the client. It's Don who encourages Pryce to arrange a sit-down with the client's father to make sure that he knows how his son is spending his inheritance. The father is unconcerned and sees no reason why Sterling Cooper shouldn't profit from his son's foolishness. Even after getting the go-ahead from Horace Sr., Don feels the need to make one last attempt to discourage Horace Jr. and tells him: "You should take this decision more seriously . . . we will take all your money . . . reevaluate this particular obsession" ("The Arrangements," episode 304).

For all his noble statements, in the end Don does what he is asked. He drops Mohawk Airlines and he takes on Horace Jr. as a client. Despite his efforts to change the situation, Don eventually goes with the flow. This would suggest that Don is not nearly as ethical as his words would suggest. Similarly, his enlightened attitudes seem to have their limits, and he certainly does not raise a public stink when someone speaks in a denigrating fashion about anyone who is not a white, middle-class male. When you add in his more glaring faults (the adultery and the stolen identity), it seems hard to call him a good man.

Adultery and Lying on a Major Scale: That's Not Good, Right?

There seems to be a difference between a good person who slips and a bad person. Following Aristotle, the difference would be whether something was done in the heat of the moment or as a long-standing habit.[3] In the case of Don Draper, it seems difficult to deny that his adultery is habitual. He has not had just one affair. We know of several lengthy affairs (Midge the Greenwich Village artist, Rachel Menken, Bobbie Barrett, and Sally's teacher Suzanne Farrell) and that he has had one-night stands with various women (like the flight attendant in Baltimore). Having affairs seems to be part of who he is. Even after he is caught, he eventually returns to philandering. That sounds like the behavior of someone for whom adultery is a part of his life. In the same vein, Don has been lying about who he is to everyone, including his wife, for about a decade, and he only confesses the truth when he is faced with incontrovertible evidence.

Based on what we have seen, it seems like Don is a mixture of good and bad character traits and, therefore, we just need to decide whether the bad traits are more important than the good ones. Moral philosophers since the time of Plato have argued that we need to be more careful in calling someone a good person. According to Plato, we need to regard virtue as something that comes as part of a package—to be a good person you need to have all the virtues, not just enough of them. This idea has become known as the Unity of the Virtues thesis because it holds that true virtue only exists when you have the whole set of virtues. In the dialogue *Protagoras*, Plato explores the Unity of the Virtues thesis. As Socrates asks Protagoras in the dialogue: "Is virtue a single thing, with justice and temperance and piety its parts, or are the things just listed all names for a single entity?"[4] In Socrates' question we have two separate things that both fall under the Unity of the Virtues. The Reciprocity thesis is the idea that virtue, like a bicycle, is composed of parts and, unless you have all the parts working together, you don't really have a bicycle (or virtue). The other aspect is the True Unity thesis, which claims that all virtues are really one thing.

You might question the Reciprocity thesis by pointing out that you know lots of people who possess some admirable qualities, such as honesty, but lack other admirable qualities, such as reliability. The argument for the Reciprocity thesis is that no person can really be called "honest" if they lack certain virtues, because those character flaws could interfere with their attempts to be honest. Don's behavior is a clear example. His adultery interferes with many aspects of his life. When Betty has a car accident, Don isn't there for her because his secretary didn't know that he was off having an afternoon delight with Midge ("Ladies Room," episode 102). In addition, when his brother, Adam Whitman, wants to reopen a relationship with him, Don refuses because that would threaten the life he has built as Don Draper ("5G," episode 105). These are just two examples of how his vices make it difficult for him to always do the right thing. If he can't always do the right thing, then it is not right to say that he has the virtue associated with those actions.

The True Unity thesis goes a step further. It doesn't claim just that our vices interfere with our capacity to be virtuous. It also claims that we can never act virtuously in a situation unless we are simultaneously displaying all the virtues. As Socrates asks, "Does someone who acts unjustly seem temperate to you in that he acts unjustly?"[5] To be a fair person, one must have self-control (so that other temptations don't interfere with our attempts to be fair), wisdom (so that we know what the fair result is), and courage (to be fair when being fair threatens our livelihood). In making sense of this idea, Socrates arrives at the conclusion that all virtue boils down to one thing—knowing right from wrong. When discussing courage he says, "The wisdom about what is and is not to be feared is courage."[6] Courage is the knowledge of the things that are good for us (and should not be feared) and bad for us (which should be feared). Similarly, honesty is the knowledge of what it is good to say and what it is bad to say. And so on. Anyone who fails to always do the right thing clearly does not understand what virtue really is. One interpretation of Don's infidelity is that he really doesn't understand what is important in life. By his own admission, he lives for today because he doesn't think there is a tomorrow ("Marriage of Figaro," episode 103). That kind of nihilism suggests that he doesn't understand the true meaning of human existence.

Plato's assumption seems to be that if people really know what is good for them, then they will always do it (because it's good for them). Many philosophers have been reluctant to embrace the True Unity thesis because it seems very difficult to say that knowing the right thing to do is the same as doing the right thing. It seems that certain habits have to be developed. Nonetheless, even philosophers who recognize this, like Aristotle, argue that the truly virtuous person has to have a certain kind of wisdom (what Aristotle calls "phronesis") that ensures that they are properly habituated. So even if we reject the True Unity thesis, the Reciprocity thesis is still before us.

Is Don Really a Bad Person?

When confronted with the Reciprocity thesis, most people resist it. That's probably because most of us recognize that we are a mix of good and bad qualities and we don't like the idea that we are not virtuous. This kind of thinking gets ahead of the philosopher's point and actually puts us at risk of saying something ridiculous. The philosopher is trying to understand what it means to say that someone is virtuous. A virtuous person should not be defined in such a way that they mostly do good things, but occasionally do something horrendous (or that they have a strange mixture of qualities—like homicidal impulses and a generosity with charitable causes). But there is a difference between not being a virtuous person—which could be a reality for most of us (much like most of us will never be rich)—and being a vicious person. Presumably our real concern is with whether we are truly a bad person.

If the Reciprocity thesis is true of the virtues, it should also be true of the vices. No one would be a bad person if they contained any virtuous qualities. The question, then, becomes whether we can explain Don Draper's behavior in terms of a Unity of the Vices. The fact that we have found character traits that undermine certain virtues—as adultery undermines honesty—means that Don can't possess a completely virtuous character. It is not unthinkable, however, that we could make his positive traits be consistent with a vicious character. For example, sadists might join an army in a just war and act in a manner that would be deemed courageous. The good that such a person does, however, might be an unintended by-product of a desire to cause others to suffer. Could Don's egalitarian attitude and business ethics also be the expression of an underlying vicious character?

Let's start with Don's negative qualities to see if we can find some underlying connection. Don's affairs are usually very carefully conducted—he does not sleep with anyone in the office and he does not brag about his conquests. His deception is also done in such a manner that it is hard to catch him in a lie—mainly because he avoids saying too much that is actually false about his background. When answering questions about his past, Don Draper seems to use the childhood of Dick Whitman. Usually he tries to avoid such questions by changing the subject or giving very vague answers, so that he doesn't actually end up telling a lie. Don's care in not doing anything that would easily get him caught suggests that he could be a "sensible knave." David Hume (1711–1776) used "sensible knave" to refer to any individual who obeys the rules of justice as long as it is in his interest to do so and takes advantage of opportunities where there is lax enforcement to do things that are unjust. Don's business ethics may stem from a belief that violating those rules will undermine long-term business and therefore aren't examples of sensible knavery. However, if anyone pressures him to break those rules, he will ultimately do so in order to benefit his career. In a similar vein, Don's egalitarian attitude may also be a way of covering his butt. Don might recognize that what goes around comes around and so it is best to treat everyone well (a lesson he may have learned from the hobo who visited his homestead in "The Hobo Code," episode 108).

Don's behavior could be further explained by a kind of egoism. His adultery shows a lack of regard for anyone's feelings but his own. His deception is also an attempt to be whomever he wants to be without any baggage from his previous life. As mentioned earlier, Don claims he lives only for today, and the several instances where he seems prepared to leave it all behind and start anew indicate that he is not too concerned about how his actions will impact his family or friends. Even his approach to advertising reflects the same attitude. He sees advertising as the art of selling someone happiness, but he regards happiness as a purely subjective thing for each individual. Another name for the "sensible knave" might be "sociopath."

Is There No Such Thing as a Good (or a Bad) Person?

Before we go so far as to conclude that Don is really a sociopath, we should take a look at a major objection to the kind of virtue talk that Plato, Aristotle, and many other moral philosophers engage in. The objection was formulated by the philosopher John Doris in *Lack of Character* and is an objection to the idea that humans possess anything resembling the kinds of character traits we label as virtues or vices. His argument begins with a rejection of the Reciprocity thesis:

> It's not crazy to think that someone could be courageous in physical but not moral extremity, or be moderate with food but not sex, or be honest with spouses but not taxes. . . . Would things were so simple. With a bit of effort we could imagine someone showing physical courage on the battlefield, but cowering in the face of storms, heights or wild animals. . . . Things can get still trickier: Someone might exhibit battlefield courage in the face of a rifle but not in the face of artillery fire.[7]

Doris's argument begins with something that we readily accept: everyone has flaws. Think of Peggy Olson—despite her many admirable qualities as a woman trying to make a name for herself in a male-dominated field, she evidences poor judgment with men like Pete and Duck. On the flip side, everyone has some positive qualities. Roger Sterling seems to be largely a jerk, but he does know the right things to say in order to smooth over tensions. He normally uses that ability to gain clients for Sterling Cooper, but sometimes he uses it as a force for good, as when he gets the guests at his daughter's wedding in the right frame of mind after the Kennedy assassination ("The Grown Ups," episode 312). However, Doris takes the denial of the Reciprocity thesis even further. He's not just claiming that it is possible to be an adulterer and a man of his word when it comes to everything other than sex. He's also claiming that one can be an adulterer only in certain circumstances—such as Pete, who only seems prone to starting adulterous affairs right before his wedding or when his wife is away for a month during the summer. The idea that specific environmental triggers can be responsible for a particular behavior is known as "situationism" in psychological circles. In making his arguments, Doris relies upon the situationist literature in psychology. For example, one study showed that people were more likely to help someone after finding a dime in a pay phone. Finding the dime seemed to be the only relevant predictor as to whether someone would help.[8] This and other experiments are meant to show that we are all manipulated by environmental factors, and so even the most honest man will have a circumstance in which he can be manipulated into dishonesty.

Don Isn't That Bad, Is He?

John Doris attacks what he calls "global character traits," but he does allow for what he calls "local character traits," which include things like "helps-someone-pick-up-their-papers-after-finding-a-dime." The problem is that Doris defines local character traits in such a narrow fashion that they are not really traits of someone's character; instead they merely identify a relatively specific environmental stimulus response. More to the point, they do not give us a very helpful picture of the people we deal with. The concern that we have very unrealistic notions of character is worth taking seriously. After all, there is no reason why nature designed us to be truthful. However, it seems that our behaviors may be reliably guided in a way that supports the main insight of the True Unity thesis.

Let's compare Don's adulterous ways with those of his coworkers Pete Campbell and Roger Sterling. Pete has had sex with at least two women other than his wife, Trudy: Peggy and the German au pair in his building. Pete went to Peggy right before his wedding and had sex with her a few times thereafter. Although Peggy seems to have had feelings for him, Pete only appears to care about Peggy when she has something he wants. Pete seems even more indifferent toward the au pair, having forced himself on her after she refused his advances ("Souvenir," episode 308). Pete seems to think she owed him after he helped her out earlier in the episode. Roger seems to get involved only with his subordinates, and he treats them as his property. In contrast, Don seems to get involved only with women with whom he forms a real relationship and whose opinions he values. Some of Don's dalliances have been one-night stands, but even then the women approach him. Don doesn't try to force himself on anyone. In some cases he has even turned down propositions, as he did with the Asian American waitress after he broke things off with Mohawk Airlines ("Flight 1"). Don is not a "horndog" like Roger or a user like Pete; he seems to get involved only with women he finds genuinely interesting. More than once, he even tries to convince his current paramour to run away with him and start a new life.

Don's reprehensible behavior is somewhat restrained by a set of rules he follows. If our actions were the product of local character traits that were keyed to specific circumstances, then that would be an amazing coincidence. It would make more sense to think that something was shaping his behavior. Instead of connecting it to a vague characteristic like honesty, however, we should consider more specialized faculties like the ability to resist temptation or a desire to be a certain kind of person. These regional character traits may not always yield the best behavior, but it is possible that some traits are admirable (even when they lead to less than desirable behavior) and others are contemptible (even when they lead to desirable outcomes). For example, Roger's way with people seems pretty smarmy and manipulative.

Nonetheless, Don Can Be a Real Heel

It seems, then, that Don has some good regional characteristics—a respect for people in general, a desire to follow a code of conduct even when it might not get him what he wants, and an interest in finding happiness. It's possible that all of his bad behaviors are the result of these characteristics. For example, his philandering might reflect dissatisfaction with the ideas of happiness that society seems to be pushing on him. Though this might be tempting because it means that Don is basically a good guy, it flies in the face of his own actions.

Roger offers the most concise assessment of Don's failings as a person when he tells him, "You're no good with relationships because you don't value them" ("Shut the Door. Have a Seat," episode 313). There is a difference between valuing people as individuals pursuing their own happiness and valuing the relationships we form with them. Don clearly does a terrible job of valuing his familial relationships. Although he is discreet in his affairs (saving Betts lots of embarrassment), Don does not consider the ways in which his involvement with other women make him unavailable to his family. Even when he isn't having an affair, he behaves in ways that ignore the needs of his family. A classic example is when he goes to get the cake for Sally's birthday party, but then drives past the house and doesn't come home until the party is long over ("Marriage of Figaro").

His treatment of his brother is even more tragic. Adam really seems to want to have his brother back in his life, but Don tries to bribe him into forgetting that he was ever Dick Whitman. Don's refusal to be a brother to Adam contributes to Adam's decision to take his own life. Don's difficulty with family relationships is encapsulated in his attempts to help Pete after Pete finds out that his father died. Don tells Pete to go home and be with his family. When Pete asks why, Don's answer is, "Because that's what people do" ("Flight 1"). Don's understanding of family relationships seems to be based on a code of conduct that he follows as opposed to a genuine depth of feeling. Don is treating family relationships the same way that he treats business relationships. Of course, Don is not much better with his coworkers. When Pete comes back later for more support, Don brushes him off. Presumably Don felt that he had done his duty in expressing sympathy the day before and is preoccupied with his own problems.

In the end it seems that Don possesses some very admirable character traits in terms of his respect for others and his desire to try to live with integrity, mixed in with a real blind spot when it comes to personal relationships. Looking at these character traits, it would seem appropriate to say that Don is a good person insofar as his positive character traits have developed in environments that are hostile to them, while his real major character flaw could be seen as the result of a cold home environment. It's true that Don could be a much better person, but what most of us like and admire about him is that he does a lot better than many other people in his situation.

NOTES

1. Aristotle, *Nicomachean Ethics*, 2nd ed., translated by T. Irwin (Indianapolis, IN: Hackett Publishing, 1999), 1103a25.

2. His record with homosexuals is mixed—he doesn't fire Sal after finding out, but he fires Sal for not sleeping with Lee Jr., even dismissing him with a sneering "you people" ("Wee Small Hours," episode 309).

3. Not every ancient philosopher would agree with this statement. The Stoics, who believed that the only good thing in the world was virtue and the only evil thing was vice, were notorious for the claim that there is no difference between someone who falls just short of moral perfection and someone who has lots of vices. For the Stoics, you were either a sage, who embodied moral perfection, or you were not.

4. Plato, *Protagoras*, translated by S. Lombardo and K. Bell (Indianapolis, IN: Hackett Publishing, 1992), 329d.

5. Ibid., 333b.

6. Ibid., 360d.

7. John Doris, *Lack of Character: Personality and Moral Behavior* (Cambridge, UK: Cambridge University Press, 2002), 62.

8. A. M. Isen and P. F. Levin. "Effects of Feeling Good on Helping: Cookies and Kindness. *Journal of Personality and Social Psychology* 21 (1972): 384–388.

DON DRAPER, ON HOW TO MAKE ONESELF (WHOLE AGAIN)

John Elia

Don Draper is a Madison Avenue ad exec, a mad man. He exudes creativity, charm, and coolness under pressure. Beneath his confident exterior, however, Don is tormented. He's got a secret. He isn't really the decorated war veteran and rising star that people believe he is: he's Richard "Dick" Whitman, farm boy, son of a prostitute, identity thief. Don's true identity is largely hidden from his coworkers, his wife, his children, and his myriad lovers. Because of his deceit, Don Draper is not at home in the world. He's always on his guard, covering up the truth, locking away his secrets. He turns to women and drink to heal himself, though we all know that's no salve for a soul.

Don Draper lives at an important time in the American story. Though traditional sources of identity, morality, and self-understanding had long been eroding, the 1960s revealed new and difficult challenges, including the civil rights movement, the assassination of JFK, Vietnam, and, yes, the growth of television (which, as *Mad Men* also attests, can be a medium for appreciating the past as much as ignoring or distorting it!). Dick Whitman's re-creation as Don Draper presents an extreme case of freedom from the past, to be sure. Few of us so completely bury our earlier selves. The thing is, Don's condition is still very much our own. We are confused about who we are and what we want. We flee from our pasts, choosing change for change's sake, or out of fear, anxiety, or fleeting desire rather than a sense of purpose. We, too, lack a kind of deep integrity or wholeness about our lives. So, let's ask, what does Don Draper need in order to become whole again? And since Don is made in our image, what can we learn from him about the reconciliation of freedom, goodness, and identity in our own complicated lives?

From Roger Sterling to Don Draper: Modernity in Transition

Modernity is a period of social and intellectual change characterized by, among other things, a departure from medieval models of church and political authority, the rise of science and the scientific method, and broad appeal to individual judgment and autonomy in moral, spiritual, economic, and political matters. Modernity probably began, depending on the scholar you choose to ask, sometime in the sixteenth or seventeenth century, prompted by the religious, scientific, and philosophical work of figures such as Martin Luther (1483–1546), Galileo Galilei (1564–1642), René Descartes (1596–1650), and John Locke (1632–1704). The eighteenth-century Enlightenment further defended and entrenched the values of freedom and autonomy while engaging in increasingly direct moves toward secularism and the authority of reason in ordering human affairs. The writings of the philosopher Immanuel Kant (1724–1804) express some of the defining elements of these Enlightenment ideals.[1]

The modern story is complicated, however, as these ideals are never univocally endorsed. Moreover, by the early twentieth century, confidence in reason as a source of human progress was withering, largely due to the devastation wrought by World War I (consider, for example, the fragmentation of T. S. Eliot's [1888–1965] poem *The Waste Land*, published in 1922). The mid-twentieth century was a time of deepening crisis in modernity. Its events are crucial to the tone and authenticity of *Mad Men*. With the devastations of World War II and the Holocaust hardly behind them, our characters will face the Cuban Missile Crisis ("Meditations in an Emergency," episode 213), the civil rights movement ("The Fog," episode 305), Kennedy's assassination ("The Grown Ups," episode 312), and the Vietnam War ("The Arrangements," episode 304). We better understand the confusion of the modern period as the characters' perceptions of and prospects for realizing the American Dream evolve in response to these events.

Not only are the difficult events of this period marked for *Mad Men*'s audience by targeted strikes into the show's unfolding narrative, the characters also display the challenges to tradition and authority stirring in an increasingly pluralized 1960s social milieu. The traditional posture shows up in Roger Sterling. Roger is aristocratic, blue-blooded, *noblesse oblige*. He deploys his forbearance rarely and asserts his power often, especially over underlings and competitors. Witness Roger's blackface performance at his country club party with Jane ("My Old Kentucky Home," episode 303).

The other characters on *Mad Men* offer a veritable roster of social challengers. For instance, Pete Campbell signifies bourgeois privilege losing its hold. After his father dies in a plane crash, Pete discovers that his inheritance is lost. Though his parents regarded his work as indecent and he once approached it with a sense of undue entitlement, Pete comes to respect his work and actually becomes good at it. Peggy Olson is part of a rising women's movement, working her way from answering phones and typing up dictation to copywriting, eventually landing an office of her own. Paul Kinsey is a hipster: pot-smoking, interracially dating, and part of a young urban movement ready to join a cultural revolution.

Mad Men is about the power and allure of modern freedom and the costs of choosing it. Beat poetry (such as Frank O'Hara's [1926–1966] *Meditations in an Emergency*) and Eastern philosophy (in the eccentricities of Bertram Cooper) make appearances on the show. The ideas of existentialist writers such as Albert Camus (1913–1960) are implied if not apparent. Camus rejected external codes of morals, social mores, and politics in his work, while embracing the consciousness of liberation such a rejection makes possible. His work helps us to understand *Mad Men*'s central character, Don Draper, as an iconic, modern figure and to better articulate Don's strategy for dealing with the confusion of the modern world.

An Outsider on the Inside

Don Draper is an upper-middle-class, thoroughly establishment achiever of all kinds of "objective" successes: a beautiful wife, three children, a nanny, a Cadillac, a great house in the suburbs. Yet, like Clamence, the former Parisian lawyer who does the talking in Camus' novel *The Fall*, Don Draper's life is not what it seems. Of his own life, Clamence says:

> Yes, few creatures were more natural than I. . . . In particular the flesh, matter, the physical in short. . . . I was made to have a body. . . . I was at ease in everything, to be sure, but at the same time satisfied with nothing. Each joy made me desire another. . . . At times, late on those nights when the dancing, the slight intoxication, my wild enthusiasm, everyone's violent unrestraint would fill me with a tired and overwhelmed rapture, it would seem to me—at the breaking point of fatigue

and for a second's flash—that at last I understood the secret of creatures and of the world. But my fatigue would disappear the next day, and with it the secret. I would rush forth anew. I ran on like that, always heaped with favors, never satiated, without knowing where to stop, until the day—until the evening rather when the music stopped and the lights went out.[2]

Recovering in the trenches from a round of mortar shots targeting their camp during the Korean War, Richard "Dick" Whitman and Donald Draper light their cigarettes. Tragedy strikes as they realize that they're covered in gasoline. Draper is killed in the explosion; Dick survives. Pondering his situation for a moment, Dick reaches down and steals Draper's dog tags. Later, a Purple Heart with Draper's name in hand, this new Donald Draper proceeds to sever himself from his previous identity. But for a few papers and memorabilia that he stows away in his desk at home, he does so completely. Eventually he meets Betty and has kids and gets a job on Madison Avenue. Like Camus' character Clamence, Don's life is not nearly as charmed as others think. His objective success is tarnished by constant fear and guilt, which he self-medicates with women and drink. As a result, his marriage suffers; his children hardly see him; his coworkers know him more as a myth than a man. Don has chosen freedom, and continues to do so with abandon. This is why he objects so vehemently to signing a contract with Sterling Cooper, even after Conrad Hilton makes it a condition of further business dealings ("Seven Twenty Three," episode 307). If Don keeps his future open, he can always re-create himself again, as he once even proposes to do with Rachel Menken, the Jewish department store heiress ("Nixon vs. Kennedy"). Freedom from the past is Don's blessing as well as his curse.

Existentialist thinkers such as Camus did not advocate carefree escapism. Theirs is a philosophy with deep respect for personal responsibility. Thus, Don Draper is not an existentialist hero. Had Dick Whitman made his choice of a new life as Don Draper with a conscious awareness of the stakes, perhaps he might have been a Sisyphus, whom Camus declares happy even while rolling his boulder up a hill for eternity, or a Meursault, the absurd hero of Camus' *The Stranger,* who discovers his happiness even as he awaits his own beheading.[3] Yet such heroism wouldn't have healed Don's wounds, grounded as it is in a thin notion of what little life an alien world has to offer. Nor is it the happiness that Don seeks.

When we think about human goodness and happiness, we tend to have something more in mind than the philosophical recognition of freedom or our capacity to make meaning for ourselves even in the shadow of the guillotine! In particular, we tend to see our pasts and our identities, including culture, tradition, religion, and relationships, as making our choices significant. This doesn't mean that we should become nostalgic for the past. But nor should we treat the past as meaningless. For example, at a crucial point in Don's story, when he chooses not to travel with the wealthy, cosmopolitan "nomads" he meets in California and instead returns to his first wife, Anna ("The Jet Set," episode 211; "The Mountain King," episode 212), he is reestablishing himself *through* his past. Don doesn't really want more freedom, whatever its type. He wants integrity. Only by bringing his past and his present together into some new whole can Don begin to approach happiness.

Integrity in a Mad World

At the end of *After Virtue,* Alasdair MacIntyre suggests that modern communities are faced with a decision between two moral models, Nietzsche (1844–1900) and Aristotle (384–322 BCE).[4] The decision he has in mind is between Nietzschean values-creation (and destruction) and an Aristotelian notion of the embeddedness of values in particular historical communities, cultures, or traditions. Whether these are our only choices is a matter of contention.[5] But MacIntyre is right that this is a central tension in modern moral life. We have seen it already through Camus's characters and in Dick's choice to become Don Draper. Are we going this life alone, creating values as we choose and act, making meaning for ourselves, or are our values significant primarily as a product of a history, background culture, and community?

Like us, Don simultaneously wants freedom *and* a past. He doesn't want to choose between Nietzsche and Aristotle, and yet he hasn't arrived at any reconciliation of these values. Don thus lacks the crucial virtue of integrity. Integrity is a moral virtue that involves choice informed by one's deepest values or core commitments. Persons of integrity have characters that reflect self-understanding and propensities to choose and act in patterns that express these deep values. Modernity frustrates the pursuit of integrity because it casts doubt on our received stories about who we are or what we should do. Modern identity, however, is compatible with integrity. If anything, as we see in the case of Don Draper, it actually elevates integrity's value, since the personal, moral project under modernity becomes centrally that of working out a complex view of identity and agency.[6]

Integrity is compatible with breaks in one's life narrative, charting a new course or stretching our selves in some ways. Integrity, however, calls for breaks in one's narrative identity to be justified in light of one's understanding of still deeper personal or social commitments. Don's break with his past wasn't justified in this way, and he suffers because of ongoing disintegration of his character. Are Dick's and Don's core values the same? How do they compare? Why does Don's behavior seem to be determined by the role he's filling at the time? Why is there so much difference among Don's personae with a client, a lover, or Betty and the children? For the sake of contrast, compare Don's choice to Peggy's choice to move out of her mother's home. It might conflict with some of her core Catholic values, and yet it is of a piece with her desire to be an independent woman. Or take Joan's decision to leave Sterling Cooper. Though it is not without costs, especially given her love for Roger Sterling, she also desires not to be a "runner-up," a mistress rather than a wife, with no family to call her own. Perhaps, one might say, Don has made the same kind of choice: freedom from the past was his deepest impulse. However, freedom from one's past is not a value to integrate oneself around. As Don discovers, the past is a moving target, freedom from which leaves one always wanting greener pastures, never finding a point of integration.

Integrity's demands work from the inside out, attempting to shelter our selves and values from fracturing influences while leaving room for innovation and change. When we succeed in organizing our lives around these values, we can be said to be integrated or whole (acknowledging that it is likely to be imperfect). Those times in *Mad Men* when Don seems most at home are when his life is the most integrated. They are often those moments when he has recently ended a relationship with another woman and in which he is most identified with his family. After breaking off his relationship with Bobbie Barrett, for instance, Don buys a new car and takes his family to the park ("The Gold Violin," episode 207). Betty lays back and says, "We should do this more often." Don, stretched out on the picnic blanket, replies, "We should only do this." Some signs of Don's integration are also evident in the aftermath of his confrontation with Betty about his past ("The Gypsy and the Hobo," episode 311). Though he had not chosen this time or this way to make his admission, in the moment he consents and explains. Don's previously hidden life is now out in the open—he doesn't have to hide his shoebox of memorabilia any longer. He sleeps in, sits on the couch comfortably, naps, not evidently feeling the need to escape to a lover, even while the world is shaken by JFK's assassination ("The Grown Ups").

Don is at home, literally and metaphorically, and however odd the timing, it has everything to do with the partial reconciliation of his present and his past.

Don has moments in which he can embrace his identity, moments in which the good of integrity and wholeness seem within his grasp and which result in an otherwise uncharacteristic—temporary peace. Don wants an integrated life. That Don lacks integrity doesn't mean that he lacks other values, however. This may be important for us, too, given the fractures we find in our own lives and the difficulty with which we keep our lives integrated. The virtue that Don seems to display most reliably is that of justice.

Just at Work, a Heel at Home

For all of Don Draper's faults, he is not evil. One of Don's most striking characteristics is his sense of justice or fairness. Thus, while integrity may be important for well-being and meaningful choice, lack of integrity does not apparently keep one from acting justly, at least in some sense. Thus, there is hope that living in a fractured world or with a torn identity may not completely deplete one's capacities for moral goodness.

Justice, traditionally, is giving each person his or her due. This is not a matter of what is now called distributive justice, that part of political theory concerned with the distribution of offices, resources, or privileges (Don is not a Kennedy).[7] Instead, it's a personal kind of justice, justice as a virtue. For Don, however, and this is ever so fitting to his condition, justice is not about one's past. It's a matter of merit. A few examples come immediately to mind. Don has no regard for Pete's pedigree. Pete has to prove his value to the firm by recruiting and retaining clients. Don punches Jimmy Barrett one night in a bar because Jimmy suggested to Betty that Don had been messing around with Bobbie, Jimmy's wife. Don doesn't care about Jimmy's earnings potential. He deserves to get decked.

In Peggy Olson, Don sees talent, though everyone else in the office sees just another girl trying to find a husband in the city. Rather than reinforcing these attitudes, Don challenges them. He gives Peggy, who was then his secretary, a shot at ad writing. Don is not a feminist or an activist (although his own liberation from the past makes a shared liberation perhaps easier). He's merely applying his principles of merit-based justice.[8]

Or consider Don himself. He works hard to merit his increasing responsibility and wealth. As a self-made man (more literally than anyone suspects), Don's focus is on doing and creating tangible benefits or successes for Sterling Cooper. He treats himself, in this sense, no differently than he treats Peggy or Pete. When he scolds them and other junior associates, he does so because they haven't created or managed well. Their work doesn't merit his praise; it hasn't *earned* his esteem. Don also realizes his indebtedness to Anna Draper, his first wife and the wife of the Don Draper whose identity he had taken on in the war; he's been supporting her financially since their divorce ("The Mountain King").

In all of these cases, interestingly, Don's justice is an extension of business, "earning" and "repaying" in some kind of accounting model of morality. Not surprisingly, it functions well at work, where capitalist notions of merit are at play, where office personas dominate private lives, and where a person is more or less his accounts. In a merit-based system, identity and context are secondary matters. Awards and penalties are determined on the supposition that it is one's effort or skill that makes one deserving of an office with a view rather than one's walking papers, as in the case of Freddy Rumsen, whose office Peggy will eventually take over ("The Mountain King"). At work Don is playing a role, but it's okay, since, in some fashion, so is everyone else.

Don's record of justice in his relationships at home or with his assorted lovers, however, is far less impressive. Perhaps in an economy of sexual gratification, all his bills are paid, but that isn't what love or personal justice is all about. In virtue of his fatherhood role, Don owes his children more time and attention. In virtue of Betty's loyalty and support, he owes her greater fidelity and respect. As a philanderer, he may even owe his dalliances freedom from the emotional baggage that he constantly lays at their doors.

Why doesn't Don apply his own principles more broadly? Perhaps it is because he wants these relationships to be grounded in something other than a thin, role-based justice. Don wants something deeper but founders on his self-imposed lack of depth and identity. A fractured personal life will threaten the justice of one's personal relationships, and it will threaten the love that initiates and sustains these relationships, as well. In these relationships identity matters, as do context sensitivity, history, and deep, core values. Don seems to know this. He simply can't bring himself to act on it. Integrity evidently means more to justice than a disintegrated self would like to acknowledge.

California Dreams

Don Draper's life is not what it seems. He is a tortured soul, inhabiting a life that is real but not true. Don has hidden his past from virtually everyone who matters to him. Don harbors deep desires for integrity, as we have witnessed in his moments of comfort between affairs and after he's revealed his past to Betty. The link between these moments of peace and his confession is his trip with Pete Campbell to California ("The Jet Set").

From the days of the nineteenth-century gold rush to the flourishing of the movie industry in the 1930s, California has been manifest destiny. With Pete, Don is supposed to be cultivating new business. At the bar, he is approached by a handsome count, Willy, who introduces him to a beautiful young woman, Joy, who, Willy says, would very much like

Don's company. Don is interested, but he declines her dinner invitation. His purpose in going to California is to escape for a while, but not necessarily in his typical, libidinal fashion.

Later, as the young woman waits for her car, they cross paths again. Don abandons Pete in a flash; he doesn't even bring a suitcase along. He and Joy drive to a house in Palm Springs that is temporarily occupied by wealthy, cosmopolitan Europeans of various ages, accents, and relationships. Don stays for a few days, perhaps charmed like Odysseus by Circe. Don is a charmer though, too, and wily like Odysseus. The nomads will be leaving California soon, heading for other gorgeous locales, no doubt. Joy invites Don along. He'll be taken care of, she says. This is Don's chance to fully satisfy the desire to be liberated from his past. But Don can't seem to get his family out of his head. He dials a number on the house telephone: "Hello. It's Dick Whitman. I'd love to see you . . . soon" ("The Jet Set"). The audience has never before heard Don refer to himself so naturally as Dick Whitman. In reconnecting to his past, Don's longing for integrity has, temporarily at least, won out over his desire for freedom.

Don leaves the jet set and finds his way back to Anna Draper, with whom, we discover, he had a friendship and a marriage of convenience ("The Mountain King," episode 212). Anna is the only part of Don's life before Betty that he seems to harbor any real sense of fidelity to. Don ignored even his own half-brother, Adam, who had spent years trying to track Don down and ended up, lonely and abandoned, committing suicide in a seedy hotel room in Manhattan ("Indian Summer," episode 111). Only on his trip to California do we fully understand that because of Don's suppression of his past, he longs for moral responsibilities that draw on history and that are deeply responsive to relationships and needs (he articulates this longing in "The Wheel," episode 313; in California, he finally owns up to it); and yet, by this same pattern of suppression, he cannot have what he longs for.

Don: I've told you things that I've never told Betty. Why does it have to be that way?

Anna: You love her. You don't have to tell her everything.

Anna [a little later]: So what are you going to do?

Don: I don't know. I have been watching my life. It's right there. I keep scratching at it, trying to get into it . . . I can't.

It's not surprising that in response to Don's greatest temptation—a nomadic life of freedom and play—the lost Don Draper would run to Anna. Perhaps this is where he was headed all along. We can't know for sure. But it is where he ends up. As soon as Don sees Anna, he enters into a confessional mode. He evidently spends a few days reminiscing with her and recovering. The former Mrs. Draper really knows him. He can be truly himself here. Because he isn't running from his past, we see Don more at home, more natural, more grateful and loving, more whole, than we've ever seen him before and will, quite possibly, ever see him again. "The Mountain King" ends with Don entering the ocean, purified by his contact with Anna.

We're Not in California Anymore . . .

Don Draper is plagued by his inability to be fairer to his wife and children. He sees the harm he's caused them and others around him, such as Adam. He longs to be at home in the world the way he is, or was, with Anna in California. Don's happiness and goodness may not be doomed, however. Don will have to give up parts of his life while working to grow others. But this growth will only be realized by a serious reconciliation of Don's complicated and duplicitous identity with his deepest values and responsibilities. Maybe Don should quit Sterling Cooper and take a different job, one where he doesn't spend his days manufacturing the desires that will keep others alienated from themselves. Or perhaps Don needs to sell his suburban home, which allows him to further split himself between work and family (Betty wouldn't mind living in the city).

And, indeed, we find Don changing jobs and moving to Manhattan at the end of season three of *Mad Men* ("Shut the Door. Have a Seat," episode 313), though sadly not because Don has realized what integrity demands. More likely, Don starts his own firm with Sterling, Cooper, and Pryce as a way of realizing his father Archie's desire for self determination (a flashback reveals Dick Whitman as a young boy, watching helplessly as a horse kicks his father in the head and kills him as he prepares to abandon the local co-op and sell his wheat at market). And Don is moving to the city because Betty is leaving him: she is going to Reno for a divorce with her new beau, Henry Francis, right beside her.

Don may not need to give up his borrowed, constructed identity altogether. But wholeness will require that he bring his life together under the umbrella of some relatively consistent, stable set of core values, whether as Don or as Dick, whether as playboy or as devoted father and husband. Perhaps these latest events in Don's story will reveal to him that he never wanted a family to begin with—that it was his suburban self that was alien rather than true. But that is doubtful. More likely, Don will rediscover what he had been somehow groping for all along: a deep desire to be with Betty and the kids, to be open, to be confessional and intimate. Fortunately, he's already begun this reconciliation process. As we know from Don's difficult disclosure to Betty, reconciliation will be painful, even while providing him some relief. Don's problem is the sheer depth of his deceptions, for while Betty had intimations of his infidelities, she had no reason to think that he might not be Don Draper. Consider this exchange from "The Gypsy and the Hobo," episode 311:

Don: I can explain.

Betty: I know you can. You're a very, very gifted story-teller.

Don: I need a drink.

[Don walks to the sink and splashes his face with water.]

Betty: Are you thinking of what to say or are you just looking at that door?

Betty [slightly later in the conversation]: You obviously wanted me to know this. . . . Say something.

Don: I didn't think I had a choice. And, I don't know what the difference is. This is our house. Those are our children.

Betty: There's a big difference. You lied to me every day. I can't trust you. I don't know who you are.

Don: Yes you do.

The news so shocks Betty because to her it means their whole life has been a lie. Don wants her to see him as her husband, the father of their children. Don appeals to the roles he plays in the family. Betty isn't so much nonplussed about Don's ethics—she really isn't sure who she's married. Don's confession seems to bring some renewed affection in the marriage at first, but the stakes are different here than they were in California, confessing to Anna about stealing her husband's identity. Don doesn't yet see what long-term effects his disclosure will have. His relationships will worsen before they improve. His first dose of this comes after Betty's drive to clear her head following the shooting of Lee Harvey Oswald ("The Grown Ups"):

Betty: I don't know where to begin. I want to scream at you for ruining all this. . . . I don't love you.

Don: Betts, don't. You're distraught.

Betty: It's true. I don't love you anymore. I kissed you yesterday. I didn't feel a thing.

Don leaves the room, continuing to treat her as if she's simply responding to recent events, though he walks to their bedroom, sits down, and holds his head with both of his hands. Things don't work out. Betty pursues a relationship with Henry and files for divorce; Don changes jobs and moves to the city. Though it's too soon to know for sure, Don's prospects for reconciling his present with his past seem dim. His lack of integrity may make him incapable of salvaging the best parts of his recent, Don Draper life.

Reconciliation Doesn't Come in a Bottle

Modernity saw the growth and protection of new freedoms: political, economic, and social. It also saw the development of narrative-shattering political, economic, and social upheaval. The two seem to be inextricably related. The mid-twentieth century is a critical juncture in this history, as freedom is challenged and defended, even as its costs and benefits are revealed and complicated. Don Draper is an icon of this time—freed by a negation of his past, remaking himself in pursuit of his dreams, and tortured by it all. This suffering is ours as well. Don shows us that our schizophrenic modern lives may not be doomed to moral incompleteness if, before it's too late, we drop what's unnecessary, increase our investments in one another, and figure out how to reconcile the remaining contradictions. This is why integrity is the most important value for late modernity. However painful it may be, we need to reclaim the past without granting it oppressive authority; we need to practice justice based on fuller understandings of people's identities and needs;

and we need to develop communities with an appreciation for the difficulties and demands of integrity and wholeness.

We can't live our parents' or grandparents' lives, but neither are we wise to forget them. Thanks to *Mad Men*, drinking classic cocktails is one of the easiest and best parts of our reconciliation project. Like Don Draper, however, much more difficult negotiations lay ahead.

NOTES

1. Not only are dates hard to come by, disagreements about how to define or understand modernity abound as well. I use the term *modern* somewhat loosely here to indicate the last four hundred years or so of Western history, as well as a variety of attitudes that take special hold in it, especially a concern for individual freedom in an increasingly fragmented world. For an accessible introduction to modern philosophy up to roughly Kant, pick up a copy of Anthony Kenny's *The Rise of Modern Philosophy: A New History of Western Philosophy*, vol. 3 (New York: Oxford University Press, 2008). For a richer but much more demanding story about modern identity, try Charles Taylor's *Sources of the Self: The Making of the Modern Identity* (Cambridge, MA: Harvard University Press, 1992).

2. Albert Camus, *The Fall*, translated by Justin O'Brien (New York: Vintage Books, 1956), 28–30. Clamence will find his own solution to his situation, which involves giving up his former life for that of self-proclaimed public confessor. Needless to say, this is not the answer we hope to get from Don Draper!

3. Albert Camus, *The Myth of Sisyphus, and Other Essays*, translated by Justin O'Brien, 1st Vintage International edition (New York: Vintage Books, 1991); Albert Camus, *The Stranger*, translated by Matthew Ward, 1st Vintage International edition (New York: Vintage Books, 1989).

4. Alasdair MacIntyre, *After Virtue: A Study in Moral Theory*, 2nd ed. (South Bend, IN: University of Notre Dame Press, 1984).

5. Robert C. Solomon, *Living with Nietzsche: What the Great "Immoralist" Has to Teach Us* (New York: Oxford University Press, 2003), 128.

6. This is similar to Jeffrey Stout's response to MacIntyre's work in *Ethics after Babel: The Languages of Morals and Their Discontents*, 1st Princeton edition (Princeton, NJ: Princeton University Press, 2001). Stout appropriates Lévi-Strauss's (1908–2009) notion of bricolage to express the complicated, contingent nature of our moral talk, always working from "whatever is at hand" (74) socially, culturally, historically, and so on. Thanks to my colleague, David True, for pointing this out.

7. Some of the same tensions I've noted here can be found in political theory, as well. Consider John Rawls's famous "veil of ignorance" thought experiment in *A Theory of Justice* (Cambridge, MA: Belknap Press, 1971), where justice results from limiting knowledge of one's life situations and personal histories in deliberations about how to distribute society's resources.

8. In an uncharacteristic moment ("Wee Small Hours," episode 309), Don fires Sal after a run-in with a client from Lucky Strike over Sal's work (the real problem wasn't Sal's competence, but that he had rebuffed the client's sexual overtures). Though Don had previously kept Sal's homosexuality a secret—consistent with his approach to merit—he here not only fires Sal, but does so while expressing some kind of disgust at "you people," perhaps implying that Sal's homosexuality overrides the quality of his work. I'm inclined to see this as an expression of Don's fear of losing the Lucky Strike account ("Lucky Strike can shut off our lights," he says) more than a twist to Don's approach to justice, though admittedly Don is a complicated character to make out.

PART FOUR

"NO ONE ELSE IS SAYING THE RIGHT THING ABOUT THIS": *MAD MEN* AND SOCIAL PHILOSOPHY

"AND NOBODY UNDERSTANDS THAT, BUT YOU DO"[1]: THE ARISTOTELIAN IDEAL OF FRIENDSHIP AMONG THE *MAD MEN* (AND WOMEN)

Abigail E. Myers

Relationships between characters on *Mad Men* are rarely what they seem to be. The picture-perfect couple is unhappy, distrustful, adulterous; the giggling gal pals are sharpening their knives with their white-gloved hands; the sweetly submissive secretary is the one really running the show. Nearly all of the characters use relationships with others to their own ends, of course—*Mad Men* is a show that seems to almost celebrate manipulation and subterfuge. But some characters in some situations use their particular gifts to subvert expectations of relationships during this time period, particularly between genders, to craft new relationships based on honesty and mutual admiration; in short, relationships that even Aristotle (384–322 BCE) would recognize as friendships.

Aristotle was hardly unique among the ancient Greek philosophers in his search for what represents goodness in human life and, like Socrates (469–399 BCE) and Plato (428–348 BCE) before him, his work in the field of ethics remains relevant today. Aristotle believed that the best and truest friendships exist among equals; specifically, between those who are at equal stages of moral development. So, to examine the friendships of *Mad Men* through an Aristotelian prism requires the following: an understanding of the Aristotelian ideal of friendship; an understanding of how morally developed our characters are; a sense of which characters are morally equivalent and why; and, finally, which of our characters form relationships with each other that fit this bill. Oh, and maybe just a dash of your favorite Belle Jolie lipstick.

Friendship According to Aristotle: "I'll Tell You Right Now, Don, I Don't Like Being Judged"

So says Roger Sterling to Don Draper as they powwow in a barbershop in season three's "Guy Walks into an Advertising Agency" (episode 306). The scene provides the initial thaw to what has been a frosty relationship indeed between Roger and Don for the first half of season three. Roger knows that Don has been silently judging him, chiefly for his fling with and eventual marriage to his young secretary Jane, and Roger, of course, feels that Don has no right to do so. Roger may not know everything about our hero, but he knows enough to know that Don shouldn't play holier-than-thou with him. What Roger doesn't know (but, given his fondness for philosophy, Bert Cooper might) is that Aristotle would have agreed with him.

In *Nichomachean Ethics*, Aristotle discusses the various types of friendships available to people: friendships based on pleasure, friendships based on profit, and friendships based on similar moral outlook or values. "For to the rich, and to those who possess office and authority, there seems to be special need of friends," Aristotle muses, "for what use is there in such good fortune, if the power of conferring benefits is taken away, which is exerted principally . . . towards friends?"[2] He eventually settles on his ideal of friendship: a relationship between two persons equal in moral development.

> The friendship of the good and of those who are alike in virtue is perfect; for these wish good to one another in the same way. . . . [T]hose who wish good to their friends for the friends' sake are friends in the highest degree, for they have this feeling for the sake of the friends themselves.[3]

Like Roger, Aristotle must have sensed that a friendship in which one person consistently judges the other for what he views as imperfect or unethical behavior will be an unsuccessful one. For Aristotle, friendship is "perfect" when it exists between people who are similar in goodness—that is, equivalent in moral development—and who wish good to their friends *because it is good*, not because it will benefit themselves in some way.

Well, this is a tall order for the men and women of *Mad Men*. Almost every character is constantly on the lookout for how they can spin a situation to benefit themselves. Rather than help each other as codirectors of accounts, for example, Pete Campbell and Ken Cosgrove (especially Pete) jealously protect their own account "territories" ("Out of Town," episode 301). When Sal Romano, a loyal and productive employee, is put in a terribly unfair position by a client's lies, he is quickly cut loose by Don so as to placate the client and not lose his business ("Wee Small Hours," episode 309). Who among these characters is morally developed at all, when you look at it that way? Fortunately for us (and for Don, Roger, and the rest of the gang at Sterling Cooper), Aristotle's discussion of moral development and friendship gives us some flexibility.

Moral Development and Friendship as Understood by Aristotle

As Aristotle continues his discussion of friendship, he notes that all friendships, even those based primarily on seeking pleasure or profit from another person, possess an element of mutual well-wishing. If they didn't, he observes sensibly, they could hardly be called friendships at all.[4] The challenge, he goes on to say, is to develop a friendship in which mutual well-wishing is maximized and the mutual well-wishing minimizes any other motive, even though, of course, the most altruistic friendships have an element of a utilitarian ethos to them: "You scratch my back and I'll scratch yours." As Aristotle says, "Each [friend] is good absolutely and also relatively to his friend, for the good are both absolutely good and also relatively to another."[5]

Any kind of friendship, Aristotle explains, must be based on similarity of some kind—chiefly, similarity in values. Moreover, the best kinds of friendships must develop over time after friends have had the opportunity to prove themselves as having the right intentions in the relationship. "It is to be expected that such would be rare,"[6] Aristotle concedes, but they are the best kind of friendships, the kind for which we all should strive.

Now we're getting somewhere. We have some characters in *Mad Men* who have proven concern and loyalty for each other, despite other mistakes large and small; we have some characters who value similar things, despite other values being perhaps somewhat lacking. How, now, do we judge whose values are most similar and whose friendships qualify as the most Aristotelian? To answer these questions, the staff of Sterling Cooper will go up against two more contemporary thinkers in moral philosophy: Lawrence Kohlberg and Carol Gilligan.

Contemporary Understanding of Moral Development in Kohlberg and Gilligan: "You Want to Be Taken Seriously? Stop Dressing (or Making Moral Decisions) Like a Little Girl."

Joan Holloway Harris, as usual, provides us with one of the series' most memorable lines, a sharp rejoinder to Peggy Olson's plea about how to be taken seriously by her male coworkers. Surely that one must have stuck in the proverbial craw of Peggy for quite some time, or at least long enough to get her to put on a tight little dress and head over to a strip club to meet the boys, as she does in that same episode ("Maidenform," episode 206). Joan's advice rings true because it *is* true—not necessarily or only in terms of fashion, but in terms of leveling the playing field between people by forming relationships based on some sense of equivalence or similarity.

How can this equivalence or similarity be measured? Lawrence Kohlberg (1927–1987), who developed his scale of moral development based on work by Jean Piaget (1896–1980) and John Dewey (1859–1952), believed that there were six identifiable stages of moral development through which individuals progress in a linear manner one at a time. Taking the time to understand each stage is a worthwhile endeavor, but for our purposes here, it is most crucial to understand that Kohlberg believed that, at their highest level of moral development, people make moral decisions based on universal principles of justice. At other, lower levels, people might make decisions based on instrumentalism and exchange; on the desire to be viewed as a "good boy" or a "good girl"; or on a social contract.[7]

Kohlberg's work, however, seems to assume that these universal principles of justice are indeed universal. Moreover, his work was based entirely on studies of adolescent men. Carol Gilligan, a contemporary psychologist, has found Kohlberg's theory lacking, based on her studies of how *women* develop morally. Gilligan's *In a Different Voice* (1982) was born from her dissatisfaction with the moral development theories of Kohlberg, which had been formulated from studies examining only men. Gilligan's study found that women's motivations for moral decisions were based less in laws and societal conventions, and more in their personal relationships and the emotions attached.[8] While, in Kohlberg's theory, this would be seen as immature and underdeveloped, Gilligan argued that this could simply be an alternative mode for moral decision making, which in its highest form could be as sophisticated and complex as Kohlbergian morality.[9]

How do these two theories apply to the world of *Mad Men*? The show gives contemporary viewers a glimpse into a time in which men and women were differentiated much more sharply in the workplace and in the home than they are today, and in which women's roles were more narrowly and traditionally defined. But the female characters in *Mad Men* spend as much of their time subverting traditional gender roles as they do fulfilling them. A hybridization of Kohlberg's and Gilligan's theories, then, may serve us well as we continue to consider the ethics of friendship.

We can use the moral development of our (anti)hero, Don Draper, as a case study. Don seems in many ways to be a reprehensible human being. He steals the identity of his brother-in-arms in Korea, abandoning his family; he maintains this stolen identity indefinitely, using it to marry the beautiful Betty and begin his professional ascent in advertising; he routinely cheats on his obviously troubled wife, who is struggling to manage their two—and eventually three—children despite having every material comfort. Yet any viewer could just as easily argue that Don has redeeming qualities of compassion, foresight, and professionalism. He cares for the widow of the real Don Draper; he tries (though he fails) throughout the series to renew his fidelity to Betty; he puts his considerable talents to work for the great benefits of Sterling Cooper's clients; and, most crucially, he enables Peggy to go on with her professional ambitions by keeping the secret of her child and encouraging her to come back to work.

Sometimes, then, Don acts ethically in his relationships. He cares for the people in the relationships he values—the real Don Draper's widow Anna, Peggy, even Betty to a certain extent. This is why Roger's stinging indictment of Don in the closing episode of season three—"You're not good at relationships because you don't value them"—does indeed sting. And Don seems to realize that Roger is right. He has not properly cared for the relationships he values the most. By Gilligan's measure of moral development, Don has failed, and he spends the rest of the episode attempting to make amends for this failure (though whether he is truly making amends or making arrangements for the success of Sterling Cooper Draper Pryce remains to be seen at the end of season three).

Despite his faults, Don seems to cling to certain universal principles of justice. His military service and his grief at President Kennedy's death both speak of a certain patriotism, to say nothing of how often and approvingly he invokes the American dream in his advertising work. He admires people who embody the advice given to Peggy by Bobbie Barrett: "This is America. Pick a job and then become the person who does it" ("The New Girl," episode 205). And his singular vision at Sterling Cooper is to not only promote his own work and the work of his creative team but to make clients realize that they've been given exactly what they wanted and needed all along. These qualities speak of a certain consistency and idealism, and Don does seem to strive to live up to them.

Neither by Kohlberg's standards nor by Gilligan's is Don a fully morally developed human being. But he certainly is not a sociopath. He is flawed, complex, and occasionally likeable; and, crucially, because he has been known to act correctly in situations in which he does not necessarily stand to benefit, he is capable of meeting Aristotle's standards for the ideal human friend.

Since no one on *Mad Men* has much of a claim to being a better person than Don, it's not hard to imagine this case study with another character. All of the characters can shock us with their callowness, greed, and insensitivity, only to surprise us at another turn with moments of pathos, honesty, and compassion. The challenge is to find characters who, due to their similar values, shortcomings, and triumphs, could enjoy the most equitable, and ideal, of friendships.

Morally Equivalent Characters in *Mad Men*: "Kids Today, They Have No One to Look Up To, Because They're Looking Up To Us"[10]

Ain't that the truth, Don. Everyone on *Mad Men* at least seems to realize that he or she is flawed. Whether it's Peggy's palpable discomfort in church, Don's look of terror when he realizes that Betty knows his secret, or Roger's heartfelt toast to his seriously wronged ex-wife at his daughter's wedding, every character not only faces tangible moments of moral discomfort, but fights guilt from various poor decisions throughout their lives. Several characters who have evolved uniquely affectionate, respectful, and honest relationships—what we might call Aristotelian friendships—throughout the series seem to possess some equivalence in terms of their secrets, mistakes, shortcomings, and eventual moral development and possibly even something that could be called progress. The Aristotelian friendships in *Mad Men* are those that are shared among moral equivalents: Don and Peggy, and Joan and Roger.

What makes Don and Peggy moral equivalents? Each values his or her career and gives his or her best effort at work at all times; each loves his or her family in the abstract but struggles to take the individuals that comprise it seriously; and each has a nebulous sense of faith. Most important, each character is hiding a dark, painful secret. Don hides his past as bastard child and identity-thief Dick Whitman, while Peggy hides her own illegitimate child with Pete. Even if Peggy eventually reveals her secret to Pete, she's hardly about to wrench him away from Trudy and bring their child into the picture. She may be concerned to protect Pete, but she's more concerned to protect her budding career and her privacy.

By the end of season three, as previously noted, even Roger takes Don to task for devaluing nearly all of his relationships. He has taken advantage of Betty shamelessly, of course (though, to be fair, Betty has certainly played Don more than once); he went as far as to make Cooper agree to keep Roger away from him; and, most devastatingly for this viewer, he has taken Peggy's work and genuine admiration for him very much for granted. Indeed, Peggy is so disillusioned with her work and her position at Sterling Cooper that she runs into the arms (literally) of Herman "Duck" Phillips and is almost tempted to join him at Grey ("Seven Twenty Three," episode 307). But although Don has begun to make amends with everyone he has wronged by the end of season three, his reconciliation with Peggy is especially resonant.

Peggy and Don have always had a unique relationship. Many viewers may have almost forgotten, by this point, that sharp-tongued, tireless Peggy started off as Don's naive, sheltered secretary. "I liked your girl Peggy," Betty mentioned to Don when she met her. "She's fresh." "As the driven snow," Don drily replied ("New Amsterdam," episode 104). But perhaps Peggy was not so naive—she's bold enough to make a move on Don in the very beginning of the series. Perhaps Don fostered that bold streak, as Peggy quickly proved herself as a more-than-competent secretary and, with the Belle Jolie campaign, won herself a position as a copywriter. Don mentors her in this new position—not always gently, tactfully, or even especially helpfully, but he does mentor her. And one of the series' most unforgettable moments comes in Peggy's flashback to her time in the hospital in which Don comes to visit her and persuades her to give up her baby: "Move forward," he tells her in "The New Girl" (episode 205). "This never happened. It will *shock* you how much it never happened." Crucially, in this episode, Peggy is flashing back to that time period as she nurses Bobbie Barrett, who encourages her to stand up to Don more frequently and hold her own in the workplace. Ironically, Peggy's cover-up, which may seem to be a subservient and tacit reinforcement of Don's games, is actually what puts Peggy and Don on a more equal footing. Peggy is no longer merely grateful to Don for keeping her secret. Rather, she has the opportunity to do for Don what he did for her. This newfound equality, rather than Bobbie's pep talk alone, enables Peggy to go back to Don with a new sense of confidence. Bobbie is right about this much, though: Don's respect for Peggy clearly grows as a result.

One might argue that Don's friendship with Peggy is based much more on a desire for profit rather than on mutual goodwill. However, by the end of season three it is clear that mutual goodwill is the primary basis for their relationship. Don doesn't need Peggy's work to keep him or Sterling Cooper afloat. His cutting remark that she hasn't "done one thing here that [he] couldn't live without" is not necessarily untrue, unkind though it may be ("Seven Twenty Three," 307). Peggy might be a good copywriter, even an excellent one, but the place would survive without her if it had to.

For her part, Peggy no longer needs Don for professional advancement (if a sharp girl like Peggy ever really did); Duck Phillips is trying to (literally) woo her away from Sterling Cooper into a job with his agency, Grey. But when Don aims to convince her to join Sterling Cooper Draper Pryce, he tells her—and you believe him—that "nobody understands that, but you do," speaking of their intuitive understanding of the

American dream ("Shut the Door. Have a Seat," episode 313). Obviously, they understand it because they, more than anyone else on the show, are living it, for better or worse. By the end of season three, Don's genuine (if belated) respect for Peggy and her work, coupled with Peggy's genuine admiration for him, keep them hurtling into the future together at Sterling Cooper Draper Pryce. Their relationship, bound as it is by their secrets and the favors they've done for each other as well as the friendship they have developed, will surely continue to prove an interesting one.

Joan and Roger, on the other hand, are moral equivalents in very different ways. Both Joan and Roger enjoy pre- and extramarital sexual and emotional dalliances, for example, though Joan shows considerably more discretion in doing so. Both show at least a nodding respect to the outward trappings of family life. Both are clever and shrewd in the workplace but, unlike Don to a certain extent and Peggy to a great extent, they make their jobs look so easy that they seem to be almost an afterthought to the thrilling social opportunities the office provides. But, like Don and Peggy, their relationship portends a future in which men and women might interact on a more equitable plane.

"Look," Roger slurs memorably at the end of season one's "Indian Summer" (episode 111), "I want to tell you something, because you're very dear to me and I hope you understand it comes from the bottom of my damaged, damaged heart. You are the finest piece of ass I ever had and I don't care who knows it. I am so glad I got to roam those hillsides." Well, you could do worse for an endorsement from Roger Sterling, whose unbridled appreciation for the female form is a recurring theme in his own life and in *Mad Men* as a whole. But it's clear from Roger's behavior toward Joan, particularly in the latter half of season three after she leaves Sterling Cooper (only to join Sterling Cooper Draper Pryce), that he has a deep and abiding affection for her wit, competence, and company.

He phones her in the middle of the night after his daughter's poorly attended wedding in "The Grown Ups" (episode 312), saying, simply, "I had to talk to you." When she admits to him in the previous episode, "The Gypsy and the Hobo," that she needs to find a new job, he quickly offers to help, saying, "I'm glad that you thought to ask me." And when season three's final episode reveals the cloak-and-dagger founding of Sterling Cooper Draper Pryce with a liberal poaching of Sterling Cooper's clients, it's Joan whom Roger trusts to sort through the paperwork and organize the new firm so it can hit the ground running. Bringing in Joan isn't just efficiency and profit-seeking on Roger's part. After all, as a partner, he surely could have ordered Harry, Peggy, or anyone do the work. And it's not just altruism because Joan needs a new job. It's a combination of Roger's respect for her work and concern for her well-being along with the genuine esteem he feels for her that leads him to ask her back.

Joan, meanwhile, has always kept her cards closer to her vest. Far from trying to hoard the attention of the males in the office, she frequently encourages the other female employees to flirt and dress attractively.[11] She is the epitome of discretion during her affair with Roger, and, when it becomes clear that it has to come to an end, she moves on briskly, making it clear that her agenda is to marry—indeed, she is engaged a few scant months later.[12] It's hard to know what she really feels for Roger because of her reticence when it comes to herself and her emotions. But her actions late in season three make it clear that Roger's affection for her is mutual. How do we know? One thing that we know about Joan is that if she doesn't like you or doesn't want to waste one more moment of her precious time on you, you'll know it. Memorable indeed is her seething at Jane, Don's secretary turned Roger's paramour and eventual wife: "What on God's green Earth do you think you're doing here?" after Joan had personally fired her ("The Gold Violin," episode 207). She often has a pithy and withering word for Peggy, who, despite her greater ambition, lacks Joan's considerable savvy around the office.[13] So when Roger calls her after his daughter's wedding and she bends her ear to him, the viewer knows that his attentions are welcome. When Joan comes back to Sterling Cooper Draper Pryce at Roger's behest, it's not just about the job—she wants to be there and wants Roger to want her there.

So with Don, Roger, Joan, and Peggy all casting their lots with Sterling Cooper Draper Pryce, we might wish to return to Aristotle for his prognosis of the agency. What does he say about friendship as a unifying force for a government, or, say, an advertising agency? Well, he says this:

> Friendship also seems to hold states together, and leg-islators appear to pay more attention to it than justice; for unanimity of opinion seems to be something resem-bling friendship, and they are most desirous of this, and banish faction as the greatest enemy. . . . It is not only necessary, but also honourable.[14]

So if the friendships between Don and Peggy, and Joan and Roger, are genuine—and, through thick and thin, they appear to be—perhaps their new venture has a better-than-average chance of success.

"To a Place Where We Know We Are Loved"

These friendships, then, against all odds, uphold the Aristotelian ideals of friendships that are based on mutual goodwill between moral equivalents. In the cutthroat world of advertising and, perhaps more important, in all of these characters' increas-ingly dark personal lives by the end of season three, Don and Peggy and Joan and Roger have come to count on one another and trust each other's presence in their lives. To borrow Don's words from the final episode of season one ("The Wheel"), these friends provide one another with "a place where we know we are loved."

None of these characters is perfect, and perhaps you or I wouldn't want any of them as our best friends. (All right, I'd want Joan as my best friend, but just so I could borrow her clothes.) But in the world in which they find themselves, these friendships are as good as it gets. They are, in the changing tides of advertising, not for sale and not for selling—they are based on mutual goodwill and some shared moral vision. Aristotle might wish that our friends at Sterling Cooper Draper Pryce were perhaps more honest and less deceitful, more compassionate and less greedy—but their friendships seem to show some potential.

NOTES

1. "Shut the Door. Have a Seat." (episode 313).

2. Aristotle, *Nicomachean Ethics*, translated by R. W. Browne (London: George Bell and Sons, 1905), 203.

3. Ibid., 207.

4. Ibid.

5. Ibid., 208.

6. Ibid., 209.

7. For a full yet concise explanation of Kohlberg's stages of moral development, see Robert Barger, "Kohlberg's Theory of Moral Development" (2000). Available at http://www.csudh.edu/dearhabermas/kohlberg01bk.htm.

8. Carol Gilligan, *In a Different Voice: Psychological Theory and Women's Development* (Cambridge, MA: Harvard University Press, 1993).

9. Gilligan was careful to point out that the ethical theory she presented, which came to be known as "care ethics," was not *necessarily* gendered; although women more frequently employed it, men could and did employ it as women sometimes employed more masculine ethics. "The title of my book was deliberate," she reminded her critics, "it reads, 'in a *different* [emphasis Gilligan's] voice', not 'in a woman's voice'" (Carol Gilligan, "Reply to Critics," from *An Ethic of Care: Feminist and Interdisciplinary Perspectives*, edited by Mary Jeanne Larrabee (New York: Routledge, 1993), 209.

10. "New Amsterdam" (episode 104).

11. For example, in "Smoke Gets in Your Eyes" (episode 101), Joan says to the then brand-new Peggy: "If I had those darling little ankles, I'd find a way to make them sing."

12. "The New Girl" (episode 205).

13. Another great Joan line: "This isn't China, Peggy. There's no money in virginity" ("Shoot," episode 109).

14. Aristotle, *Nicomachean Ethics*, translated by R. W. Browne (London: George Bell and Sons, 1905).

MAD WOMEN: ARISTOTLE, SECOND-WAVE FEMINISM, AND THE WOMEN OF *MAD MEN*

Ashley Jihee Barkman

Peggy Olson, Betty Draper, and Joan Holloway (later Harris) portray the various obstacles women faced in the 1960s as second-wave feminism was coming on the scene. Clearly demarcated as second-class citizens, these women tolerate sexual harassment in the workplace, adulterous husbands, and even nonconsensual sex. But as the forbidden fruit of self-awareness remains on their palate, the injustices these intelligent, competent, beautiful women suffer become more apparent even to themselves. As the series unfolds, the middle-class white women of *Mad Men* are shown coping in an era fraught with what Aristotle, in a qualified sense, would deem "injustice." This is especially appropriate for the time, as second-wave feminism addressed both official (legal) and unofficial inequalities in the home and in the workplace.

Aristotle thought justice meant treating each person or thing as it ought to be treated: equals should be treated as equals, superiors as superiors, subordinates as subordinates.[1] Now if we ignore Aristotle's belief that women are incomplete men,[2] and rather say that women, to the same degree as men, have rational souls (endowed with free will, rationality, creativity, and so on), then, *in this respect at least*,[3] women—including the women of *Mad Men*—ought to be treated the same as men, and for them not to be treated so is unjust. To the extent that they stand up to male-instigated oppression, repression, and suppression, Peggy, Betty, and Joan are "mad women" in the best sense. To the extent that they don't stand up for themselves, they may simply go mad.

Peggy the Initiator: Dealing with Oppression at Work

In the series, Peggy starts out as a mousy, servile secretary. Whether she is naive or determined, we cringe as she awkwardly tries to seduce Don Draper in the pilot episode ("Smoke Gets in Your Eyes"), suggestively laying her hand on his in gratitude for standing up for her. It's hard to blame her for verging on sexual harassment on her very first day at work, though. Her day begins with Ken Cosgrove's chauvinistic comments in the elevator, followed by Joan's suggestions about what men want, Pete Campbell looking her up and down and suggesting how she should dress, and (only halfway through the day) Nanette suggesting she show more leg. It's clear that women are sexually objectified. And this, according to my qualified Aristotelianism, is unjust, since such objectification fails to acknowledge that Peggy is more than a piece of meat, but has in fact, a rational soul.

Nevertheless, first impressions are deceptive. The honest girl from Bay Ridge who blushes at sexual innuendos will undergo the greatest transformation of all. She turns out to be the most "progressive" of the leading female characters. But then again, maybe we shouldn't be so surprised. Attempting to initiate an inappropriate relationship with her boss on her first day at work may have signified some of the things to come. Her ambition overshadows what appears to be an awkward or timid nature.

In a work environment where a male employee is cheered on by his coworkers to chase down a female employee to find out the color of her panties ("Nixon vs. Kennedy," episode 112), Peggy's obstacles to success seem overwhelming. But the evolution of Peggy in ponytails to Peggy with the shoulder-grazing flip, from a girl timidly asking for her own desk ("Indian Summer," episode 111) to a woman who receives Don's apology ("Shut the Door. Have a Seat," episode 313), Peggy is a dynamic individual.

The "basket of kisses," which quickly launches her career as a copywriter, enables her to put her talents to use. Of the three women analyzed in this chapter, Peggy is the lone individual who not only receives due justice—that is, she is treated as a person possessing a rational soul—but seeks it out as well. She knows where her abilities lie, and she is willing to vocalize what she deserves.

Peggy's talent is evident in her various impromptu creative inputs. When Don argues that feelings, not sex, sell products, Peggy blurts, "What did you bring me, Daddy?" as a tag line for Mohawk airlines ("Flight 1," episode 202). Or when Don disapproves of Paul Kinsey's idea for an Aquanet commercial, Peggy modifies it on the spot to meet Don's approval ("The Color Blue," episode 310). Though she holds the position of copywriter, she recognizes her exclusion from certain events by her colleagues and looks for a way to be a part of that group. She takes initiative and tells Freddy Rumsen that she wants to be part of any after-hours outings, expresses frustration that she wasn't told about the casting call for bra models, and, having overheard that the Playtex execs are taking her colleagues to a strip club, shows up at the outing elegantly dressed.

Peggy recognizes her merits and isn't shy about going after what she thinks she deserves: she asks Roger Sterling for Fred's old office after he is let go, noting that she landed the Popsicle account ("The Mountain King," episode 212). Further emboldened by "Duck" Phillips's offer to join his firm, she asks Don for a raise in pay equal to that of her male coworkers, and when he turns her down, stating that he's "fighting for paper clips" these days, she states the injustice: "You have everything and so much of it" ("The Fog," episode 305). Peggy is right. Don has everything she wants and in excess, and to turn down her reasonable request—she does equal work, so why not equal pay?—is unjust. She leaves, contemplating the alternative, which is to accept Duck's offer. Peggy finally puts her foot down when Don simply assumes that she'd follow him to his new company and declines his proposition. Later, Don, a man of great pride who would neither admit to his adultery nor concede to blackmail by Pete or Jim Hobart, humbly apologizes and states that even if she turns him down, he would "spend the rest of [his] life trying to hire [her]" ("Shut the Door. Have a Seat."). As Bobbie Barrett suggested, treating Don as her equal takes her a step closer to acquiring that corner office ("The New Girl," episode 205).

Though Peggy is aware of what she deserves, she never attempts to get it by acting unjustly (that is, by treating rational souls as anything less). Pete blackmails Don with his past, but Peggy keeps Don's affair with Bobbie (and earlier on, with Midge) to herself. Peggy never blackmails Don or anyone else; she never resorts to unjust tactics. When she makes requests for a desk, a raise, an office, or a promotion, she sticks to the facts and keeps it all about business and *her* merits, not the moral shortcomings of others. She is unlike her colleagues. Pete and

Paul can be whiney, emotional, resentful tattletales, but Peggy never is. She never stoops to their level.

Peggy is selective about the men she dates, turning down Paul and Carl, but choosing to be intimate with Pete and later Duck. Pete abuses their relationship, taking Peggy for granted. He sleeps with her, then turns her down later on the dance floor ("The Hobo Code," episode 108). Eventually, though Peggy has feelings for Pete, she is frank and breaks off their relationship, saying, "Every time I walk by I wonder, are you going to be nice to me—or cruel?" ("Long Weekend," episode 110). She knows where to draw the line and chooses to be in control of the situation rather than letting her emotions get the best of her.

Peggy quickly makes her way from a shunned woman to a confidante. The underlying assumption that women have it easy, with their limited responsibilities, is shattered in *Mad Men*. Pete assumes this, alluding to the overwhelming stress he feels about flying, the objections to adoption from his mother, and the responsibilities he has at work. He implies that women can't understand what men go through, but Peggy corrects him. "It's not easy for anyone, Pete" ("The Inheritance," episode 210). This is obvious for the viewer. Peggy breaking conventions, getting pregnant and giving the baby up for adoption, and keeping this all to herself seems far more of a burden to bear than Pete's trivial musings. But because of Peggy's approach to the status quo—namely, her outspokenness toward injustice in the workplace—she is able to overcome the obstacles that are before a working woman in the 1960s. The strength of her character is reflected when she discloses to Pete, who implicitly professes his love for her, that she could've shamed him into her life forever if she'd wanted to by the very fact that he got her pregnant ("Meditations in an Emergency," episode 213), but instead chose the higher ground. Her resilience is profound, but perhaps shockingly profound when we must consider her sterile attitude toward the whole pregnancy: it shocks us all how much "this never happened" ("The New Girl").

Betty's Reaction: Dealing with Repression at Home

Straight out of every boy's fantasy (just ask Helen's son), Betty Draper, who "looks like a princess" ("New Amsterdam," episode 104), is the kind of woman every man would want to marry. Beautiful, educated, and elegant, she also happens to be a doting wife. Or that's how the story begins. An idyllic house in suburbia, a housekeeper, financial stability, a daughter and a son (and later another son), and a pairing of two unbelievably attractive individuals—could life be more perfect? Apparently, it could.

We discover the deception even before we learn of Prince Charming's castle in Ossining. The end of the pilot episode ("Smoke Gets in Your Eyes") reveals that Don is an unfaithful husband. Every season has been speckled with one-night stands and serial mistresses like Midge, Rachel, Bobbie, and Suzanne. Don's injustice toward Betty—that is, his treating her as less than a rational soul with all its entailed dignity—is overwhelming. His reluctance to disclose information about his past—from his upbringing to his true identity, from his situation at work to his infidelities—is detrimental to his marital relationship. Whether the details are minor, like when she purchases the Heineken for their dinner guests, unknowingly and embarrassingly falling into a demographic pattern, or major, as when Roger asks her to persuade Don to sign a contract (a contract she has never even heard of), Don treats Betty like a mere accessory at home. Betty wants to be an intimate part of Don's life, not just a prized pony to show off when the occasion arises. But every time she is called for, it's for appearances, to "be shiny and bright . . . [to be the] better half" ("The Benefactor," episode 203).

Consider her tearful jubilation when she is able to participate in Don's life by attending the dinner to get an apology out of Jimmy Barrett: "I'm just so happy. When I said I wanted to be part of your life, this is what I meant. We make a great team" ("The Benefactor"). Even when they are having marital difficulties and Betty is not feeling up to it, Don insists that she attend the party honoring him because everyone is expecting him to bring her: "I want to show you off, Betts" ("The Color Blue"). She desires to grow with Don and contribute to his life, and thereby her family's life, by playing a bigger role than that of a bored housewife. In short, Betty wants Don to acknowledge her true worth—as an equal in terms of possessing an Aristotelian rational soul. Only in this way could the two of them have a healthy marriage, a marriage grounded in justice.

Though there are temptations, Betty is loyal to Don. When Roger makes a pass at her, she is quick to rebuff him. When Bob Shaw (the door-to-door air conditioning salesman) arouses her fantasies, she forces him to leave (though she does fantasize about him while steadying a washing machine). When Arthur Case makes persistent passes at her at the stable, she changes her riding times to avoid him ("Maidenform," episode 206). Betty resists temptations and remains faithful to Don, who is often at work (or in the arms of a mistress) until unreasonable hours, and whose mind is often elsewhere. Summing up her frustrations after a failed lovemaking attempt, she tells him, "I wish you'd just tell me what to do" ("For Those Who Think Young," episode 201).

For the sake of his career, Don is willing to humble himself toward Roger, Pete, and Peggy. And certainly he is willing to fight for his clients' businesses. But he becomes passive and complacent when it comes to his relationship with his wife. The one aspect of his life for which he should fight the hardest—his family—he concedes too easily. When Betty kicks him out for not admitting to having had an affair with Bobbie, he is so stubborn that right up to the end, he never explicitly confesses his exact wrongdoing. Likewise, when Betty tells him she wants a divorce, he again passively states that he won't fight her ("Shut the Door. Have a Seat."). Betty's response to their first attempt at separation is a double-edged sword: "I thought you can talk anyone into anything" ("Six Month Leave," episode 209). Clearly, this sarcastic remark speaks not only to his failure to convince her but also to his passivity. Don is unjust to Betty, not only for his infidelity but also for his complacent, negligent attitude toward keeping the family together.

"She Seems Consumed by Petty Jealousies and Overwhelmed with Everyday Activities. We're Basically Dealing with the Emotions of a Child Here."

It's pretty much all gossiping and smoking; few consequential things seem to occupy Betty's time. Her children are babysat by the television, and her chores are done by the housekeeper. We see her taking riding lessons, organizing some fundraisers, and going to the salon, but aside from loving Don, few passions or genuine hobbies occupy her life. Betty's father, Gene, tells his granddaughter, Sally, that she "can really do something" with her life. Betty, by contrast, is mostly a spectator ("The Arrangements," episode 304).

Betty empowers her husband to the extent that she has no voice of her own. Reality, security, and identity all seem to be grounded in her husband. When contemplating divorce, she tells Helen, "Sometimes I think I'll float away if Don isn't holding me down." Helen replies that the most difficult part about divorce "is realizing you're in charge" ("The Inheritance").

Though she is educated (she studied anthropology at Bryn Mawr and speaks fluent Italian), she does nothing to expand her mind, to satisfy her intellectual needs as an Aristotelian rational soul. Everyone recognizes how pretty she is. Even Conrad Hilton tells Don, "By golly, you are an indecently lucky man" upon his first encounter with Betty ("Souvenir," episode 308). Perhaps her beauty muffles her chance at self-actualization. As she fiercely defends her mother to Dr. Wayne, she says her mother wanted her to be beautiful so that she could find a man and that there is nothing wrong with that ("Ladies Room," episode 102). She clearly maintains this view as she tearfully relays to Don that if her car accident had been more serious and Sally had gotten a scar on her face, she'd be guaranteed a sad and lonely life ("Ladies Room"). She believes that the outward appearance of a woman solely determines her future, though Peggy could tell her otherwise.

"I Want to Scream at You for Ruining All This"

Betty's numb hands are obviously a psychosomatic response to her repressed feelings of marital distress and general discontentment at home. Likewise, shooting at her neighbor's pigeons with a rifle is a great way to express her deep frustration ("Shoot," episode 109). Is she lashing out in anger for losing what she may deem to be her one last shot at being defined outside the home (by getting replaced at the Coca-Cola photo shoot)? Unable to repress her suspicions any longer, she kicks Don out when she is convinced that he had an affair. Though they briefly show a united front when her father has a stroke, she tells Don, even after they've slept together, that it was all pretense ("Six Month Leave").

Once the seams of their marriage begin unraveling, Betty chooses to do things for herself that she would never have done before. She confides in Helen about the separation; she initiates an intimate relationship between Arthur and Sarah Beth; she has sex with a random stranger at a bar; and she buys a fainting couch fraught with erotic connections to Henry Francis, a man with whom she later pursues a relationship. Her repressed emotions reach their limit as she tells Don she wants a divorce. When Don says she should see a doctor, obviously pinning the problem on her, she replies, "Because I'd have to be sick to want out of this? I didn't break up this family" ("Shut the Door. Have a Seat."). With all that Don has done to her, she realizes that she doesn't love him anymore, and she tells him so. The threshold of injustice she can bear has been reached. The pain and humiliation of never having been enough for Don are too much for her to bear: "I'm going to Reno, and you're going to consent" ("Shut the Door. Have a Seat").

Sassy but Passive: Joan and Suppression at Work and Home

If Betty is every boy's fantasy, Joan must be every teenager's. With her fiery red hair and unmatchable curves, she is Botticelli's Venus come to life. Joan is not a Marilyn (Monroe); Marilyn is a Joan. Never a hair out of place, her words and actions are as smooth and sugary as her voice. First impressions may lead us to think that she's a redheaded vixen, but she turns out to be quite a likeable and charming individual. And as such a sassy woman of the world, it's a surprising turn to discover that she is the least progressive of the three women. She neither initiates like Peggy, nor reacts like Betty, but patiently waits for her due. Joan is a woman comfortable and content in the values and expectations of those in the pre-second wave world (of feminism).

As the office manager at Sterling Cooper, Joan is not just highly competent, she is also great with people—her superiors, her clients, even her subordinates. She's not power-hungry or egocentric, in need of boosting her self-esteem by preying on the weak and newly initiated. On numerous occasions, she helps Peggy fit into her environment. Joan suggests that Peggy take herself seriously, stop dressing like a girl, speak the language of the creative and accounts team ("Maidenform"), and not disclose private information; and by loaning her a spare outfit, saves her some embarrassment (when her skirt rips) ("Red in the Face," episode 107). Even when Roger undermines her authority and tells Jane that she isn't fired, Joan is able to brush it off, rather than dwell on it ("The Gold Violin," episode 207).

Joan, far from being petty or immature, is a level-headed person. She doesn't seem to hold grudges. She genuinely cares about Roger, and even when he marries Jane, she doesn't hold any resentment or ill will toward him. In fact, she remains his confidante and friend ("The Grown Ups," episode 312; "Shut the Door. Have a Seat.") and though she owes him nothing, she chooses to help Roger form Sterling Cooper Draper Pryce, which will likely become a mutually beneficial enterprise. In her highly competent manner, Joan comes to the office fully prepared (movers ready to go) and efficiently delegates the necessary tasks: what they need to take and where to find it ("Shut the Door. Have a Seat."). She's an invaluable part of the ad agency, and on numerous occasions we see her coolly keeping things under control. Cooper calls her for help to assure their clients that business will go on uninterrupted in light of Roger's heart attack. She remains professional, even though she is clearly distressed. When Guy MacKendrick's foot is cut off by a lawn mower, Joan doesn't miss a beat and quickly applies a tourniquet to stop the bleeding ("Guy Walks into an Advertising Agency," episode 306).

Though she is an efficient and proficient multitasker, she suffers a blatant form of injustice when she is overlooked for the position of script reader, though she has proven highly successful at it ("A Night to Remember," episode 208). Typical of the times, Harry Crane is unable to conceive of Joan being anything other than an office manager.

"You Don't Know What It's Like to Want Something Your Whole Life, Plan on It, and Not Get It"

With a worldview rooted in stereotypical gender roles, Joan doesn't try to fight the restrictions, hurdles, and injustice that face a woman of her time. She doesn't disagree with her husband that a woman should be eating bonbons and watching the shows, even though she enjoyed script reading. Her goal in life, as she relays in the pilot episode ("Smoke Gets in Your Eyes"), is to achieve what Betty has achieved: marry a wealthy enough man so that she can be a full-time housewife. Her hopes for this are dashed when she discovers that her husband, Greg Harris, has been passed over for chief resident ("Guy Walks into an Advertising Agency").

Though she is always congenial, accommodating, and encouraging, her husband is immature. We discover this even before they marry, when he forces himself on Joan in Don's office, even though she tells him to stop ("The Mountain King"). Greg violates and humiliates her by this act: he treats her as a piece of meat, as a physical being endowed with a mere vegetative or animated soul, and not as one possessing a rational soul or one with the same dignity as men (that is, other rational souls). But per her usual self, she doesn't lose her composure, and acquiesces. When they hold a dinner party for Greg's superiors, Joan keeps the mood jovial. From serving food buffet-style to solve the seating arrangement problem (Who should sit at the head?) to playing the accordion and singing for their guests (as Greg attempts to deflect attention from a mishap at surgery), she saves the day. And though Greg's being passed over for chief resident affects her as much as it affects him, he, in his state of self-pity, tells her curtly to "get another [job]" (she has already quit Sterling Cooper). But Joan consoles, "You are still a doctor. I married you for your heart, not your hands" ("Guy Walks into an Advertising Agency"). She is Greg's biggest supporter, helping him prepare for his interviews, giving him vital and appropriate feedback on a most professional level. Greg, however, is childish and sulky when his interview goes poorly, telling her, "You don't know what it's like to want something your whole life" and not get it. We see the first instance of Joan acting justly—acting as a suppressed rational soul is entitled to act—when she bashes his head with a vase. How humorously shocking and refreshing! The vase acts as a wake-up call to Greg, a reminder that every-thing Joan wants in life is what Greg has to offer her, and his failure affects her as much as it does him. The only difference is that Joan deals with unfortunate circumstances as an adult, whereas Greg sulks like a child. Fortunately, Greg realizes his selfishness and later apologizes to her and tells her that he's joined the army (to work as a surgeon) so that Joan won't have to return to work ("The Gypsy and the Hobo," episode 311).

Greg and Joan seem to have a similar philosophy on life and how women should be treated. He believes that he is doing her a favor by joining the army to alleviate the necessity for a second source of income; Joan appears to be happy with Greg's decision. At the end of season three, however, we see Joan back at work at Roger's request. There is no indication that this is an act of defiance against her husband's will. It doesn't seem con-trary to what has been Joan's modus operandi: going with the flow and taking what she is given. And this time, we're happy for her chance at moving up and putting her talents to better use. Maybe Joan will discover that her previous aspiration to marry rich and not work is not her cup of tea. Clearly her stint as a script reader hinted at her enjoyment of work.

Joan has the same misconception that Betty has: a wom-an's greatest value is in her physical appearance. Although she is an extremely competent and intelligent individual, she doesn't value herself as a rational soul, only as a physical being. Consider what she advises Peggy: "Go home, take a paper bag, cut some eyeholes out of it. Put it over your head, get undressed and look at yourself in the mirror. Really evalu-ate where your strengths and weaknesses are. And be hon-est" ("Smoke Gets in Your Eyes"). Rather than suggesting an assessment of Peggy's relevant skills and talents and how best to apply them at work, Joan recommends that Peggy evaluate her physical appearance, as if accentuating those strengths will be of the utmost importance to Sterling Cooper. Her continual advice to Peggy reveals that a woman's worth is determined by how men perceive her physically. Clearly, she has no qualms with this, especially considering that she has no problems getting the kind of attention from men that she wants. She doesn't mind perpetuating this expectation of women, advising Peggy to show those darling little ankles ("Smoke Gets in Your Eyes").

Don't Go Mad

We already see the flaw in Joan's life goal. As a rational soul, a woman can't be satisfied through superficial means. Peggy becomes aware of the fact that attracting men doesn't guarantee a happy outcome. We see her growing comfortable with herself as she defines herself by her own merits on her road to self-actualization, trudging along and setting a new path for other women in the second wave. Betty, the woman who seems to have it all, is "profoundly sad" not only because of her husband's infidelity, but because she doesn't treat herself as a rationally developing being. And Joan, who seems so worldly-wise, is blinded by conventions and false ideals. Not only are these women treated unjustly, but the latter two perpetuate the injustice. While Peggy is a mad woman in the best sense, Betty and Joan may ultimately go mad from injustice.

NOTES

1. Aristotle, *Ethics*, translated by Hugh Treddenick (Toronto: Penguin, 2004), 1129a17–1131a9.

2. Aristotle, *On the Generation of Animals*, translated by David Ross (Oxford: Oxford University Press, 2002), 737a25.

3. I'm not arguing that women are equal to men in all respects, only that they are so in respect to the basic faculties of the rational soul.

"WE'VE GOT BIGGER PROBLEMS TO WORRY ABOUT THAN TV, OKAY?": *MAD MEN* AND RACE

Rod Carveth

In "The Fog" (episode 305), Pete Campbell is stunned while reviewing research for a meeting with the Admiral TV people. "Atlanta, Oakland, Chicago, Detroit, Newark, D.C. Is it possible that Negroes are outbuying other people two to one?" he asks incredulously.

To validate his interpretation of the research reports, Pete asks Hollis, the black elevator operator, probing but unsophisticated questions about the shopping preferences of "Negroes." Because he doesn't want to get into trouble for speaking freely with one of the white elevator riders, Hollis is reluctant to say anything. Even when Pete assures Hollis that it's okay to talk to him, Hollis is not particularly helpful about the TV buying habits of African Americans. He really doesn't even watch

TV. When Pete asks him why he doesn't watch TV, Hollis responds, "Why should I? We've got bigger problems to worry about than TV, okay?"

This scene demonstrates the verisimilitude of *Mad Men* when it comes to race relations in the 1960s. Minorities live in Pete Campbell's world, but they might as well live on another planet. He does not understand them as people, and he certainly does not understand their issues. As we'll see, the societal changes occurring in 1960s America will force the mad men at Sterling Cooper to undergo a paradigm shift in their thinking about race.

The Evolution of Race on *Mad Men*

As the series has developed, *Mad Men* has evolved its depictions of race.[1] The portrayal of blacks in the first season is best exemplified by a scene in the series premiere, "Smoke Gets in Your Eyes." The scene opens with Don sitting in an upscale restaurant. A black busboy gives him a light for his ever-present cigarette. Don then engages the busboy in a conversation about his smoking and brand preferences. While Don and the busboy are talking, an older white waiter comes over and asks Don if he is "being bothered." Don dismisses the white waiter and continues his conversation with the busboy. The scene is instructive, as it shows how blacks were to serve the white power structure, and to do so without "bothering" the white elite. Let's not be fooled, though. Don isn't offended by the white waiter's racism; Don's on a mission to gain marketing information from the busboy. After all, he has a meeting with Lucky Strike to prepare for.

So in season one, blacks are occasionally seen, but rarely heard. Carla, the Drapers' maid, not only cleans the house and cooks the food, but also babysits the Draper children. Yet, she is portrayed as doing all of this without being heard. Similar circumstances exist for Hollis, the elevator operator at the building where Sterling Cooper is housed. Hollis is sometimes seen, never heard.

By season two, however, the events of the 1960s begin to have an influence on the all-white world of Sterling Cooper. And in "Six Month Leave" (episode 209), the virtual invisibility and silence of African Americans begin to dissolve. As will be discussed later in this chapter, Hollis and Carla have significant lines in this episode. And in the next episode, "The Inheritance," Viola, the maid working for Betty's father, Gene, calmly fends off Betty's anger at her father's declining health ("You wanna give me your temper?"), then provides Betty with comfort ("The minute you leave, you'll remember him as he used to be. It's all good outside that door.").

Meanwhile, back at Sterling Cooper, copywriter Paul Kinsey resists accompanying his African American girlfriend, Sheila, to register black voters in Mississippi, telling her that he'd rather go to the Rocket Fair in California than "face Mississippi, and those people screaming at me, and maybe getting shot." But Paul later agrees to go to Mississippi when Don lets him know he won't be going to California. One of the final scenes of the episode shows Paul, the only white face on the bus, providing a pseudo-Marxist analysis of advertising. Paul pontificates: "We must include everyone. The consumer has no color." Paul later describes the trip as the adventure of a lifetime, though his relationship with Sheila ended during it.

The portrayal of blacks in season two is best summed up by an exchange between Don and Roger at a bar after breaking the news to account man Freddie Rumsen that he is being let go (the alcoholic Rumsen had urinated himself moments prior to a client meeting). Roger notes, "You know, BBDO hired a colored kid. What do you think of that?" Don responds, "I think I'm glad I'm not that kid."[2] In other words, blacks made some progress in being visible during season two, but you would still not want to be one.

During the first two seasons of *Mad Men* race is portrayed in a mostly ancillary fashion—the black characters are presented sparingly, underscoring just how insulated and out of touch with the times the folks at Sterling Cooper are. But the portrayal of race changes significantly in season three. To be true to the times, the increasing visibility of blacks on *Mad Men* is only natural. Season three opens in 1963, a year of historic events affecting the civil rights movement: John F. Kennedy was assassinated, four young African American girls were killed in a bombing in Birmingham, Malcolm X was becoming popular, and Dr. King delivered his "I Have a Dream" speech.

Early in the season, in "My Old Kentucky Home" (episode 303), Roger Sterling and his fiancée Jane throw a Derby Day party at Roger's country club. Roger, on his knees in blackface, sings "My Old Kentucky Home" to Jane. Roger revels in his performance, relating how he "did it with shoe polish and she just laughed and laughed." The performance, and the comments, illustrate Roger's perception of blacks. Reactions of the partygoers range from mild amusement to blatant discomfort. Don, for example, wants to leave, but Betty wants to stay. Among other staff at Sterling Cooper, only Pete Campbell seems disdainful of Roger's actions.

The scene reflects how the world is about to undergo major changes concerning race. However, just as in the real world, those changes will prove slow to implement. Two episodes later, in "The Fog," Pete Campbell, preparing a pitch for Admiral television, notices that while overall sales of Admiral TVs among whites are flat, sales among blacks are up. Nothing if not ambitious, and pitted in a competition with Ken Cosgrove to become head of accounts at the agency, Pete sets out to see if these results can bear fruit to a new marketing approach that will impress the folks at Admiral.

Throughout the series, Pete, more than his colleagues at Sterling Cooper, is aware of his times. For example, in the "The Marriage of Figaro" (episode 103), Pete alone among his fellow ad men saw the humor in the acclaimed

Volkswagen "Lemon" ad designed to promote the 1961 VW Beetle. So it's not surprising to see Pete take a more modern approach to audience demographics in his pitch to the men from Admiral TV. He presents the sales data and proposes an innovative strategy for boosting sales—targeting blacks in black media such as *Ebony* magazine: "This is *Ebony*. By Negroes, for Negroes."

Because the men from Admiral had not yet stopped Pete in his tracks, Pete drops a bombshell: as a cost-saving cornerstone of the campaign, ads can feature both whites and blacks and be used for all media. This "integration" pitch is too much for the men from Admiral. "Negroes," they assert, buy Admiral TVs because they are trying to emulate whites—"Monkey see, monkey do." Further, they fear that by appealing to black consumers, they will drive away white consumers. For the good folks at Admiral, blacks at best possess no original thinking skills and at worst represent a threat to business. Pete may not be a force for civil rights, but for the higher-ups from Admiral, blacks are best when they are Invisible Men.

It is bad enough for Pete that the client strongly resists the campaign. But to add to his defeat, he is roundly criticized by both Sterling and Cooper. Cooper goes so far as to say, "Admiral has no interest in becoming a 'colored' television company." Still, Lane Pryce, the financial officer installed by Sterling Cooper's new British parent company, Putnam, Powell and Lowe,[3] observes that he sees an evolving attitude toward race in the United States, one that should be taken advantage of, even if with another client. Thus Lane sees what viewers already know: Pete has lost his battle, but mad men like him will win the advertising war over time.

"We Thrive at Doing Business with People Who Hate Us"

In a 2007 interview for *AdWeek*, the *Mad Men* series creator Matthew Weiner noted, "The men of that period had a different code and a lot of it is sexist and racist and selfish."[4] As noted elsewhere in this book, Weiner has certainly captured the sexist and selfish part of that code.[5] Mal MacDougall, who was a BBDO copywriter on the Lucky Strike account in the 1960s, said about *Mad Men*, "The booze, the sex, the cigarettes, the suits, the haircuts, the harassment, the office politics, the 'we own the world' attitude—even the offices—are absolutely dead-on true."[6] Yet the racist part of the mad men code is treated gingerly. For example, though characters such as Pete Campbell or Roger Sterling have no problem in letting their misogynistic comments fly freely, they are never heard uttering a racial epithet.

Unlike its understated treatment of racism, however, *Mad Men* has had no problem portraying the overt anti-Semitism of the period. In the series premiere episode, Don and Roger prepare to meet with a potential new client—Rachel Menken, the daughter of the Jewish owner of a major department store. As they ponder whether they should have a Jewish employee present to make her think they're a Semite-friendly firm, Roger asks, "Have we ever hired any Jews?" Don replies, "Not on my watch." He then jokes, "Want me to run down to the deli and grab somebody?" The two settle for pretending a Jewish mailroom employee is part of their account team for the Menken department store.

In "Babylon" (episode 106), Don turns to Rachel for information about Israel and its importance to Jews around the world. Of course, he's not trying to broaden his cultural horizon; he's preparing a pitch for the Israel Department of Tourism. Don admits to Rachel that he's "having a hard time getting a handle on it." Rachel replies snarkily, "And I'm the only Jew you know in New York City?" She continues, "I'm sorry. I'm not an expert on this and something feels strange about being treated like one."

When Don persists in getting something beyond Israeli Ministry "propaganda," Rachel says in favor of her "tribe" that despite years being in exile, "We've managed to make a go of it. Maybe it has to do with the fact that we thrive at doing business with people who hate us." Don protests, "I don't hate you," to which Rachel fires back, "No, individuals are wonderful." Translation: for Don, "some of his best (girl)friends are Jewish."

The exchange, interestingly, serves as a metaphor for Madison Avenue in the 1960s. While it is true that Jewish advertising agencies such as Doyle Dane Bernbach (DDB) served Jewish clients, they didn't limit their messages to Jewish consumers. DDB, for example, produced one of the twentieth century's most noted advertising campaigns, "You Don't Have to Be Jewish to Love Levy's Real Jewish Rye."

One-Dimensional Characters

Whereas the treatment of anti-Semitism in *Mad Men* is multi-dimensional, the portrayal of blacks is largely one-dimensional. Most black characters don't just lack any identifiable faults, they lack backstories altogether. The most regularly occurring black characters—Carla, the Drapers' maid, and Hollis, the elevator operator—usually get one or two lines, and we don't ever learn their last names. They are shown doing their jobs and knowing their place: serving—and suffering—in silence.

But then there is Sheila White, Paul Kinsey's girlfriend, seen primarily in the season two episode "The Inheritance" (episode 210). While her character gives the show an opportunity to explore interracial romance, Sheila turns out to be more of a plot device to show that Paul is a "rebel." As Joan observes, Paul is "falling in love with that girl just to show how interesting [he is]."

But as much as Paul may think he is liberated, when Sheila protests Paul's backing out of going to register voters in Mississippi for a chance to go to an aeronautics convention in California, Paul orders her not to speak about this issue at the office. In effect, Paul silences Sheila in much the same way other black characters on *Mad Men* are silenced. When Paul returns from the Freedom Ride, noting that he and Sheila have broken up, it is clear that rather than taking an opportunity to delve more deeply into the era's most controversial topic, the series plays it safe.

Disappointingly, *Mad Men* portrays the racial discord outside the office at Sterling Cooper as occurring primarily in the South. The characters watch TV news events, such as the Freedom Rides in the South, suggesting that racism was far worse in the South than in the North. Yet in the 1960s, racial strife was not confined to states south of the Mason-Dixon Line. Race riots broke out in Chicago, Boston, Washington, D.C., and San Francisco. But in *Mad Men*, northern racism consists simply of rude comments and a failure to see blacks as equal to whites. In *Mad Men*, northern racism does not include employment and educational discrimination, steering prospective black home owners away from white neighborhoods, blacks harassed for simply being in the wrong place after dark, or whites arbitrarily and capriciously venting their anger on blacks in subordinate positions. In reality, things were quite different.

The portrayal of blacks on *Mad Men* illustrates *differential racialization*.[7] Black characters are there to support white characters, not to challenge their privileged positions. For example, in "Six Month Leave," Carla begins to offer marital advice to her employer, Betty. Betty will have none of it—"This is not a conversation I am going to have with you." In other words, stay in your place; you are black and thereby subordinate to me in terms of societal power.

The one time that Carla appears to openly challenge a white person is in season three's "My Old Kentucky Home." When Betty's dad, Gene, now living with the Drapers, thinks someone has stolen five dollars from him, Carla tears apart his room looking for the missing money. When Gene asks what she was doing, she protests that she is doing the task to prove she didn't take the money. Gene says that he didn't accuse her of taking the money, to which she responds, "Not yet." Gene then mistakenly calls her "Viola," his former domestic servant. "I'm not Viola. I'm Carla," Carla snaps. Gene then asks, "Do you know Viola?" Carla responds, "No. We don't all know one another." Thus, Carla challenges a white person twice, first in correcting him on her name (her very identity) and then pointing out that not all black people know one another, no matter what this old white man thinks. Of course, Gene is stroke-addled—his lack of cognitive power lowering him to Carla's social level.

Similarly, in "Six Month Leave," Hollis laments the death of Marilyn Monroe to passengers Don and Peggy: "You hear about Marilyn. Poor thing." Hollis not only knows that Don and Peggy are part of the dominant white culture that has lost one of its icons, but also relates to Marilyn being a victim of the male power structure of Hollywood.

Peggy then observes, "You just don't imagine her ever being alone. She was so famous." Hollis replies, "Some people just hide in plain sight." Hollis should know—he's been hiding in plain sight of the people of Sterling Cooper for a number of years.

Yet while Hollis can talk to his white riders about the death of Marilyn Monroe, he is silent when the black civil rights icon Medgar Evers is assassinated. Maybe Hollis knows that his riders will be uninterested, or even offended, if he mentions Evers' passing. Or maybe it is because *race is a social construction*, a product of social interactions, social thought, and political relations.[8] If Hollis talks about Evers to others, especially those in the dominant power structure, then he sees reflected back his own subordinate status. Thus, being silent on issues of race is a defense mechanism for Hollis. He doesn't have to be reminded of his being on the lower rung of the societal food chain.

Overall, then, the picture of race as seen through the lens of *Mad Men* is one where oppressed blacks are there to serve the dominant white power structure.

What's on the Horizon?

Mad Men is a fictional series airing on AMC, not a documentary on the History Channel. And the series creator, Matthew Weiner, certainly exercises creative license. As Troy Torrison, the creative director for WPP Group's Grey Worldwide, told *Advertising Age*, "I think [the show] did a better job of accurately capturing the era (the smoking, sexism, sense of entitlement, etc.) than it did at portraying 'the work.'"[9] Yet the show fails to deal with the institutionalized apartheid in the industry at the time, and does little better in developing fully realized black characters.

But maybe there's hope for how blacks are portrayed on the series. In the season three finale, when Roger and Don visit Pete at home and offer him a role at their new agency, Roger states that not only do they need Pete's accounts, they also need his talent. "I want to hear it from him," Pete insists, glaring at Don. Don concedes, "You've been ahead on a lot of things. Aeronautics, teenagers, the Negro market. We need you to keep us looking forward."[10]

On the Draper home front, it appears from the last episode of season three that Carla's role will become more important for Sally and Bobby Draper. Betty has left Don to go to Reno with baby Gene and new lover Henry Francis (an aide to Governor Nelson Rockefeller) in order to get a "quickie" divorce. With Don immersed in getting a new agency off the ground, Carla is going to assume more maternal duties while Betty is away. Perhaps with Carla's more important role will come increased airtime (or, at least, the revelation of her last name).

Given the events that will happen in the time period in which season four will open (post-1963), we can at least hope that in terms of portrayals of race, *Mad Men* will keep moving forward as well.

NOTES

1. When we are talking about race in *Mad Men*, we are talking about African Americans. During the series first three seasons, no Latinos were portrayed in the series, and Asian Americans only appeared as comic relief for a practical joke fellow Sterling Cooper peers played on the recently married Pete ("The Marriage of Figaro," episode 103) and as a waitress who wants to know if Don wants her to come to his place after work. He declines ("Flight 1," episode 202).

2. "Six Month Leave," episode 209.

3. "Meditations in an Emergency," episode 213.

4. Kamau High, "On the Spot," *AdWeek*, June 23–30, 2007, 28.

5. See chapters 5, 7, and 10 of this volume.

6. Mal MacDougall, "A Real Mad Man," *AdWeek*, June 23–30, 2007, 14.

7. Richard Delgado and Jean Stefancic, *Critical Race Theory: An Introduction* (New York: New York University Press, 2001).

8. Kimberle Crenshaw, Neil Gotanda, Gary Peller, and Kendall Thomas, *Critical Race Theory: The Key Writings That Formed the Movement* (New York: The New Press, 1996).

9. Brian Steinberg and Andrew Hampp, "Did the Admen Watch 'Mad Men'?," *Advertising Age*, July 23, 2007, 4–5.

10. "Shut the Door. Have a Seat," episode 313.

"NEW YORK CITY IS A MARVELOUS MACHINE": *MAD MEN* AND THE POWER OF SOCIAL CONVENTION

James B. South

This is your brother. We don't know who he is yet,
or what he's gonna be. And that is a wonderful thing.

("Guy Walks into an Advertising Agency," episode 306)

In a pivotal moment early in the first season of *Mad Men* ("New Amsterdam," episode 104), Don Draper learns the limits of his authority at Sterling Cooper. Pete Campbell, a young account executive, has overstepped his place by pitching an idea directly to the owner of Bethlehem Steel. Don fires Pete as a result of this bit of insubordination, but Bert Cooper explains to Don that Pete is too important to Sterling

Cooper to be fired over such a matter and orders Don to keep him on. In one obvious way, Don has run up against his limits as an employee of Sterling Cooper. Bert Cooper is the boss, and what he says goes. So, too, Pete almost ran up against his limits in that Don is clearly higher up on the Sterling Cooper food chain.

What is especially interesting, though, is that the real authority had nothing to do with the corporate food chain. It turns out that the real authority had to do with some larger social dimension of the world within which Sterling Cooper has to survive, namely, the city of New York, with its rich history. As Bert Cooper explains to Don, "New York City is a marvelous machine filled with a mesh of levers and gears and springs, like a fine watch, wound tight. Always ticking." The clear message here is that Don is just another lever, gear, or spring, although it is also clear that Bert sees himself in much the same position.

There is a social, and even a political, dimension to authority. Both Don and Pete find themselves forced to recognize that there are features of their individual lives to which they must answer that are not simply claims to authority by another person (for example, a boss) and to which they are not willing parties in a contract. This fact suggests that these social dimensions crucially shape their identity, though they are not as easily recognized as one-on-one assertions of authority.

The issue that is most pressing, once one accepts the various ways that the social and political dimensions limit the possibilities of pursuing life projects, is the question of human agency. Obviously, in one-on-one expressions of authority, the persons on both sides are clear on the line of authority and clear on how to address it. In this chapter, I will refer to "agents" and "agency" quite a bit in a somewhat technical way, and these terms should not be confused with either those who work at an advertising agency or the agency itself. For my purposes, an agent exercises her agency when she is able to effect the change she desires and does so with some degree of transparency about her desires. That is, in order to act as agent, the person must know what she wants and why she wants it. If Don is unwilling to accept the authority of Bert Cooper, he can walk away, assuming there's no contract to hold him. When, though, the mechanisms of authority are less apparent, the issue of agency achieves a different level of urgency. How can the agent be sure that her actions are not being coerced in ways that are unknown to her?

While *Mad Men* occasionally tackles explicit political issues, most notably the Kennedy-Nixon election, it is not easy to discern the political views of the show. Indeed, it is not obvious that there is a particular political viewpoint advanced within the show, though characters occasionally espouse political claims. It is more fruitful, then, to consider the way that the show prompts us to think about the connections between the individual and the social/political, and "New Amsterdam," with its obvious allusion to the rich history of New York City, is a good place to begin. After all, one of the first philosophical discussions of the relationship between individual identity and social identity occurs in Plato's (428–348 BCE) *Republic*, where the explicit connection between the "psychology" of the individual and the influence of the city is a central theme.

"You're Going to Need a Stronger Stomach If You're Going to Be Back in the Kitchen Seeing How the Sausage Is Made"

When Plato first introduces the notion of the relationship between the city and the soul, he does so rather causally. The basic idea is that it is easier to see what makes a just city than it is to see what makes a just individual. The further idea is that once we see what makes a just city just, we'll be better able to see what makes a just individual.[1] By the time Plato gets to the end of his discussion of the relationship between individual souls and the city, though, the soul is increasingly described in explicitly political terms. He speaks, for example, of the way an individual's appetites can take over the "Acropolis of the soul,"[2] and he describes the political order set forth in the *Republic*, the ideal city, as the constitution (*politeia*) of the philosopher's soul.[3]

At least one important lesson of the *Republic*'s account of the relationship between the individual and the city is the reminder that our individual identities, the hopes, desires, fears, and interests that we possess, are shaped by social forces outside us—ones that we often fail to notice. Consider this conversation from the *Republic*:

> "Contravention of established custom in this sphere [music]," Adeimantus said, "all too easily insinuates itself without people being aware of what is happening."
>
> "Yes," I [Socrates] said, "because it is taken to be nothing but a form of play, which does no harm to anyone."
>
> "Naturally enough," he said, "because all it does is to make itself at home little by little, until it overflows ever so quietly into people's character and pursuits. From these it emerges, grown larger, into their dealings and associations with one another, and from dealings and associations it proceeds against laws and constitutions (so great, Socrates, by this stage is its insolence), till it ends up overthrowing everything in private and public life."[4]

Over the course of the first three seasons of *Mad Men*, we see some of these gradual, perhaps unnoticed changes play out. At the end of season three, for example, talking with Pete Campbell, Don points out just how often Pete has been right about things that Don could not see: "It's not hard for me to say, Pete. You saw this coming, we didn't. In fact, you've been ahead on a lot of things: aeronautics, teenagers, the Negro market. We need you to keep us looking forward. I do, anyway" ("Shut the Door. Have a Seat," episode 313). That is, Pete seems to have noticed how various aspects of the social world were changing, which is something Don failed to do. What is at stake if we fail to notice the gradual changes in the social world around us?

"People May See Things Differently, but They Don't Really Want To"

Toward the end of "New Amsterdam," after Roger has lied to Pete and told him it was Don's idea to let him stay at Sterling Cooper, Don and Roger have a conversation. Roger says, "I bet there were people in the Bible walking around, complaining about 'kids today.'" Don replies, "Kids today, they have no one to look up to, 'cause they're looking up to us." In this exchange, we are reminded that it is possible for a society to be made up of people who do not have, in Plato's words, "characters and pursuits" that are worthy of emulation. Don seems on to a fairly substantive critique of a society in which there are no plausible models leading to education for "kids." In such a society, presumably, those "little by little" influences will be unchecked and unacknowledged, leaving the younger generation as adrift as the older generations. But if there are no role models for the younger generation, how will they develop characters and pursuits? One possible response to this question is to accept that the younger generation will remain as characterless as the older one, subject to social forces that coerce them in unnoticed ways. Another possible response is that there may be some way for people to establish characters even if there are no obvious models to emulate.

Plato teaches us that we need not be mere passive receptacles for social influences. Of course, it would be strange to look to *Mad Men* for a Platonic approach to the issue of passivity. Plato's own account of the way we escape being subject of external forces involves a complex account of the objects of knowledge and a nondemocratic political theory that involves rule by philosophers. But Plato does point to the need for there to be a way to relate to social influences with a higher degree of agency and autonomy. It is precisely the failure to notice those "little by little" influences that can take agency away from us.

In "New Amsterdam," and throughout the series, the characters constantly run up against roadblocks to the development of character. Over and over, we see how they are constantly buffeted by history and customs to which they haven't consented. Indeed, the very title of the episode, "New Amsterdam," suggests just how old some of the customs are. We are shown what Don cannot know: that Pete's motivation for going over Don's head was not just a matter of Pete trying to show off—testing the limits of Don's authority, say—but rather was a result of his having come up against the limits of his own authority and agency. The other authority he is made to recognize is not related to work, though. Instead, he is forced to come to terms with his place within his family. And it turns out that it is quite a family.

Let's look closely at the scene in which Pete finds out the ultimate limit of his authority. He has gone to ask his father for money to help buy an apartment his wife, Trudy, has found. Pete's father expresses contempt for what Pete does: "I run into you at the club, you're working. At a restaurant, you're working. Taking people to dinner, wining and whoring? That's not a job for a white man." Pete responds that there is more to it than that, but his father does not agree. There are two interesting features of this exchange. One is the sheer straightforwardness with which Pete's father exemplifies a form of racism. It is an interesting shortcut into his character. We learn later in the series that he married into money and then managed to squander it. The racism and the lack of character involved in losing a fortune suggest that the lack of character and the unthinking acceptance of a racist attitude somehow go together.[5]

The other feature worth noting in this conversation is that we see the way that history and social forces shape identity. Pete's parents are in the process of closing up their city house and going to a summer house on Fishers Island. They are "old money"—a family with a long history in New York City. The father, who has married into the wealth of Pete's mother's family, shows nothing but contempt for the day-to-day work of business. The distance between Pete and his father is palpable. Their outlooks on the world are inconsistent. This is not to say, of course, that Pete is without flaws. The way he treats and mistreats women shows him to be less than forward-thinking in all areas. Pete nonetheless exhibits a healthy attitude toward work, seeing a value in it that his father does not.

After Pete's father rejects his request for money, Pete complains that his parents never give him anything. His father responds, "We gave you everything. We gave you your name—and what have you done with it?" Pete gives his father an angry look, but says nothing. Later that same night, Pete tells his wife that he did not ask his father for the money because "My dad has been having some health problems." When Trudy asks what's wrong with his father, Pete responds: "Nobody knows."

"Nobody" refers to Pete, who fails to understand his father's words or his attitude about the advertising business. Given the machine that is New York, though, Pete's father is not exactly wrong. Indeed, it's that gift that spares Pete from being fired by Don. He's needed by Sterling Cooper. After Roger has explained to Bert how Pete broke a rule about pitching a campaign directly to a client, Bert replies: "There are other rules." As Bert goes on to explain, "His mother is Dorothy Dyckman Campbell." That's the name Pete was given, and it accounts for his value to Sterling Cooper. Of course, Pete is not aware that that is the source of his value.

"Madison Square Garden Is the Beginning of a New City on a Hill"

In the very next scene of "New Amsterdam," Don pitches his idea to the Bethlehem Steel magnate. The idea seems straightforward and effective: "New York City—Brought to You by Bethlehem Steel." When the magnate demurs, Don explains that "the sentiment, the idea—it's so basic, you feel like you know it, you just haven't thought of it lately." The complaint, though, is that it looks like an ad for cities, not for steel. The steel man seems to think that steel has some intrinsic value, not just the instrumental value of being a basic building block of cities. He can't articulate exactly why he doesn't like the campaign and its artwork, simply saying that it "bothers me."

In these two encounters—Pete with his father and Don with the steel man—we are confronted by people who lack significant understanding of what is in front of them. In Don's term, they're missing something "basic." He makes it very clear to the steel man that steel is not the sort of thing that can be advertised directly; it's not something that can be bought at the grocery store. The magnate still thinks, though, that steel ought to be advertised as that sort of product. So, too, Pete is unable to appreciate his father's claim that he's been given something very valuable, a name. But could it be that Don is also missing something basic?

Later that evening, after Don's unsuccessful pitch, Pete has both a humiliating experience and a triumph. The humiliation comes when he and Trudy are out having dinner with her parents. She asks them for money for an apartment, and they readily agree to help, despite Pete's protestations. In this conversation, Pete seems deeply uneasy with taking Trudy's parents' money, though he had not been ashamed to ask his own father. Perhaps Pete sees his manhood threatened in this deal, missing the fact that other families are not like his. The triumph comes later in the evening when Pete meets up with the steel man for a bit of what his father would call "wining and whoring." Pete brings along a young blonde as a date for the magnate. Over drinks, Pete pitches an idea for the account: "Bethlehem Steel—The Backbone of America." This rather simple change, putting the product first and highlighting its role, goes over very well indeed. The next day, meeting with Don again, the magnate picks this slogan over Don's.

Of course, from Plato's perspective, Don had it right. What's important is the city with its customs and laws, not the ingredients used to make its structural underpinnings. The steel man has simply endowed his product with something that is not intrinsic to it. But we see here a very important fact about Pete: he really is good at his job. He figured out what the client wanted and gave it to him. We see again and again in the series that Pete is often right in ways his co-workers, perhaps especially Don, can't see. For example, later in the first season Pete compares Kennedy to Elvis, a fact that annoys Bert Cooper but shows how wrong the other characters were in assessing the Kennedy-Nixon election.[6] In season three, we see Pete reading *Ebony* magazine in an effort to understand the importance of the "Negro" demographic.[7]

"I Have Been Watching My Life. It's Right There. I Keep Scratching at It, Trying to Get into It. I Can't."

If Pete's primary obstacle to developing agency is his lack of understanding of the way family constrains him and helps him, Don's obstacle is rather different. In Don's case, we have the almost too obvious symbolism of starting from no history at all. Don Draper is not really Don Draper, but Dick Whitman. When Draper was killed in Korea, Dick took over his identity. Throughout the series, though, we see Don get more and more constrained by the choices he's made since assuming this new identity. He's living a suburban life with a beautiful wife and two children. He has a corporate job. There is no doubt that he sometimes feels trapped by these decisions. What caused him to make them? We can't know, obviously, but one plausible answer is that in thinking about how to live a life he simply took the path he saw so many others taking. We might say that he decided to emulate the average upwardly mobile member of the late-1950s middle class. In short, he takes no agency at all, instead settling into a kind of social conformity. That this is not who Don is seems clear. One need only think of the remark Don makes at the end of season three's "Shut the Door. Have a Seat." As he and Roger are leaving the Sterling Cooper office for the final time, Roger asks, "How long do you think it'll take us to be in a place like this again?" Don replies, "I never saw myself working in a place like this." Don may not have seen himself working in a place like Sterling Cooper, but he spent several years doing so anyway.

In the season two "The Jet Set" (episode 211), we see Don think about leaving the baggage of his life behind. On a business trip to California, he is tempted by Joy, a rich young woman staying at a house in Palm Springs. She is with a group of people who are rootless. Don spends time with them and sleeps with Joy. Don's rootlessness as an adult is not so much a choice as an impulse. When Don Draper was killed, Dick almost immediately took over his legal identity. With Joy and her companions, though, the story is a bit different. These are people who revel in being rootless. Sensing a kindred spirit, they invite Don to join them. Don is obviously attracted to this, but at the moment of decision he sees two children who are part of the group. This seems to give him pause. Is this what he wants for *his* children? Can he abandon the responsibility he has for them? In the next episode, "The Mountain King," we see Don go back to the beginning of his Don Draper identity as he spends some time with the original Don's wife, Anna Draper. Though he stays for a while in California, he eventually returns to New York, Sterling Cooper, and his family. But one must wonder about his commitments. Before leaving California, we see Don walk into the Pacific Ocean—a symbolic gesture, perhaps signifying a new life starting. What, then, are we to make of Don's claim to Anna that "People don't change"? One can't help but think that Don is returning to New York a changed man, or at least one open to change.

"Maybe I'm Not as Comfortable Being Powerless as You Are"

The trajectory of Don's character after this symbolic scene of rebirth is initially surprising. He finds various aspects of his life disorienting. Sterling Cooper has been bought by a British company. Betty gives birth to another child. Don starts an affair with his daughter's teacher, Miss Farrell. He seems more powerless at work, recommitted to a routine at home, and yet still looking for happiness outside both. Indeed, at one point in the season, he is forced to sign a contract with Sterling Cooper. If the Pacific Ocean scene is supposed to represent change, the contract surely represents the closing-off of possibilities. Yet by the end of season three, we see Don starting a new work life. He breaks off the affair with Miss Farrell and hatches the plan to start a new company. We see him and Betty split; as his new life in New York starts, Betty is flying to Reno. At the end of the season, he's decided that "I want to build something of my own." With the help of Bert Cooper, Roger Sterling, and a few other former Sterling Cooper coworkers, he thinks he's going to build something.

To do so, he has to talk both Bert and Roger into leaving Sterling Cooper, the company with their names on it. He has to explain to Pete that he has valued his forward thinking, his understanding of the small changes that would have such a big effect on the years to come. He has to explain to his protégée Peggy that she understood the ways that the world was changing, that Kennedy's assassination was something truly significant. Here's Don's pitch to get Peggy to come work at the new start-up agency: "There are people out there who buy things. People like you and me. Then something happened, something terrible. The way that they saw themselves is gone. Nobody understands that. But you do, and that's very valuable. With you or without you, I'm moving on, and I don't know if I can do it alone. Will you help me?"

Don and Peggy recognize that the Kennedy assassination changed everything because the social and political verities were shaken. While the long-term effects of the assassination seem unnoticed by many, Don knows that what is at stake are peoples' souls. But this speech to Peggy is also a bit unsettling. While Don may recognize that things have changed, at some very basic level *he* hasn't. Don is staying in the business of selling products to people. As he puts it in the final episode of season two, "I sell products, not advertising."

"I'm Enjoying the Story So Far, but I Have a Feeling It's Not Going to End Well"

Let's conclude this chapter on a cautionary note. It seems that at the end of season three, Don has figured out how to assert his agency, by figuring out that he wants to build something, something that's going to be called Sterling Cooper Draper Pryce. But it may be that things are not always as they seem. Consider Conrad Hilton, a recurring character throughout season three. In the season finale, it's Hilton who lets Don know that Sterling Cooper will be absorbed by McCann Erickson, a company Don calls a "sausage factory." Don is understandably upset that he's about to have a new boss. Hilton responds: "This happens all the time, Don. It's business." Once again, Don is brought up against the reality of the wider dimensions of social reality, dimensions that threaten his agency and autonomy. Hilton's message to Don is that "I got everything I have on my own. It's made me immune to those who complain and cry because they can't."[8] Maybe that's the only way to navigate the constraining powers of the city, to go it alone, to build something on one's own. Plato, though, is not so optimistic that one can go it alone, because the city is always there. Nor is *Mad Men* especially optimistic.

At the end of season three, we see a core group of series characters starting out on a new venture. Things look hopeful for Don to "build something of his own." But we need to place two features of the world highlighted by the series up against our optimism. The first is the sheer power of the intricate working of the city and the way it constrains agency, including ways that are unknown to those trying to exercise agency. The show has given us no reason to think that individual agency can overcome that. "The city" understands the significance of Pete's name even if Pete does not. Second, there is Don's claim that "People don't change." It may be that the world has changed; Don says as much to Peggy. And if that's the case, then it may be that the constraints on Don's agency will change such that he can build something for himself. But the little-by-little changes in the social world will have their effect on Don, even if he's not aware of them. Perhaps he can become as self-sufficient as Conrad Hilton. But the show's decision to use Conrad Hilton as the exemplar of the self-made man is interesting. After all, it brings to mind a person to whom he gave a name—Paris Hilton. And her example, at least, suggests that the city continues to work as it always has irrespective of anyone's effort to build something of his or her own.

NOTES

1. Plato, *The Republic*, Books II–IV, translated by G. M. A. Grube and C. D. C. Reeve (Indianapolis: Hackett, 1992).

2. Ibid., 560B.

3. These examples come from the excellent essay by Myles Burnyeat, "Culture and Society in Plato's Republic," in *The Tanner Lectures on Human Values*, vol. 20, edited by Grethe B. Peterson (Salt Lake City: University of Utah Press, 1999), 215–324.

4. Plato, *The Republic*, 424D–E, quoted in Burnyeat, 251.

5. Another example of this unthinking racism is the completely nonironical blackface that Roger Sterling wears in "My Old Kentucky Home" (episode 303).

6. "Red in the Face" (episode 107).

7. "The Fog" (episode 305).

8. "Shut the Door. Have a Seat." (episode 313).

APPENDIX

It's Not a List of Titles and Air Dates;
It's an Episode Guide

Season One

Episode	Airdate	Title	Writer(s)
101	7/19/07	"Smoke Gets in Your Eyes"	Matthew Weiner
102	7/26/07	"Ladies Room"	Matthew Weiner
103	8/02/07	"Marriage of Figaro"	Todd Palmer
104	8/09/07	"New Amsterdam"	Lisa Albert
105	8/16/07	"5G"	Matthew Weiner
106	8/23/07	"Babylon"	André Jacquemetton
			Maria Jacquemetton
107	8/30/07	"Red in the Face"	Bridget Bidard
108	9/06/07	"The Hobo Code"	Chris Provenzano
109	9/13/07	"Shoot"	Chris Provenzano
			Matthew Weiner
110	9/20/07	"Long Weekend"	Bridget Bidard
			André Jacquemetton
			Maria Jacquemetton
			Matthew Weiner
111	10/4/07	"Indian Summer"	Todd Palmer
			Matthew Weiner

Season One

Episode	Airdate	Title	Writer(s)
112	10/11/07	"Nixon vs. Kennedy"	Lisa Albert André Jacquemetton Maria Jacquemetton
113	10/18/07	"The Wheel"	Matthew Weiner Robin Veith

Season Two

Episode	Airdate	Title	Writer(s)
201	7/27/08	"For Those Who Think Young"	Matthew Weiner
202	8/03/08	"Flight 1"	Lisa Albert Matthew Weiner
203	8/10/08	"The Benefactor"	Matthew Weiner Rick Cleveland
204	8/17/08	"Three Sundays"	André Jacquemetton Maria Jacquemetton
205	8/24/08	"The New Girl"	Robin Veith
206	8/31/08	"Maidenform"	Matthew Weiner
207	9/07/08	"The Gold Violin"	Jane Anderson André Jacquemetton Maria Jacquemetton
208	9/14/08	"A Night to Remember"	Robin Veith Matthew Weiner
209	9/28/08	"Six Month Leave"	André Jacquemetton Maria Jacquemetton Matthew Weiner
210	10/05/08	"The Inheritance"	Lisa Albert Marti Noxon Matthew Weiner
211	10/12/08	"The Jet Set"	Matthew Weiner
212	10/19/08	"The Mountain King"	Matthew Weiner Robin Veith
213	10/26/08	"Meditations in an Emergency"	Matthew Weiner Kater Gordon

Season Three

Episode	Airdate	Title	Writer(s)
301	8/16/09	"Out of Town"	Matthew Weiner
302	8/23/09	"Love among the Ruins"	Cathryn Humphris Matthew Weiner
303	8/30/09	"My Old Kentucky Home"	Dahvi Waller Matthew Weiner
304	9/06/09	"The Arrangements"	Andrew Colville Matthew Weiner
305	9/13/09	"The Fog"	Kater Gordon
306	9/20/09	"Guy Walks into an Advertising Agency"	Robin Veith Matthew Weiner
307	9/27/09	"Seven Twenty Three"	André Jacquemetton Maria Jacquemetton Matthew Weiner
308	10/4/09	"Souvenir"	Lisa Albert Matthew Weiner
309	10/11/09	"Wee Small Hours"	Dahvi Waller Matthew Weiner
310	10/18/09	"The Color Blue"	Kater Gordon Matthew Weiner
311	10/25/09	"The Gypsy and the Hobo"	Marti Nixon Cathryn Humphris Matthew Weiner
312	11/01/09	"The Grown Ups"	Brett Johnson Matthew Weiner
313	11/08/09	"Shut the Door. Have a Seat."	Matthew Weiner Erin Levy

CONTRIBUTORS

Some Real Mad Men and Women

Adam Barkman is an assistant professor of philosophy at Redeemer University College, Ontario. He is the author of *C. S. Lewis and Philosophy as a Way of Life* and *Through Common Things*. He is the coeditor of *Manga and Philosophy* and has written more than ten articles in philosophy and popular culture books. Besides the men routinely imbibing Scotch in the A.M., Adam's most striking memory of *Mad Men* is giving his son, Tristan, his bottle while adding the lyrics "Daddy, Daddy, feed me, feed me" to the beat of the theme song.

Ashley Jihee Barkman is a lecturer in English at Yonsei University, Seoul. She holds two M.A.s (in English and Theology) from the University of Toronto and lives far from Ossining with her husband and two small children. After going home, taking a paper bag, cutting some eyeholes out of it, putting it over her head, getting undressed, looking at herself in the mirror, and really evaluating where her strengths and weaknesses are, Ashley decided to write a few articles instead. She has contributed to *Manga and Philosophy* and *30 Rock and Philosophy*.

Raymond Angelo Belliotti is SUNY Distinguished Teaching Professor of Philosophy at the State University of New York at

Fredonia and the author of ten books. He steals snappy one-liners from Roger Sterling and spews them at unsuspecting colleagues and students.

Rod Carveth is an assistant professor in the Department of Communications Media at Fitchburg State College in Massachusetts. The author of more than forty journal articles and book chapters, Rod is also coeditor of *Media Economics: Theory and Practice*. Rod sees himself as a composite of the principal characters in *Mad Men*—the ego of Don Draper, the white hair of Roger Sterling, and the rotundity of Bertram Cooper.

George A. Dunn is a jet-setting philosopher who teaches at the University of Indianapolis, Indiana University–Purdue University in Indianapolis, and the Ningbo Institute of Technology in China. He is an editor of *True Blood and Philosophy* and a contributor to several other volumes in the Blackwell Philosophy and Pop Culture Series. No longer a smoker, he has had to seek other outlets for his "death wish," such as flying American Airlines. An avid music lover, he hopes to be reincarnated as Joan Holloway's accordion.

John Elia is the Therese Murray Goodwin '49 chair and assistant professor in philosophy at Wilson College, in Chambersburg, Pennsylvania. His primary areas of research include ethics and political philosophy. He has also contributed to *The Office and Philosophy*. John's thinking about *Mad Men* was inspired as much by his love of rye whiskey, vintage threads, and mid-century furniture as by his love of wisdom.

John Fritz is a Ph.D. candidate at Duquesne University in Pittsburgh, where he teaches and studies ancient and contemporary philosophy. He wishes he had Don Draper's charm for his upcoming comprehensive examinations, where he suspects that his inability to remember anything of importance will prove disastrous, despite speaking well of his psychic health. He watches *Mad Men* when he should be studying, and tries to emulate Peggy Olson in his daily life.

Kevin Guilfoy has been a fan of advertising ever since he learned as a child that happiness and popularity could be bought at the toy store. Many of his fondest childhood memories involve public tantrums begging his parents for "just this one new toy." Most of his youth was spent accumulating debt. He is currently an assistant professor of philosophy at Carroll University in Wisconsin, but he knows that true happiness can be achieved if he buys a big-screen TV in time for the new season of *Mad Men*.

Ada S. Jaarsma is an assistant professor of philosophy at Sonoma State University in California. Her research interests include continental philosophy, feminist philosophy, existentialism, and the philosophy of culture. Like Don Draper, she is beginning to realize that the powers of Madison Avenue extend into the realms of desire, domesticity, and daydreams. She can't help but wonder: If Draper were operating his magic today, what inventive pitch would he make to attract new philosophy majors?

Abigail E. Myers earned her B.A. in English and philosophy from King's College and her M.S.Ed. in adolescent education from St. John's University. She is also the author of "U2, Feminism, and the Ethic of Care" (with Jennifer McClinton-Temple) in *U2 and Philosophy* and "Edward Cullen, Bella Swan: Byronic Hero and Feminist Heroine. Or Not" in *Twilight and Philosophy*. Abigail has started taking Facebook quizzes seriously ever since the *Mad Men* quiz informed her that she was a Joan.

Andreja Novakovic and Betty Draper used to dance around the "mayhole" in white dresses every spring and chant "Anassa kata kalo kale ia ia ia Nike!" in unison. But since graduating from Bryn Mawr, they have gone their separate ways. While Betty went on to become a woman of leisure, Andreja is still a Ph.D. student in philosophy at Columbia University in New York City, writing her dissertation on G. W. F. Hegel and spending far too much time analyzing *Mad Men*.

Landon W. Schurtz has never worked in advertising, but he does occasionally enjoy vodka martinis. He received his B.A. in English from Tennessee State University and is currently a graduate student pursuing a Ph.D. in philosophy at the University of Oklahoma. A lifelong lover of bowling, cars with fins, and Formica-and-chrome furniture, he feels that *Mad Men* is the television show he never knew he couldn't live without.

James B. South is an associate professor of philosophy, and chair of the department, at Marquette University in Milwaukee, Wisconsin. He publishes essays on late medieval and Renaissance philosophy when he's not writing about popular culture. He edited *Buffy the Vampire Slayer and Philosophy* and coedited (with Jacob Held) *James Bond and Philosophy*. James wants things he hasn't seen—where's that Hilton Hotel on the moon?

Andrew Terjesen is currently a visiting assistant professor of philosophy at Rhodes College in Memphis, Tennessee. He has previously taught at Washington and Lee University, Austin College, and Duke University. His philosophical interests center around business ethics and moral psychology. He has written essays exploring these topics for other volumes in the Philosophy and Pop Culture series, including *The Office and Philosophy*, *Twilight and Philosophy*, and *Iron Man and Philosophy*. According to his wife, Andrew is totally lamer than Don Draper—but then again, aren't we all.

Gabrielle Teschner is an artist living and working in the San Francisco Bay Area. She received her M.F.A. in sculpture from the California College of the Arts, where she was fascinated by the combined power of language and image. She has work in the permanent collection of the De Young Museum, and her Draperian tendencies were evident in a solo showing of her work titled "Everything You Think Is True." She coauthored a chapter of this book with her father, a philosopher with whom she has a long-standing door-slamming wrangle over whether art follows copy or copy follows art.

George Teschner is a professor at Christopher Newport University in Virginia, where he regularly teaches courses in contemporary philosophy, comparative philosophy, and philosophy in popular culture. He did his graduate work in New York City at the time when *Mad Men* takes place and resonates with its values and characters. He had the choice of advertising or teaching philosophy and has come to believe there is little difference between the two.

Robert White is an assistant professor of philosophy and ethics at the American University in Bulgaria. He teaches a course on business ethics in which he uses *Mad Men* to illustrate how social conformity and a lack of intellectual independence sustain unethical conduct, such as racism and sexism. He previously taught at the University of Auckland, New Zealand, where he earned his Ph.D. Unlike Don Draper, White is a productive and rational man and, in the end, completely self-interested.

Tyler Whitney studies German literature and media history at Columbia University in New York City. He agrees with Joan Harris and Marshall McLuhan that the medium is indeed the message. If the academic job market does not improve in the near future, Tyler would consider working with Harry Crane in the television department at Sterling Cooper Draper Pryce.

INDEX

Client Files Lifted from Sterling Cooper